China and Mozambique

From Comrades to Capitalists

Edited by Chris Alden and Sérgio Chichava

First published by Fanele, an imprint of Jacana Media (Pty) Ltd, in 2014

10 Orange Street
Sunnyside
Auckland Park 2092
South Africa
+2711 628 3200
www.jacana.co.za

© Chris Alden and Sérgio Chichava, 2014

All rights reserved.

ISBN 978-1-920196-94-3

Cover design by publicide
Set in Bembo 10.9/14pt
Printed and bound by Inside Data
Job no. B000001

See a complete list of Jacana titles at www.jacana.co.za

China and Mozambique

Contents

Contributors vii

Acknowledgements xi

Introduction An Overview of China and Africa Relations
(Chris Alden and Sérgio Chichava) xiii

Chapter 1 China in Mozambique: Caution, Compromise and
Collaboration (Chris Alden, Sérgio Chichava and Paula
Cristina Roque) 1

Chapter 2 Assessing Chinese Investment in Mozambique
(Sérgio Chichava) 24

Chapter 3 Chinese Banking in Mozambique: The Macanese
Connection (Ana Cristina Alves) 39

Chapter 4 All Part of the Master Plan? Ethnographic Encounters
with the Chinese in Mozambique (Mikkel Bunkenborg) 50

Chapter 5 How *Not* to Build a Road: An Analysis of the
Socio-economic Effects of a Chinese Infrastructure Project
in Mozambique (Morten Nielsen) 67

Chapter 6 Myth and Reality: Chinese Involvement in Mozambique's
Agricultural Sector (Sigrid-Marianella Stensrud Ekman) 84

Chapter 7 The Chinese Agricultural Technology
Demonstration Centre in Mozambique: A Story of a
Gift (Sérgio Chichava, Jimena Durán and Lu Jiang) 107

Chapter 8 Chinese Rice Farming in Xai-Xai: A Case of
Mozambican Agency? (Sérgio Chichava) 120

Chapter 9 Mozambican Perspectives on the Chinese Presence: A
Comparative Analysis of Discourses by Government, Labour
and Blogs (João Feijó) 146

Chapter 10 Migrants or Sojourners? The Chinese Community in
Maputo (Sérgio Chichava and Jimena Durán) 188

Conclusion Reflections on a Changing Relationship (Sérgio
Chichava and Chris Alden) 199

Index 210

Contributors

Chris Alden is a professor of International Relations at the London School of Economics and Political Science (LSE) and heads the Global Powers in Africa Programme at the South African Institute of International Affairs (SAIIA). He has published widely on China-Africa relations as well as on Mozambican politics, including *A Mamba e o Dragão: Relações Moçambique-China em perspectiva* (IESE/SAIIA 2012; edited with Sérgio Chichava), *China in Africa* (Zed 2007) and *Mozambique and the Construction of the New African State* (Palgrave 2003). *j.c.alden@lse.ac.uk*

Ana Cristina Alves is a senior researcher with the South African Institute of International Affairs (SAIIA) and an expert on emerging powers and Africa. Her publications include *China and Angola: A marriage of convenience?* (Fahamu 2012) and articles in numerous internationally recognised journals. She has a PhD from the London School of Economics and Political Science (LSE). *ana.alves@wits.ac.za*

Mikkel Bunkenborg is assistant professor of contemporary China studies at the Department of Cross-Cultural and Regional Studies, University of Copenhagen. Trained in Chinese and anthropology, he has published on bodies, medicine, politics and religion in China and, more recently, been engaged in a collaborative research project on Chinese infrastructure construction, resource extraction, and trade in Mongolia and Mozambique. *msn512@hum.ku.dk*

Sérgio Chichava is a senior researcher at the Instituto de Estudos Sociais e Económicos (IESE), Mozambique and a lecturer in Political Sociology and Political Studies at Eduardo Mondlane University (UEM), also in Maputo. He obtained his PhD from the Institute of Political Studies of Bordeaux, France. He works on Mozambique's relations with rising powers, particularly on China and Brazil. He is editor of *A Mamba e o Dragão: Relações Moçambique-China em perspectiva* (with Chris Alden; 2012), *Cidadania e Governação em Moçambique*

(with Luís de Brito and others; 2009), *Desafios para Moçambique 2010* (2010), *Desafios para Moçambique 2011* (2011), *Desafios para Moçambique 2012* (2012) and *Desafios para Moçambique 2013* (2013).
sergio.chichava@iese.ac.mz

Jimena Durán has a master's degree in International Politics from SciencesPo, Bordeaux. She has done research concerning China and Brazil South-South Cooperation and the Chinese Community in Mozambique with the Agence Française de Development and the Instituto de Estudos Sociais e Económicos. She has also collaborated with Future Agriculture Consortium on publications about Brazil and China's cooperation in Mozambique. At this moment, she is a consultant for the Ministry of Education of Colombia on internationalisation, South-South Cooperation and knowledge management.
jime.duranp@gmail.com

Sigrid-Marianella Stensrud Ekman is a researcher specialising in China-Africa affairs, currently working as a consultant on the 'Chinese Trade and Investment in Africa' project for the Center of International Forestry Research. She holds a master's degree in Chinese Political Economy from Fudan University and a bachelor's degree from the University of Cape Town.
sigrid.ekman@gmail.com

João Feijó has a degree in Sociology of Organisations, University of Minho, Portugal, a post-graduate degree in Intercultural Communication from the University of Jyväskylä, Finland, a master's degree in Intercultural Relations from the Open University in Portugal and a PhD in African Studies from the Higher Institute of Enterprise and Labor Sciences, Lisbon. He has published several research papers related to identities and social representations, to human resources management in Mozambican contexts and the Chinese presence in Mozambique.
joaofeijo@hotmail.com

Lu Jiang is a PhD candidate in International Relations at the London School of Economics and Political Science (LSE). She got her master's and bachelor's degrees from Fudan University in Shanghai, China. Her research interests revolve around China's foreign policy, and particularly China's foreign relations with Africa. Her master's thesis was about China's oil engagement in Sudan. She is now working on Chinese agricultural aid and investment in Africa and has chosen Mozambique as her case country.
l.jiang4@lse.ac.uk

Contributors

Morten Nielsen has a master's degree (2002) and PhD (2009) in Social Anthropology from the University of Copenhagen. From 2009–2010 he was a research fellow at the Centre for Cosmopolitan Studies, University of St Andrews, and post-doctorate at the University of Copenhagen. Since 2012 he has been associate professor at Aarhus University and was in 2012 Head of the Ethnographic Collections at Moesgård Museum. Based on ethnographic fieldwork in Brazil (2001–2002), Mozambique (2004–2012) and Scotland (2013–), he has published a number of articles and book chapters on the relationship between time and materiality as reflected through processes of urban planning, house-building and large-scale infrastructure projects. His book *Bricks of Time: Inverse governmentality through informal house building projects* is forthcoming with Berghahn Books.
etnomn@cas.au.dk.

Paula Cristina Roque is a political analyst finishing her PhD at Oxford University in International Development. She currently holds the position of research director of the South Sudan Centre for Research and Policy Studies, as well as consulting regularly on Angola and South Sudan. Roque is a former senior researcher at the Institute for Security Studies (Pretoria) and was previously with the South African Institute of International Affairs (SAIIA) working on China in Africa.
pcroque@gmail.com

Acknowledgements

The authors would like to gratefully acknowledge the support of the Instituto de Estudos Sociais e Económicos (IESE) in Maputo and the South African Institute of International Affairs (SAIIA) for this book project and the assistance of the following individuals, who shepherded it into publication: Alexandra Begg, Thabiso Mahlape, Judy Smith-Höhn.

Introduction
An Overview of China and Africa Relations

Chris Alden and Sérgio Chichava

China's rising position in African affairs, from that of quiescence to open activism at the centre stage of events, is changing the dynamics of the post-colonial system (Broadman 2007; Bräutigam 2009; Taylor 2006). Since the onset of the domestic reform process starting in 1978, Maoist faith and revolutionary altruism have given way to the consciously self-interested commercial entrepreneurs and advocates of forms of market capitalism. The emergence of China as Africa's top trading partner and leading source of foreign direct investment in 2009, surpassing the United States and key European Union states still struggling in the aftermath of the global financial crisis, has sharpened the focus on Chinese aspirations and conduct in Africa.[1] Two-way trade is surging, from just over US$1 billion in 2000 to US$198 billion in 2012, and is predicted by a leading South Africa financial institution, Standard Bank, to rise to US$300 billion by 2015 (Ministry of Commerce 2013; Freemantle & Stevens 2011). Backed by the world's largest foreign exchange reserves and a desire to seek out long-term strategic positions in key resource markets, Chinese are investing in key sectors across the continent from energy in Angola, Sudan and Uganda to mining in Zambia and the Democratic Republic of Congo (DRC). Between 2009 and 2012, Chinese foreign direct investment (FDI) grew from US$1.44 billion to US$2.52 billion, reaching a cumulative FDI stock of US$21.23 billion (Ministry of Commerce 2013). Though African resources still dominate its exports to the Chinese economy, at over 80% of the total in 2010, there is evidence of a diversification in trade taking place, albeit reflected more readily in the bilateral trade in selected countries. For instance, Chinese telecommunications firms like Huawei and ZTE are increasingly penetrating this important market while Chinese financial institutions are entering into partnerships with banks in South Africa, Nigeria and Kenya. Small and medium enterprises are investing in light industry in countries like Mali and Uganda while thousands of individual investors are setting up businesses in retail, wholesale, services and even farming

---

1 According to the US Commerce Department, US-Africa trade fell by US$55 billion in 2009 from a high of US$141 billion in 2008 to a total of US$86 billion while Chinese Ministry of Commerce figures put China-Africa trade at US$106 billion in 2008. It had only dropped to US$90 billion in 2009.

(Ministry of Commerce 2013). And, the launching of Chinese *reminbi* currency conversion in a sprinkling of important African economies like Zambia, where Chinese business and migrant communities are well represented, suggests that the deepening of integration between these economies is inevitable.

African leaders have recognised, perhaps belatedly in some cases, the necessity of closer ties with the rising economic giant, calling for a concerted effort to better understand and utilise the opportunities presented by China. At the continental level, the Economic Affairs Department of the African Union, for one, has created a number of events and research reports focused on China while sub-regional organisations, like the East African Community, have actively sought to devise a strategy of engagement. Bilateral efforts are more pronounced, with countries like Zimbabwe and Namibia devising 'Look East' policies aimed at explicitly attracting Chinese (and other Asian) investment, while others like Angola, Nigeria and Gabon have been more focused on seeking 'package deals' that exchange access to resource assets for large Chinese-financed and -built infrastructure projects. Notably, there are also those states, such as Ethiopia and Egypt, without significant material resources to attract Beijing, which have nonetheless managed to develop close economic relationships with China.

Behind the remarkable success in bolstering Chinese engagement with Africa is a set of policies and a range of experiences that drew the attention of governments wary of Western donor pontifications and conditionalities. China's declared position is that its ties with Africa are based on explicit declarations of historic connectivity, political equality, respect for sovereignty, non-intervention and, in economic matters, mutual benefit. China frames the relationship in the form of a multilateral diplomatic initiative called the tri-annual Forum on China-Africa Cooperation (FOCAC), while the details of its implementation are overwhelmingly bilateral arrangements. Negotiated loans, grants and investments have allowed African governments a role in setting the agenda for the relationship, for example, in prioritising particular sectors or projects. Beijing likes to point to the constancy of Chinese solidarity with African interests, especially during the anti-colonial struggle, as well as their shared history as victims of imperialism as producing the requisite conditions for a common outlook. A pre-colonial episode, the voyages of Ming Dynasty Admiral Zheng He to Africa in the early 15th century, has been retrieved from the archives of history to underscore the constancy of China's benign intentions towards the continent.

Given the diplomatic imperative of countering Taiwan's drive – now muted since the KMT government came to power in Taipei in 2010 – for official recognition in Africa from the 1950s onwards, the Chinese government has had to ensure that it has a continent-wide approach to Africa. This has given a specific geo-strategic rationale to Chinese foreign policy in Africa that is lacking in any of the other emerging or traditional powers. At the same time, the bulk of China's economic interests are focused on the leading African resource economies, namely Angola, Sudan, Nigeria, and the DRC, as well as the more diversified South African economy. Beijing's dualist approach – multilateral through FOCAC and bilateral in terms of implementation of specific forms of cooperation and investment – is tailored to provide a means of addressing both sets of concerns for China.

At the same time, a chorus of dissatisfaction among some elements in African society – concerned primarily with the socio-economic and environmental impact of Chinese involvement on the continent – points to the growing complexities that accompany the deepening of such ties. There is a belated recognition by Chinese officials that not all Chinese economic actors have been operating in ways that promote mutual benefit for China and Africa. Official admonishments to abide by local government laws and regulations, combined with an effort to introduce aspects of the corporate social responsibility (CSR) agenda into the conduct of leading state-owned enterprises (SOEs) and major Chinese corporations are seen to be sufficient palliatives. With regard to smaller private Chinese firms, however, the ability of Beijing to control their actions is relatively limited as these operate in Africa without utilising the conventional sources of finance and consciously seek to act outside of the reach of the Chinese state. Nonetheless, the weakness of some African states' ability to enforce their own regulations is in many ways a fundamental problem in this area. This has not stopped the local media and civil society from trenchantly criticising the conduct of some Chinese firms.

Running in parallel with this problem is a growing dilemma for the Chinese government, specifically how to protect and preserve its growing and established economic interests in Africa without being seen to violate the aforementioned sacred foreign policy principles such as non-interference. One response has been to distinguish between intervention legitimised through multilateral institutions such as the United Nations with the concurrence of host governments from those actions that lack these elements. The Chinese changing position in favour of support for multilateral intervention in Darfur after 2004 marked the first full elaboration of this approach to intervention (Large & Patey 2011). This selective embrace of multilateralism can been seen in Beijing's expansive participation in UN peacekeeping operations in Africa, with its troops taking up positions in, among others, Liberia, the DRC and South Sudan (Gill et al 2007). President Hu Jintao's declaration at FOCAC V in mid-2012 officially launched the China-Africa Cooperative Partnership for

Peace and Security, a much expanded spectrum of peace and security related engagement.[2] The sending of 395 elite Chinese troops six months later with a mandate to protect peacekeeping headquarters and ground forces in Mali was one concrete expression of this more engaged approach. Ruminations as to how China might contribute to more complex forms of post-conflict peacebuilding currently occupy policy think tanks (Alden 2014).

Complementing these cautious steps into the security arena is a more concerted Chinese effort to promote public diplomacy and engage with the African public through the media. The opening of over 30 Confucian Centres across Africa and provisions for 5 500 annual scholarships are aimed not only at education, but also at improving social relations and building personal networks between the two regions (Li & Ronning 2013). Concurrently, Chinese inroads into the African media space, through the expansion of CCTV across the continental airwaves, the opening of a regional office in Nairobi (with 60 Chinese journalists and 400 local staff) and even the purchase of media groups in countries like South Africa, promise a clearer articulation of China's involvement in continental affairs to an African audience (Wu 2013).

Finally, the role of continued Chinese migration to Africa, though small compared to migration to other parts of the world, is casting its own shadow over the relationship. Data remains scarce, notwithstanding some influential studies and an endless stream of impressionistic anecdotes, but there are some indicative aspects of the migration (MacNamee et al 2013). Chinese migrants to Africa seem to be poor, ill-educated and intent on escaping the competitive environment back home. They bring little capital with them and tend to move into retail or wholesale trade, fanning out to small towns in rural Africa. Many in southern Africa are from coastal provinces like Fujian but there is evidence from across the continent that the regional sources of Chinese migration are wider. South Africa supports by far the largest community, numbering anywhere from 300 000 to 500 000, but migrants are moving into countries like Angola, Zambia and Ethiopia in large numbers as well.[3] Indeed, the rapid rise and subsequent withdrawal of Chinese migrants to Libya, numbering 35 850 at the point of evacuation in 2011, illustrates just how swiftly these infrastructure projects can swell the population of contracted and migrant Chinese in a

---

2 See the Fifth Ministerial Conference of the Forum on China-Africa Cooperation Beijing Action Plan (2013–2015), 23 July 2012, which states that China and Africa will 'strengthen cooperation in policy coordination, capacity building, preventive diplomacy, peace keeping operations and post-conflict reconstruction and rehabilitation on the basis of equality and mutual respect to jointly maintain peace and stability in Africa' (at 2.6.1).
3 For example, there are alleged to be 250 000 Chinese in Angola, according to Ji Dongye's report in 'Rule of Law Weekly', reposted in *China Africa Project*, www.chinaafricaproject.com/Chinese-people-in-africa-an-inside-view-into-their-daily-lives-part-5-angola/ (Accessed on 30 September 2013).

Introduction

country. While there is no inevitability implied in suggesting the rise in tensions between communities – indeed there is as much evidence of social harmony as there is problems – nonetheless the possibility that politicians will utilise this phenomenon to whip up support (as has been the case in Zambia) as they have with other ethnic and migrant communities seems strong. The outcome of such actions on the tone of China-Africa relations will be significant.

While all of these themes provide a framework for understanding China-Africa relations, especially as these ties have grown in depth and complexity, it is necessary to go beyond the larger palette to delve into a bilateral relationship to get a fuller sense of the ties today. For this reason this edited book chooses to explore one case in particular: that is the relationship between China and Mozambique, and the specificities that it brings to these general themes raised above about China-Africa relations.

The book opens by examining the bilateral relationship in both its historical context and more contemporary forms in a chapter written by Chris Alden, Sérgio Chichava and Paula Roque, touching on the origins of the relationship and development of closer ties. The second chapter, by Sérgio Chichava, analyses the tendencies, impacts and significance of Chinese in Mozambique investment and trade between 2000 and 2012. The period under review was marked by the increased Chinese presence in Africa, generally, trends that are evident in the Mozambican experience but tempered by Mozambican agency in managing the relationship. The third chapter, by Ana Cristina Alves, looks at Chinese investment in the Mozambican banking sector. In addition to showing its characteristics and specificities, this chapter also sheds light on Chinese and Mozambique elite business alliances. Based on a series of ethnographic encounters with Chinese entrepreneurs, construction workers, and engineers in Mozambique and contrary to the widespread Western idea of Chinese planned expansion, Mikkel Bunkenborg's chapter shows that the presence of Chinese nationals in Africa is not an orchestrated plan or even policy, but rather that it emerges from individual actions. Focused on the activities of the China Henan International Cooperation Group, Co Ltd, one of the most active Chinese construction enterprises in Mozambique, and using an ethnographic approach, the fifth chapter, by Morten Nielsen, examines the socio-economic effects of the construction of a road in the Southern Gaza province. The following three chapters focus on China-Mozambique cooperation in the area of agriculture. Written by Sigrid Ekman, the sixth chapter outlines agricultural cooperation between Mozambique and China, and the Chinese investment in this sector, providing a picture of what it is and of some of its impacts. Taking the case of Boane Agricultural Demonstration Centre, one of the most representative examples of Chinese presence in Africa, particularly in Mozambique, the seventh chapter, by Sérgio Chichava, Jimena Durán and Lu Jiang, discusses the meaning and implications of the cooperation between the two countries, and in the Mozambican institutions. The eighth chapter, by Sérgio Chichava, develops the case study of Chinese rice farming in Xai-Xai. In the ninth chapter, João Feijó looks at how the Chinese and Mozambicans perceive each other and its implications for their relationship and, for the Chinese presence in Mozambique while the tenth chapter, by Sérgio Chichava and Jimena Durán, has the aim of discussing Chinese intra-community relations and the characteristics of these communities in Maputo. In the final chapter Sérgio Chichava and Chris Alden, as a general conclusion and based on the Mozambique-China relationship, reflect on its meanings and features for our understanding of this dynamic actor in continental affairs.

References

Alden, Chris. 2014. 'Seeking Security in Africa: China's evolving approach to peace and security in Africa'. NOREF, forthcoming.

Bräutigam, Deborah. 2009. *The Dragon's Gift: The real story of China and Africa*. New York: Oxford University Press.

Broadman, Harry. 2007. *Africa's Silk Road*. Washington DC: World Bank.

Freemantle, Simon & Stevens, Jeremy. 2011. 'BRIC-Africa: The redback's rise – opportunity for Africa'. Occasional Paper, Standard Bank, Johannesburg. January.

Gill, Bates, Huang, Chin-hao & Morrison, J. Stephen. 2007. 'Assessing China's Growing Influence in Africa', *China Security*, 3(3), 3–21.

Global Times. 2011. 'State pays Libyan compensation'. Available from: www.globaltimes.cn/business/world/2011-03/639544.html [Accessed on 30 September 2013].

Ji Dongye report, in 'Rule of Law Weekly', reposted in China Africa Project. Available from: www.chinaafricaproject.com/Chinese-people-in-africa-an-inside-view-into-their-daily-lives-part-5-angola/ [Accessed on 30 September 2013].

Large, Dan & Patey, Luke. 2011. *Sudan Looks East: China, India and the politics of Asian alternatives*. Oxford: James Currey.

Li, Shubo & Ronning, Helge. 2013. 'Winning Hearts and Minds: Chinese soft power foreign policy in Africa'. *CMI Brief*, 12(3), September.

Ministry of Commerce. 2013. 'China-Africa Economic and Trade Cooperation'. Available from: www.news.xinhuanet.com/2013-08/29/c?132673093_3.htm [Accessed on 11 October 2013].

MacNamee, Terence, Mills, Greg, Manoel, Sebabatso, Mulaudzi, Masana, Doran, Stuart & Chen, Emma. 2013. 'A Study of Chinese Traders in South Africa, Lesotho, Botswana, Zambia and Angola'. Discussion Paper 2012–13. Johannesburg: The Brenthurst Foundation.

Taylor, Ian. 2006. *China and Africa: Engagement and compromise*. London: Routledge.

Wu, Yu-Shan. 2013. 'The Rise of China's State-Led Media Dynasty'. SAIIA Occasional Paper 117, June.

Chapter 1
China in Mozambique: Caution, Compromise and Collaboration[1]

Chris Alden, Sérgio Chichava and Paula Cristina Roque

China's engagement with Mozambique has taken a different form from that of other parts of Africa, and is best characterised as a relationship of caution, compromise and collaboration. While Beijing's rise has been welcomed by Mozambican officials, not the least because it offers the possibility of diversity and leverage with its traditional development partners, they have been more circumspect when it has come to actually facilitating major resources for infrastructure deals of the kind seen in Angola and elsewhere. This caution has conditioned the pace and depth of ties with China in the last decade, but since the onset of the global financial crisis in 2008, it is a trend that is beginning to change.

First, in direct contrast with China's role in Angola, where the centralised planning system is clearly in government hands, the long-standing dependency and participatory approach in Mozambique has allowed Bretton Woods institutions, Western donors and non-governmental organisations (NGOs) to have had a stronger role in influencing government decision-making on macro-economic policy (Hanlon 1991; Pitcher 2002; Alden 2003). Indeed, Maputo's established relationship with traditional donors and their presence in the country – foreign aid from traditional donors has contributed to 51% of the 2008 national budget of US$3.2 billion – adds an important structural dimension to Beijing and the Mozambican government's bilateral relations not present in China's ties with other resource-rich countries. A second factor is the relatively strong Western NGO presence – especially pronounced in Maputo – and, with that, the fostering of a local civil society. The third is the role of Frelimo, the governing party since independence in 1975, as a cohesive source of policy formulation and implementation in the country. Notwithstanding the well-founded accusations of profiteering by some of the party elite, Frelimo has proven its ability to manage an array of external actors under the direst circumstances and, in the current climate of growing prosperity, continues to

---

1 This chapter is partially based on earlier work done by Paula Cristina Roque, 'China in Mozambique: a cautious approach', SAIIA Occasional Paper 24, Braamfontein, 2009.

demonstrate this capacity. All of these factors have meant that China's approach in Mozambique, while emphasising the now familiar focus on resources and infrastructure, nonetheless has been far less significant than perhaps Beijing's aspirations would have it. This is despite the fact that, in the words of one Mozambican analyst, 'China appears in this setting when generations and generations of Mozambicans have witnessed cooperation with Europe but are yet to see the benefits' (Interview, senior Frelimo official April 2008).

Sino-Mozambican relations: from solidarity to technical and financial cooperation

The last 30 years have witnessed considerable change in Mozambique. After a lengthy armed struggle against the colonial power Portugal, the country achieved independence in June 1975 and the Front for the Liberation of Mozambique (Frelimo), the liberation movement, created a one-party state guided by socialist economic principles.

Sino-Mozambican relations date back to the 1960s when China provided important diplomatic and limited military support for Frelimo (Chichava 2008:2–6). The liberation movement, under the leadership of Eduardo Mondlane, received aid from both China and the Soviet Union, a strategy it pursued to avoiding getting involved in the Sino-Soviet ideological split and as part of its campaign to be internationally recognised as the legitimate representative of the Mozambican people (Taylor 2006). The pragmatism demonstrated then when Frelimo strived to balance foreign influence over its movement would later be seen again in its approach with international donors and development partners during the post-independence period.

At the height of the Cold War, Mozambique became embroiled in a lengthy civil war where the government fought against the counter-insurgency movement Mozambique National Resistance (Renamo) that was supported by the minority-governments of South Africa and Rhodesia (now called Zimbabwe). China provided Frelimo with important ideological inspiration, a source of military support and guerrilla training, a fact recognised by the first president of Mozambique Samora Machel during a visit to Beijing on the eve of independence in 1975 (Jackson 1995:412). China provided a US$59 million loan to the new government and the expectation was that ties would deepen in the coming years. However, Maputo edged closer to the Soviet Union, with Frelimo declaring itself to be Marxist-Leninist at the 3rd Party Congress in April 1977 that was solidified through the subsequent signing of a Treaty of Friendship with Moscow. During this period relations with China cooled, partly in reaction to its support for the National Front for the Liberation of Angola (FNLA) and other global events (Jackson 1995:415–416). Premier

Zhao Ziyang's tour of Africa in 1983 marked a conscious effort to re-engage with African states (and liberation movements such as the ANC), laying the foundation for a more pragmatic relationship. China provided Mozambique with emergency assistance in 1983, followed by the extension of an interest-free loan of US$13 million in 1985.

By 1987, Mozambique began its economic reform designed to stabilise the economy, marking a departure from ineffective socialist policies and the adoption of a market-oriented economy (Pitcher 2002). Despite dramatic improvements in the country's growth rate following these reforms, Mozambique remains highly dependent on foreign assistance.

Following on this was the opening of direct negotiations between the Mozambican government and Renamo, culminating in peace talks in Rome and the promulgation of the Comprehensive Peace Agreement in October 1992. The UN oversaw the transition from civil war, which had killed over a million Mozambicans, to democratic elections over a two-year period. The economic recovery that followed was owed in part to the reactivation of several sectors, the acceleration of agricultural production, and macro-economic stability.

After the conclusion of the UN Peacekeeping Operation and elections in October 1994, Mozambique increasingly came to be described as a model of cooperation with Western countries and donors, after having adhered to the conditions and programmes presented by the Bretton Woods institutions in 1984. Due to its economic reform and good track record, Mozambique became the first African country to benefit from the Heavily Indebted Poor Country Initiative from where it began receiving debt relief. After adopting the World Bank's structural adjustment programmes, international investment began pouring into the country, which in turn began its sweeping privatisation of formerly state-owned enterprises. Aid from Western institutions has played a significant role in Mozambique's economic and social recovery but has also been influenced by donor priorities and reduced the capacity of the government to govern itself. Official Development Assistance (ODA) continues to finance over 50% of government expenditure, mainly in the form of budget support. Although poverty dropped 22 percentage points between 1997 and 2006 (OECD-DAC 2008), Mozambique remains a poor country with 59.6% of the population living on less than US$1.25 a day (World Developemnt Indicators 2014). The country struggles to achieve significant development in the formal sector, in its export capacity, agricultural production, industrialisation process, the development of small and medium enterprises, its banking system, and integration with the Southern African Development Community (SADC). In the last decade, Mozambique has witnessed an average 8% growth rate, one of the fastest growing economies in southern Africa, driven mainly by foreign-funded mega-projects and large aid inflows. Since 2006 economic growth has also been driven by large investments in mineral extraction, agro-industry, services, the construction sector and other industries.

It is in this context that China as a newly activist economic power came to operate in Mozambique and because of these particular localised factors, it has had to tailor its approach to the country. The contemporary relationship between China and Mozambique, coming in the wake of President Jiang Zemin's ground-breaking trip to the continent in 1996, was gradually rebuilt in 1997/98 with a US$20-million fund provided by China Export-Import (Exim) Bank to provide incentives for Chinese companies to start doing business in Mozambique as well as the building of a new embassy complex and a trade centre administered by the Economic Counselor's office in downtown Maputo. From this period, technical cooperation steadily diversified and intensified. Support and training of the Mozambican military was renewed, along with the construction of housing for soldiers worth US$7 million and a further US$150 000 worth of equipment being donated by China (Chichava 2008:8). By 2011, China had provided an annual disbursement of US$3 million in non-lethal equipment and training, though a significantly lower level of engagement than with the US (Robinson 2012:9). In addition to health (medical teams and anti-malaria medicines), education and capacity building came to feature as critical dimensions of China's technical cooperation with Mozambique. Over 100 Mozambican students go every year to Chinese universities with scholarships supported by Chinese government and companies like Huawei and there is an expectation that the number of scholarships will double in coming years (Macauhub 2010; Belchior 2011:14). In addition, a Confucius Centre was established at Eduardo Mondlane University in 2012. Several hundreds of professionals have received training in China in many different areas throughout the past decade. China set up an agriculture technological demonstration centre just outside Maputo in 2009. This centre is run by Hubei Agriculture University and has the aim of disseminating rice-farming techniques and technologies to local farmers.

In 2001, the two countries set up a Joint Economic and Trade Commission after signing several agreements on trade and the protections of investment. Since 2004, China and Mozambique have signed various cooperation agreements strengthening economic, political and historical links. Agreements on debt cancellation were signed for loans dating back to the 1980s worth US$20 million. In 2006, Mozambique was added to China's official list of tourism destinations, making it the 13th African country to be given such a status. Bilateral cooperation was further cemented with President Hu Jintao's visit to Mozambique in 2007 when he pledged further support, in the form of US$170 million in loans, and cooperation in the areas of agriculture, technology, education, health, the economy, and in the exploration of natural resources. Finally, in late 2007, a military assistance protocol was signed in Beijing between the chiefs of staff of the Mozambican and Chinese armed forces stressing the importance of creating mechanisms to increase military cooperation and helping Mozambique meet future security and defence challenges. As part of this agreement, the Chinese government granted Mozambique a total of US$1.5 million towards the refurbishment of several departments of the Mozambican Armed Forces (FADM).

Specifically in the defence and security area, Mozambique and China have signed several agreements that include technical military assistance, the supply of logistical and communications material to the Mozambican army and police (vehicles, computers, uniforms and boots, among other equipment), the training of Mozambican officers in Chinese academies and the construction of housing for the various staff in this sector (Government of Mozambique 2011a; *O País* 2009a; *O País* 2009b). One of the symbols of the cooperation in this sector was the construction and inauguration of military housing on the outskirts of Maputo city in 2001. It was intended for Mozambican military personnel, and budgeted at about US$7.5 million. It should be mentioned that, in 2009, Mozambique opened an office of a military attaché in Beijing (GoM 2010). In 2011, and in the framework of the annual assistance to the Mozambican armed forces, China donated assorted military equipment valued at US$3 million (Portal of the Mozambican Government 2010). Mozambique is also banking on China to modernise its armed forces, particularly the air force and the navy, currently lacking in resources to control Mozambican air space and waters. It has requested loans from the Chinese government of US$212 million, to acquire various types of military equipment, particularly aircraft and patrol boats and to build arsenals for storing military artefacts (GoM 2011a).

There is growing Chinese involvement in the social services as well. In the health sector, since 1976 Mozambique and China have had an agreement through which Chinese doctors are sent to Mozambique every two years. There is also an agreement signed in 2007 for the training of Mozambican specialists in various areas of health care.

In education, China has supported Mozambique not only by granting scholarships to Mozambican students and by training staff from various state institutions, but also in building and equipping some schools. Between 2004 and 2006, 183 Mozambican state cadres were trained in various areas in China (MINEC 2007a). In 2007 alone, 42 students and 22 public functionaries were sent to China under agreements signed during the visit by the Chinese president to Mozambique (MINEC 2007b). This number could undergo a significant increase thanks to the five-year partnership between the Mozambican state and the private company, the China Qingho Group (an important Chinese company in the coal sector), signed in 2011 to finance a hundred scholarships for Mozambican students to study in various Chinese universities (*O País* 2010).

Chinese financial involvement in Mozambique has expanded in this period as well. As early as 2006, the Mozambican government applied to the China Exim Bank for loans of US$2 billion for the Mphanda Nkuwa dam project on the Zambezi River,[2] US$50 million to support agricultural investment in Zambézia province and another soft loan to rehabilitate the capital's airport. The loans for the Mphanda Nkuwa dam never materialised while the agricultural investment, channelled through Moza Banco, was aimed at supporting the development of three agro-processing factories in the Zambezi valley (see below). The last loan for airport construction for US$115 million was split into two phases: an initial loan for US$50 million for the international terminal (completed in 2011), followed by US$65 million approved in 2010 to finance the reconstruction of the domestic terminal of Maputo's airport by Anhui Foreign Economic Construction Group. In 2007, the China Exim Bank and the World Bank established a widely publicised venture to jointly finance projects in Mozambique, Ghana and Uganda, but no concrete project financing agreements resulted.

While the formative economic boundaries of China-Mozambique engagement were being established between 2000 and 2009, a few trends were notable. With respect to the Mphanda Nkuwa dam project, which had been rejected by Western donors and international institutions as poorly sited and environmentally suspect, Frelimo appeared to see the Chinese as a more forthcoming source of support. Though the actual reasons behind the China Exim Bank's subsequent rejection of the project are not a matter of public record, the failure of the Mozambican government to put together a package that was sufficiently appealing to the Chinese is telling. Secondly, the selection of Mozambique as a model African country around which World Bank-China Exim Bank cooperation would be built is an indicator of the esteem and significance that Mozambique has for Western donors and international institutions. This symbolic position in the development world was replicated in the use of Mozambique as a case study for trilateral development cooperation involving Mozambique-Brazil-Japan in 2011. Examining these two cases

---

2 The dam project was later awarded to a consortium of two national energy companies (60%) and Brazilian construction firm Camargo Corrêa (40%) – with financial backing from Brazilian Development Bank (BNDES).

together, the impression that one gets is of a governing elite attempting to use China to skirt the constraints of dependency on the Western donor community at the same time that the Western donors are seeking to enmesh China into the Organisation for Economic Cooperation and Develop-Development Assistance Committee (OECD-DAC) framework of development assistance. These patterns were to continue to feature in the relationship but, as subsequent events were to demonstrate, were matched by the sharpening of elite efforts to transform ties with Beijing into personal and development gains, as well as the growing complexities produced by local responses to deeper Chinese engagement in the country.

Overview of contemporary China-Mozambique cooperation

The foundation for China-Mozambique cooperation laid over the previous decade centred on high-level diplomatic visits and exchanges of legislative bodies, political parties, government agencies, and foreign policy coordination in regional and international affairs. Party-to-party links seem to play an important role in, as one observer suggests, 'catalysing' relations (Njal 2012:8). The signing of an agreement in 2008 marked the beginning of an extended period of exchanges of party personnel, even up to Cabinet level in the case of Frelimo, to learn from each other's experiences and organisational methods at party and government level (Njal 2012:7). At the same time that formal links concretised, the economic component of China-Mozambique relations deepened its focused the development of economic and trade cooperation in infrastructure, agriculture and natural resource extraction. Greater economic involvement between China and Mozambique was reflected in growing trade ties. Two-way trade increased from US$284.1 million in 2007 to US$950 million in 2011. While Chinese exports are mainly composed of electronics and machinery, imports from Maputo are largely dominated by timber. In fact, Chinese trade interests have played a critical role in the exploitation of timber in the central provinces over the past decade. China has become the largest buyer of Mozambican timber while Mozambique ranks fifth among African exporters of timber to China, though much of that is said to be shipped illegally and through third countries (see below).

According to the Mozambican government, China has invested in 69 projects in Mozambique, with the focus on infrastructure, agriculture, aquaculture and forestry. Chinese investment has been an instrument for job creation in Mozambique, with 11 214 Mozambicans formally listed as employees of Chinese firms in 2008 (Chichava 2008:11). At the same time the poor conduct of some Chinese businesses like the China Henan International Cooperation Group, a construction firm involved in building a bridge over

Table 1.1 Official visits by Chinese and Mozambican heads of state 1998–2013

Year	Visits by Chinese heads of state to Mozambique	Visits by Mozambican heads of state to China
1998		Joaquim Chissano
2004		Joaquim Chissano
2006		Armando Guebuza
2007	Hu Jintao	
2008		Armando Guebuza
2011		Armando Guebuza
2013		Armando Guebuza

Source: Compiled by authors from various media reports

the Incomati river, towards their Mozambican employees has produced strikes, aroused the ire of labour unions, civil society and protest from the government.

Chinese foreign direct investment (FDI) in Mozambique has risen considerably over the last few years, having reached US$60 million in 2007, from US$10 million in 2003, placing China as the sixth largest investor in the country (Xinhua 2008). By 2008 China had become the second largest investor in Mozambique after South Africa, up from the 26th position less than a decade ago; and by 2011 it topped the list with US$312.9 million (Chichava 2008; Macauhub 2009; Club of Mozambique 2012). Along with booming bilateral trade, the increased flow of Chinese investment into Mozambique in recent years has been one of the key traits of China-Mozambique relations. Interestingly though, despite the growing allure of Mozambique's untapped mineral resources (namely coal, natural gas and oil), Chinese investment has so far targeted retail, services, manufactures, agriculture, logging, fisheries and the nascent banking sector.

The onset of the global financial crisis in 2009 signalled a dramatic shift in the international development landscape. As was the case in other African countries, the new global conditions sparked a more decided turn to Beijing on the part of the Mozambican government, reflecting the growing trade and investment trends with China as well as Beijing's position as possessing the largest holdings of foreign currency reserves in the world. During the visit of Mozambican prime minister Aires Ali to China in late 2010, for instance, two other concessional loans totalling US$100 million were signed with another Chinese state-run bank (China Development Bank or CDB, which manages the US$5 billion China-Africa Development Fund and is more politically oriented than its counterpart, the China Exim Bank) to support the construction of a cement factory in Sofala (US$80 million) and a cotton plant in Maputo

(US$20 million). A follow-up trip to China by President Armando Guebuza in August 2011 produced a framework agreement on financial cooperation that was signed with CDB. The agreement aims to introduce commercial loans to the private sector in Mozambique as well as channel funds to public investment, which suggests greater involvement of CDB in Mozambique's financial sector in the near future. Finally, reflecting the changing financial landscape, China became Mozambique's top creditor for the year 2012, with Maputo borrowing US$1.1 billion from Beijing out of a total of US$1.9 billion.

Infrastructure
The widespread destruction of infrastructure during the war has hindered development in the country. Donor-funded infrastructure rehabilitation projects have therefore played an important role in fostering Mozambique's economic development and contributing to the county's growth. In this regard, China's explicit interest and track record in supporting infrastructure projects across the continent has made it a particularly appealing development partner. Beijing has played an important role in the construction of an array of public buildings, the rehabilitation of roads and proposed hydro-power facilities.

China has funded several public infrastructure projects in Mozambique since 1999 with the construction of the parliament buildings. From 2001 to 2004, concessional loans amounting to US$15.6 million were attributed to several public-works projects, the construction of the Joaquim Chissano Conference Centre, the new Foreign Ministry, and purchasing of police equipment, and low-income housing in Zimpeto on the outskirts of Maputo, to be repaid between 2013 and 2025 (Bila 2007). A new national stadium, seating over 45 000, was also built by the Chinese ahead of the 2010 FIFA World Cup held in South Africa, later utilised as part of the All-Africa Games in 2011 (Njal 2012). Poor construction methods have, however, already rendered some of these buildings dangerous and requiring repairs (interview, residents 2011).

Chinese construction companies are playing an important role in the rebuilding of national roads; a third of all road construction in Mozambique, amounting to 600 kilometres of roads, is being carried out by Chinese road contractors (Bosten 2006). The China Henan International Cooperation Group has, for example, built a 154-kilometre road between Muxungwe and Inchope that provides an important transportation link between the north and south of the country. Over 30 Chinese construction companies currently have offices in Maputo and normally outbid South African and other foreign construction companies in international tenders by the government or the World Bank. Chinese construction companies are also involved in rehabilitating urban water supply systems in Maputo (US$30 million), Beira and Quelimane

(US$25 million in total), through international tender procedures, and are looking at further tender opportunities in the road- and bridge-construction sectors (Bosten 2006). An interesting aspect to note is the participation of China and Chinese companies in international tenders launched by the Mozambican government, where they lose their bargaining position and the ability to impose certain conditions, like labour requirements (as opposed to those cases when agreements are made bilaterally on donations or soft loans).

China's Export and Import Bank was approached by the government to provide financial support for Mozambique's biggest infrastructure project, the construction of the Mphanda Nkuwa dam, worth US$2.3 billion, and a 1.5-megawatt hydro-electric plant. The Mphanda Nkuwa dam project is part of a larger state strategy, based upon studies initially developed in the colonial era, to harness Mozambique's hydro-power for national and regional development (CSIS invest-tripartite.org 2013:3). Four large hydro-power projects were identified, including Mphanda Nkuwa, and the Chinese were asked to consider financing them. In most cases like these, Chinese construction companies are normally awarded the project when Chinese financing is concerned but in this case the construction of the dam has been awarded to Camargo Corrêa, a Brazilian engineering company, and to their Mozambican partner Insitec (a group with close links to the Frelimo elite) (Alvarenga 2008).

For a number of reasons, the Mphanda Nkuwa project has proved to be quite controversial among environmentalists who believe that an additional dam on the Zambezi river will add to the damage caused by the gigantic Cahora Bassa dam, one of the biggest hydro-electric schemes in Africa. Some of the problems raised are the displacement of 1 400 rural farmers, and that the new dam would require that Cahora Bassa continue operating at its current destructive rate which would, as a result, make downstream restoration even harder. Moreover, the dam is located in an area considered risky due to the probability of seismic activity. Further possible impacts on the environment include the recurrence of flooding that will destroy the capacity of subsistence farming downstream, and the degradation of fisheries. Mozambican civil society has taken a lead in criticising the project. The results of the feasibility study conducted in 2001 by the Technical Unit for the Implementation of Hydro-power Projects, Mozambique (UTIP) highlighted several technical risks and negative impacts on the communities directly affected as well as potentially harmful environmental consequences. This is thought to be the reason why Western funders like the World Bank and European Investment Bank did not get involved (Jansson & Kiala 2009:10). China Exim Bank, after lengthy discussions, elected not to provide financing for the project.

A smaller project, the Moamba Major dam outside of Maputo, was also subject to consideration by the Chinese. The Ministry of Public Works and Housing and the China Exim Bank engaged in prolonged negotiations aimed at developing a US$300 million hydro-electric dam in Maputo to supply both water and electricity to the capital. Ultimately, the Chinese backed away from funding this enterprise too, again, without the rationale being made public.

In 2012, it was announced that China Exim Bank is to finance a significant part of two major infrastructure projects in Maputo. The first one is the ring-road around Maputo (74 kilometres) with an estimated cost of US$400 million and the second is the bridge linking Maputo to Catembe (US$1.1 billion). According to Chinese official sources the loans will not be fully concessional as part of that credit is to be extended in commercial terms.[3] Finally, in 2013, the same Chinese bank signed another agreement with the Mozambican government to lend US$416.5 million to finance the rehabilitation of 286 kilometres of Beira-Machipanda road over the Beira corridor, one of the most important links between Mozambique, Zimbabwe, Malawi and Zambia (*China Daily* 2013).

Energy and mining

Mozambique has, since the 1990s, concentrated on attracting foreign investment for large projects in order to jump-start the post-war economic recovery. Investments into the country's natural resources have seen the creation of mega-projects like the Mozal aluminium smelter, the Kenmare mineral sands, the Sasol natural gas pipeline, the Moatize coal mines and the Corridor Sands Titanium project. Foreign trade has, therefore, in addition to the Cahora Bassa hydro-electric facility, been dominated by these projects. Mozambique has also begun discussing the possibility of China investing in its energy sector, mainly natural gas and coal reserves (Reuters 2008), but so far no agreement has been reached.

Foreign companies are currently prospecting for oil in the Rovuma Basin, near the Tanzanian border, which is believed to have onshore and offshore deposits. In terms of other hydro-carbon exploration, there are already four proven gas fields in Mozambique, the Pande, Temane, Buzi, and Inhassoro, and the exploration of the first two is currently being conducted by Sasol. In 2010, Wuhan Iron and Steel (WISCO) signed an agreement with Riversdale Mining Ltd to purchase 40% stake of this Australian Company in Tete province. Apparently and for unclear reasons this agreement was not completed. In 2013, the Chinese National Petroleum Corporation (CNPC) acquired a stake in ENI East Africa

---

3 Interview, Chinese Economic Counselor, Maputo, 17 February 2012.

for US$4.21 billion in March 2013, giving it 20% in Area 4 and an opportunity to engage in exploration for natural gas (Silkroad Finance 2013). As of early 2012, Chinese engagement in the mineral sector was not very significant. Aside from a couple of small private miners active in gold mining and trading, there is only one company, the China Qingho Group, that holds an exploration licence for coal in Tete (they also interested in prospecting for coal in Niassa province), and none active in the natural gas sector. China Qingho is interested in building a coal power plant and has signed a Memorandum of Understanding with the government for the construction of a railway and a port facility in Sofala province. Despite the manifest interest, Chinese companies are crippled by the fact that they are latecomers and are seeking to partner up with local companies and established foreign operators in an effort to access this opportunity.

Forestry and fisheries
Mozambique's forests are one of the country's greatest resources with 19 million hectares of productive woodland where highly valuable slow-growing tropical hardwoods like umbilla, jambirre, chanfuta and African sandalwood are found. China's logging activities have become one of the most controversial aspects of its engagement with Mozambique considering how these are colluding with sustainable development and environment policies. Mozambique is currently China's lead supplier of wood in East Africa, although most of the timber is illegally exported as unprocessed logs, a strategy pursued with the assistance of locals. In the province of Zambézia alone an estimated 94 000 cubic metres of logs were exported to China in 2006 while according to one source, 85% of the timber shipped from Cabo Delgado province between 2000 and 2005 had China as its final destination. Chinese logging companies are also operating in the provinces of Nampula, Niassa and Inhambane. The partnership between local communities and Chinese timber buyers begins with the acquisition by a Mozambican national of a simple licence that allows logging to take place in small quantities in determined areas. The cost of these licences, estimated at US$15 000, is covered by the Chinese partner. The local partner then transports the logs to port cities where the Chinese buyer is waiting either with ships or in smaller vessels that will transport the merchandise to cargo ships that wait in international waters. Authorities lack the capacity to effectively patrol the 2500 kilometres of coastline.

Several policies and programmes have been adopted by the government aimed at sustainable forest management and the development of industries in the forestry sector to combat poverty. The Africa Forest Law Enforcement and Governance initiative (AFLEG) was adhered to in 2004 as a commitment to tackle illegal logging, trade and corruption. Several national institutions have also been created to handle this problem. However, the local media continues to view this problem as one where Chinese companies involved in the illegal extraction of timber are associated with groups of powerful Mozambicans and senior government officials that have concessions and are becoming partners in several of these private companies.

Local regulations regarding the unprocessed export of logs aim to compel foreign investors to set up processing facilities in the country and promote community-based enterprises. Legislation protecting the export of the main commercial species of timber therefore exists but has been undermined by the passing of a special regulation – the ministerial diploma – that reclassified commercial timber to permit their export as logs (Lemos & Ribeiro 2006). Having a licence does not therefore guarantee responsible exploitation and the enforcement of regulations. Concessions are the second type of logging licence that can be awarded to foreigners, where a large area of land can be exploited in accordance with sustainability and assessment plans. These types of licences are easier to regulate because of the bureaucratic and legal procedures required for a company to become a concession holder. The lack of incentives to follow these processes leads to many loggers opting to operate using simple licences and therefore avoid detection.

The problem is aggravated by the lack of monitoring mechanisms where reporting is rare, as are inspections and the ability to enforce quotas. Forest regulations are manipulated, bribes are common, and the falsifying of information and statistics facilitate illegal logging. In January 2008, 750 containers of logs were abandoned in the port of Nacala in the north after inspection teams began investigating allegations of corruption in customs officials. The containers belonging to Chinese companies were seized and the customs tribunal issued a fine of US$556 000 to eight of these companies. The Chinese buyers would be allowed to export the wood, worth US$7 million, after paying the fine and processing the logs. The companies opted for the cheaper option, which was to abandon the containers. This was the first fine ever awarded: an indication of greater law enforcement and that the government was becoming more responsive. Two forestry officials in the Zambézia province accused of conniving with TTTimber, a Chinese company, were arrested for the illegal export of 30 containers of unprocessed wood. When the containers were seized there was a public auction and the logs were sold for more than US$16 600. An inspection in July 2011 revealed 561 containers with illegal timber belonging to six Chinese or Chinese-Mozambican companies. (Picarra 2012:27–28) Despite the encouraging developments, illegal logging continues through poorly controlled ports in the central and northern provinces leading some to speculate that senior political interests may be involved and there is no clear evidence that fines made against the country are being paid.

According to the Environment Ministry, what is also lacking is an adequate and updated inventory of the forests, which should be conducted every five years so that there is a register of which areas are being explored and the quantities of trees being cut. This would allow the Ministry a greater ability to monitor each of the concession areas. Unfortunately, the last survey was done ten years ago and the government lacks the resources to conduct these studies, which in the past were carried out by cooperation partners (Roque 2009). What has emerged because of this is a large national campaign against illegal logging and pressure is mounting on the government to take action regarding this. Negative reactions have become widespread because this sort of practice further undermines the possibility of activating local industries and the creation of employment and is depriving the country of potential tax revenues. The result was the public seizure of 900 cubic metres of precious unprocessed hardwood in a small port in Cabo Delgado, destined for illegal export to China, in October 2008 (AIM 2008). This followed on the detention of two provincial officials allegedly involved in undervaluing and disguising timber exports.

Fisheries is also a sector that provides Mozambique with significant foreign exchange earnings, but has the potential to have a greater impact on the country's gross domestic product (GDP) with the development of shrimp, oyster, mussels, algae and pearl aquaculture. The commercial fishing of seafood, mainly shrimp, accounts for 3% of the country's GDP and employs nearly 100 000 people, most of whom are artisan fisherman. The Chinese have been accused of illegal fishing by using methods that catch turtles and sharks, like longlines and gillnets, and contribute to the degradation of coastal areas (though there are rumours that, in fact, these are Taiwanese vessels). Civil society groups claim that Chinese fishing vessels are involved in large-scale poaching of shrimp and lobster and other species of fish. Mozambican authorities struggle to patrol the coastline and enforce the law stipulating that industrial fishing can only occur 12 miles from the coast with just ten patrol boats.

Banking and investment from Macau
In early 2008, it was announced that a new bank would be opening in Mozambique with the capital from China's Administrative Region of Macau, and Portugal. The majority shareholder is Geocapital, a company created as an investment vehicle in Lusophone Africa, set up by the billionaire Stanley Ho from Macau. Moza Banco had an alleged initial capital of US$10 million and focused on investment banking although it has been given a licence to operate as a universal bank (Meyer et al 2011). There were in total 150 investors, most of

whom were Mozambican individuals who would control 51% of the bank. The former governor of the Bank of Mozambique, Prakash Ratilal, was appointed Chairman of Moza Bank (see the Alves chapter in this volume). According to Horta (2008), Geocapital established Zamcorp, Moza Capital and Moza Bank to explore potential agricultural and biofuels projects in the Zambezi valley. However, in the first months of 2013 it was announced that Geocapital sold its stake in Moza Banco to Banco Espírito Santo Africa, a subsidiary of Portuguese Banco Espírito Santo Group (Quintã 2013).

Development assistance and areas for future cooperation
President Armando Guebuza declared that China is 'a partner not a coloniser' and that he is satisfied with the relationship (Robinson 2012:7). While calling for further collaboration with China, the Mozambican president is quoted as having stated that while the current agreements between the two countries are valuable in complementing the efforts of the Mozambican people they will not address all the challenges faced in the struggle against poverty. The Mozambican government, together with its donors and international financial institutions, has vowed to take action and implement policies and programmes aimed at poverty alleviation. These include the Action Plan for the Reduction of Absolute Poverty (PARPA), the National Agricultural Programme (PROAGRI), and the passing of several recent laws and regulations citing sustainable forest management and the development of forest industries as a fundamental step towards combating poverty. One of the areas that China has expressed interest in is through promoting investment and development of the country's agricultural sector, the production of biofuels and the provision of technical expertise and capital in the creation of Special Economic Zones (SEZs).

Agriculture
With an estimated 36 million hectares of arable land, a network of 60 rivers, and a wide diversity of soil types and climatic conditions, the agricultural potential of Mozambique is massive. The majority of the population depends on agriculture for subsistence and employment but the underdeveloped sector is not yet contributing to rural development or poverty reduction. Both the Chinese and the Mozambican government agree that the large-scale production of rice in the Zambezi region would be mutually beneficial in terms of helping China address its food insecurity problem and in Mozambique's ability to tap into an underdeveloped source of wealth. Beijing is reported to have pledged to invest US$800 million towards the modernisation of the Mozambican agricultural sector, with the immediate objective of increasing the production

of rice from 100 000 tonnes to 500 000 tonnes yearly in the next five years (Macauhub 2008). The consumption of rice in China has doubled in the last 20 years, bringing annual consumption of rice alone to 75 kilograms per person, while the consumption of other crops like sugar, soya and cereals has seen a 30% increase (Abdullah et al 2005:39). Access to arable lands is therefore a priority for Beijing. China's involvement in the agricultural sector will bring several benefits for the country in terms of its export capacity (given that 90% of the Mozambican diet is comprised of cassava and maize), in terms of rural development with the rehabilitation of infrastructures, and the transfer of skills, technology and expertise.

The highly fertile Zambezi valley, located in Mozambique's central provinces, is being identified by foreign investors as a region where commercial farming can eventually take place. A Memorandum of Understanding was apparently signed in 2006 between the two governments regarding the creation of a large agricultural project that would be run by China and would involve a settler-community of 20 000 Chinese (Horta 2007), though there is as yet no evidence of it being operationalised (see Chapter 6 for details). Joint ventures in the agriculture sector are also being developed, a case in point being the joint project between Mozambique and the China Grains and Oils Group (CGOG) in a soya-processing plant in Beira, worth US$10 million. This model, combining a Mozambican partner, to supply the natural resources (fertile land or mineral-rich land), and a Chinese partner, to provide the capital, technology, knowledge and construction, was originally going to be repeated in the future but the failure of the joint venture has cast a pall over this prospect.

In terms of technical assistance, there was an agreement signed in September 2007 with the Eduardo Mondlane University to conduct research on rural development and agriculture. Subsequent to the Forum on China-Africa cooperation in Beijing 2006, China created the first pilot project in agricultural technology cooperation – the Umbeluzi Institute of Agricultural Research – in Maputo. In addition to the Umbeluzi centre there is also the possibility of building a pilot centre in agricultural technology in the province of Nampula in the north. A group of 100 Chinese experts are also reported to have arrived in Mozambique to assist with an irrigation channel network project in addition to a team from the Hunan Hybrid Rice Institute. China has also funded several other smaller agricultural schools nationwide.

In order for Mozambique to fully leverage the potential of its agriculture sector and achieve agricultural growth, it will need the expertise and investment of countries like China that have the past experience of setting up agricultural research and extension systems and can also offer a market for African exports. Strong pro-poor policies should therefore stem from boosting agricultural and rural development so that large numbers of unskilled labour can be absorbed into small farms. China can again play an important role here with expertise in mechanisation, improved seeds, fertilisers, and irrigation systems.

Special Economic Zones

In terms of expertise transfer, Mozambique has taken active steps in learning about China's Special Economic Zones and using this blueprint to attract foreign investment. Several industrial estates and scientific and technology parks are being considered, with at least one already being built. Coupled to the SADC trade policies, which enable products with 30% value-added to enter without restrictions into the South African market (as well as that of other SADC countries), there are strong incentives to open up manufacturing in Mozambique for those interested in expanding business in the region (Escobar 2011:8–9). In March 2007, a delegation from the Mozambican Ministry of Agriculture, Finance and Development, and the Central Bank spent several weeks in China learning about SEZs. The concept was approved by the Council of Ministers in March 2007 and the first SEZ will be established in Nacala. This SEZ aims to create triangular corridors (development corridors), with assistance from Japan and Vietnam, connecting to Zambia and Tanzania, aimed at maximising the potential of the coastal areas. Nacala will have an oil refinery and other processing plants where the main objective will be to import raw materials and then process them and do the value-adding in Mozambique. An additional oil refinery will be built in the deep sea port of Ponta do Bela in the south, also approved by the Council of Ministers. Chinese companies like the IT giant Lenovo have expressed interest in the creation of these industrial parks so that they can have greater representation in Mozambique with more computer assembly plants and factories.

In September 2010, Shanghai government and business interests sought to establish an industrial park in Matola, on the outskirts of Maputo, that reportedly would include an automobile assembly plant, light industry, housing for Chinese workers and a rehabilitation of the country's main port facilities. Initially, the Chinese initiative seems to have met with some resistance in Mozambican government circles, with concerns being raised about provisions for Chinese labourers, among other issues. Further negotiations with China Tong Chian Investments produced an agreement to establish an automotive plant in Matola. According to the director of the Office for Accelerated Development Economic Zones (Gazeda), the project involves a US$200 million investment, with the automobile plant producing 10 000 vehicles initially and aiming to sell 30% of these to the local market (Escobar 2011:10). More recently, a group of private Chinese entrepreneurs called Dingsheng International Investments

– some of whom are already operating on the border between Zimbabwe and Mozambique – together with a Mozambican partner, have established a special economic zone in Sofala province, in the centre of Mozambique (Trademark Southern Africa 2013) called Mananga-Mungassa. With planned investments totalling US$500 million, the zone will focus on services, as well as manufacturing and food processing (interview, Chinese Economic Counselor 2012). A cotton factory opened in Sofala in September 2012, by a joint Chinese-Mozambican venture called China-Africa Cotton, aims to purchase cotton from local producers (Belchior 2011:16). Another cotton-processing factory opened the same year in Manica province. This factory is part of three processing plants (rice, cotton and maize) that were financed by a China Exim Bank loan. The North and South also have their own SEZs: the Special Economic Zone of Nacala and Beluluane Industrial Park, which it is expected, will also attract Chinese companies.

Mozambique as China's gateway into Africa
Over the longer term, China's interest in resources, infrastructure and the development of Africa as a market in its own right argues for a more strategic engagement with Mozambique. In this regard, Mozambique's position as a key transportation corridor for its neighbouring landlocked countries of Malawi, Zambia and Zimbabwe, with the benefits of a 2000-kilometre coastline and several deepwater ports, makes it an excellent entry point for maritime access. The aforementioned creation of SEZs linked to Mozambique's ports, which themselves are currently being refurbished and upgraded with the expectation that they will become a shipping gateway for Eastern Africa, is a clear signal that Chinese officials and private investors recognise this potential. The port of Pemba could come to compete with the Dar es Salaam and Mombasa ports because of its deep harbour that does not require dredging and handles large cargo ships. The rehabilitation of the harbour infrastructure of Quelimane in the province of Zambézia and the harbour of Nacala in the Nampula province are also potential projects to be financed and constructed by the Chinese. The announcement during President Xi Jinping's visit to Tanzania in April 2013 that China would support a massive port rehabilitation scheme in Dar es Salaam suggests that Maputo may have lost a match to their neighbours.

There are other indications of Chinese interests in utilising Mozambique as a regional hub. According to the Mozambican Planning Ministry, the China Development Bank is said to want to base its regional office in Maputo with the objective of going into Zambia, Zimbabwe and Malawi. The idea is to create a centre for financial decision-making and regional integration in Mozambique by securing funds for the construction of railways to the interior and into other countries (Roque 2009). The CDB's approach confirms designs to use Mozambique as an entry platform into SADC because of its geographic location, ports and resources, and infrastructure necessary to ensure the flow of commodities for export. Certainly the rehabilitation of Maputo as a port has allowed the reassertion of exports from South Africa (which Durban had taken over post-1975) through Mozambique and this enhances its attractiveness.

Conclusion: Mozambican agency – fitting China in or using it for self-enrichment?

African agency is increasingly recognised by scholars working on emerging power relations to be a significant factor in determining outcomes of engagement at both macro and micro levels (Brown & Harman 2013; Alden 2013). The variety of understandings of what constitutes agency, ranging from an analysis of African actors exercising assertiveness in negotiations to a discussion of the formative impact of the African social context within which external powers operate, complicates its meaning without necessarily addressing its normative dimensions (Brown & Harman 2013:2–4, 8). It is bound up with the notion that accounts of African engagement with the external world have underplayed the degree to which African elites have, among other things, actively employed the outside world to accrue resources that enhance their domestic standing and serve the interest of personal accumulation (Clapham 1996; Bayart 2000).

China has, as scholars and politicians alike have noted, enabled African governments to play a more assertive role in negotiations with the Western and Western-dominated international institutions (Brown & Harman 2013:8). By shattering the donor cartel not only over certain practices but the monopoly over ideas of development, the Chinese have provided African governments with a broader range of possibilities that, carefully managed by their policy makers, can translate into new sources of innovation and revenue for development. The context within which China is operating in Mozambique is one that, until the recent discovery of offshore natural gas and other resources set off an investment boom, was dominated economically by a deep dependency on Western donors and international institutions. The institutional and normative impacts of this dependency are still significant, even if they are increasingly under stress, posing challenges for Chinese firms that are accustomed to a more loosely regulated environment at home or in other African countries. At the same time, the rise of new commercial opportunities for Mozambicans has produced a surge of excitement in official circles. The danger, recognised by Mozambicans as well as outsiders, is that these opportunities presented by China can reinforce a trend that is already in danger of transforming the political elite into a business class with predatory intentions.

Having created the new space for new thinking and possibilities, loosely framed under the rubric of 'South-South Cooperation', China's involvement in Mozambique needs to give serious consideration to participating in the economy in ways that align and reinforce the development agenda as articulated in numerous National Planning documents. The Mozambican government, bolstered by growing commercial interests and a vocal civil society, needs to ensure that Chinese resources in the country reflect and support these same development aspirations and programmes. The transformation of Mozambique, using Chinese capital and expertise, coupled with careful management of other foreign interests in the country, could pave the way for a more rapid realisation of long-standing hopes for development. But, concurrently, there is the possibility that the aforementioned African agency will find expression in the elite rent-seeking forms of behaviour. The latter scenario would, unfortunately, do more to entrench patterns of unequal development that have featured in Mozambique's past than initiate the promise of a new future for all.

References

Abdullah, bin Alias, Ito, Shoichi & Adhana, Kelali. 2005. 'Estimates of Rice Consumption in Asian Countries and the World towards 2050'. Available from: www.worldfood2.apionet.org.jp [Accessed on 30 January 2014].

Abrahamsson, Hans. 1997. *Seizing the Opportunity: Power and powerlessness in a changing world order – the case of Mozambique.* Gothenburg: Padrigu.

African Development Bank. 2011. 'Republic of Mozambique – country strategy paper, 2011–2015'. Tunis: AFDB.

Alden, Chris. 2003. *Mozambique and the Construction of the New African State*. Basingstoke: Palgrave.

Alden, Chris. 2013. 'African Agency and the New Multipolarity'. In: Chris Alden, ed. *Emerging Powers in Africa*. LSE-IDEAS Strategic Report, October.

allAfrica. 2008. 'Mozambique: Illegal Export of Logs Prevented', 1 October. Available from: http://allafrica.com/stories/200810020136.html [Accessed on 9 April 2014].

Alvarenga, Daniel. 2008. 'Mozambique-China Relations: Common trends and hints of change'. *China Monitor*, 27, April, Centre for Chinese Studies, Stellenbosch University. Available from: http://www.ccs.org.za/wp-content/uploads/2009/04/china-monitor-march-2008.pdf [Accessed on 30 January 2014].

Alves, Ana Cristina. 2012. 'Chinese Economic and Trade Cooperation Zones in Africa: Facing the challenges'. SAIIA Policy Briefing 15, Braamfontein.

Bayart, Jean-Francoise. 2000. 'Africa in the World: A history of extraversion', *African Affairs*, 99:217–267.

Belchior, Maria Joao. 2011. 'Deeping Ties for the Future: China and Mozambique'. *Macao*, 9, October.

Bila, Alberto Teodoro. 2007. 'Chinese Capital in Mozambique: Critical assessment of Chinese assistance to Mozambique'. AFRODAD.

Bosten, Emmy. 2006. 'China's Engagement in the Construction Industry of Southern Africa: The case of Mozambique'. Paper for the workshop 'Asian and Other Drivers of Global Change', St Petersburg. Available from: www.eldis.org/vfile/upload/1/document/0708/

DOC22157.pdf [Accessed on 30 January 2014].
Broadman, Harry. 2007. *Africa's Silk Road*. Washington DC: World Bank.
Brown, William & Harman, Sophie. 2013. *African Agency in International Politics*. London: Routledge.
Chichava, Sérgio. 2008. 'Mozambique and China: From politics to business?' *Discussion Paper 5*, Maputo: IESE.
Chichava, Sérgio. 2013. 'Xai-Xai Chinese Rice Farm and Mozambican Internal Political Dynamics: A complex relation'. Occasional Paper 2, LSE IDEAS Africa Programme.
China Daily. 2013. 'China Exim Bank Lends Mozambique $416.5m for Road Rehabilitation'. Available from: www.chinadaily.com.cn/business/2013-11/16/content_17110186.htm [Accessed on 20 November 2013].
Clapham, Christopher. 1996. *Africa and the International System*. Cambridge: Cambridge University Press.
Club of Mozambique. 2012. Investimento directo estrangeiro em 2011 atingiu cinco mil milhoes USD, 23 March. Available from: www.clubofmozambique.com/pt/sectionnews.php p?secao=investimento&id=21654&tipo=one [Accessed in May 2014].
Corkin, Lucy. 2012. 'Angolan Political Elites Management of Chinese Credit Lines'. In: Marcus Powers & Ana Cristina Alves, eds. *China and Angola: A marriage of convenience?* Cape Town: Pambazuka.
CSIS Invest-Tripartite.Org. 2013. 'Mphanda-Nkuwa Hydropower Project Brief', 29 May. Available from: invest-tripartite.org/wp-content/uploads/2013/06/9-Mphanda-Nkuwa-Hydgropower-Project-Brief-29-05-2013.pdf [Accessed on 22 October 2013].
Escobar, Antonia. 2011. 'Full Speed Ahead: China-Mozambique relations get a big boost from President Guebuza visit', *Macao*, 9, October.
Government of Mozambique (GoM). 2010. *Balanço do Plano Económico e Social de 2009*, Maputo: Government of Mozambique.
GoM. 2011a. *Balanço do Plano Económico e Social de 2010*. Maputo: Government of Mozambique.
GoM. 2011b. *Matriz dos projectos com a República Popular da China*. Maputo: Government of Mozambique.
Hanlon, Joseph. 1991. *Who Calls the Shots?* Bloomington: Indiana University.
Hanlon, Joseph. 2000. 'Power without Responsibility: The World Bank and Mozambican cashew nuts'. *Review of African Political Economy*, 27(83): 29-45.
Horta, Loro. 2008. 'China's relations with Mozambique: A mixed blessing'. Online Africa Policy Forum.
Jackson, S. 1995. 'China's Third World Foreign Policy: The case of Angola and Mozambique, 1961-93'. *The China Quarterly*, 142:388-422.
Jansson, Johanna & Kiala, Carla. 2009. 'Patterns of Chinese Investment, Aid and Trade in Mozambique'. Centre for Chinese Studies, Stellenbosch University, October.
Lemos, Annabela & Ribeiro, Daniel. 2006. 'Mozambique: Taking ownership or just changing owners?' December. Available from: http://www.pambazuka.org/en/category/comment/38847 [Accessed on 9 April 2014].
Macauhub. 2008. 'China and Mozambique invest in the Zambezi valley to make Chinese "grain store"', says researcher', 21 July. Statements by Loro Horta. Available from: http://www.macauhub.com.mo [Accessed on 30 January 2014].
Macauhub. 2009. 'Mozambique: China second largest investor in 2008 after South Africa', 27 March. Available from: www.macauhub.com.mo/en/2009/03/27/6795/ [Accessed on 39 April 2014.].
Macauhub. 2010. 'Grupo chinês vai pagar formação de estudantes de Moçambique na China'. Available from: www.macauhub.com.mo/pt/2010/11/09/grupo-chines-vai-pagar-

formacao-de-estudantes-de-mocambique-na-china [Accessed on 30 January 2014].
Mafalda Ferreira Picarra. 2012. 'Revisiting Sino-Mozambican Cooperation: China's inroads into the agriculture and Forestry sectors'. *African East-Asian Affairs. The China Moniter*, 72, June, Centre for Chinese Studies. Available from http://www.ccs.org.za/wp-content/uploads/2012/06/China_Monitor_JUNE_2012_FINAL.pdf [Accessed on 9 April 2014]
Meyer, Riaan, Alao, Abiodun, Alden, Chris & Alves, Ana Cristina. 2011. 'Chinese Financial Institutions in Africa'. SAIIA Occasional Paper 103, December, Braamfontein.
MINEC. 2007a. *Acta acordada da Terceira Sessão da Comissão Conjunta para a cooperação Económica, Técnica e Comercial entre a República de Moçambique e a República Popular da China*. Maputo: Ministry of Foreign Affairs.
MINEC. 2007b. *Avaliação do grau do cumprimento da implementação do Plano de Acção dos resultados da visita de S. Excia. o presidente da República Popular da China à República de Moçambique*. Maputo: Ministry of Foreign Affairs.
MINEC. 2010. *Relatório da participação de Moçambique na III Conferência para a Cooperação Económica e Comercial entre a China e os Países de Língua Portuguesa e respectiva matriz de seguimento*. Maputo: Ministry of Foreign Affairs.
Njal, Jorge. 2012. 'The "Chinese Connection" in Mozambique's Hosting the 2011 Maputo All-Africa Games'. *African East-Asian Affairs. The China Monitor*, 72, June, Centre for Chinese Studies. Available from: http://www.ccs.org.za/wp-content/uploads/2012/06/China_Monitor_JUNE_2012_FINAL.pdf [Accessed on 9 April 2014].
OECD-DAC. 2008. *African Economic Outlook*. Paris: OECD.
O País. 2009a. 'China incrementa cooperação com as FADM'. *Maputo, 25 March*.
O País. 2009b. 'Moçambique vai adquirir novo equipamento militar'. *Maputo, 20 May*.
O País. 2010. 'Chineses vão formar cem estudantes moçambicanos anualmente'. Maputo, 9 November.
Pitcher, Anne. 2002. *Transforming Mozambique: The politics of privatization, 1975–2000*. Cambridge: Cambridge Africa.
Portal of the Government of Mozambique. 2010. 'Em 2011: China concede três milhões de dólares às FADM', 29 December. Available from: www.portaldogoverno.gov.mz/ noticias/news_folder_politica/dezembro-2010/em-2011-china-concede-tres-milhoes-de-dolares-as-fadm/ [Accessed on 12 March 2011].
Quintã, Victor. 2013. 'Stanley Ho's Firm Sheds Mozambique Bank Stake'. Available from: macaubusinessdaily.com/Business/Stanley-Ho%E2%80%99s-firm-sheds-Mozambique-bank-stake [Accessed on 20 November 2013].
Reuters. 2007. 'Mozambique sees Pemba challenging African ports'. *Engineering News*, November. Available from: www.engineeringnews.com [Accessed on 30 January 2014].
Reuters. 2008. 'Mozambique Says in Talks with China for Energy Investment', 28 January. Statements by Energy Minister Salvador Namburete. Available from: http://guetalisadc.blogspot.com/2007/11/mozambique-sees-pemba-challenging.html [Accessed on 9 April 2014].
Robinson, David Alexander. 2012. 'Chinese Engagement with Africa: The case of Mozambique'. *Portuguese Journal of International Affairs*, Spring/September.
Roque, Paula Cristina. 2009. 'China in Mozambique: A cautious approach'. SAIIA Occasional Paper 24, Braamfontein.
SADC Review. 2007. 'Country Profiles: Mozambique agriculture'. Available from: www.sadcreview.com/country_profiles/mozambique/moz_agriculture.htm [Accessed on 30 January 2014].
Silkroad Finance. 2013. 'Mozambique Outlook 2013'. Available from: www.silkroadfin.com/news/mozambique-outlook-2013. [Accessed on 30 January 2014.]
Taylor, Ian. 2006. *China and Africa Engagement and Compromise*. London: Routledge.

Trademark Southern Africa. 2013. 'Beira's Special Economic Zone Boosts Relations between Mozambique and China', 27 March. Available from: www.trademarksa.org/news/beira-special-economic-zone-boosts-relations-between-mozambique-and-china [Accessed on 24 October 2013].

World Bank Indicators (2014), wdi.worldbank.org/table/2.8 http://wdi.worldbank.org/table/2.8 http://wdi.worldbank.org/table/2.8 [Accessed on 14 April 2014].

Xinhua. 2008. Tian Guangfeng, Chinese ambassador to Mozambique, interview 10 July. Available from: www.xinhuanet.com/english/2008-07/11/content_8528377.htm [Accessed on 30 January 2014].

Interviews

Senior Frelimo official, April 2008.
Residents of stadium housing, September 2011.
Chinese Economic Counselor, Maputo, April 2012.

Chapter 2
Assessing Chinese Investment in Mozambique

Sérgio Chichava

Among the so-called 'emerging countries' operating in Africa today, it is China whose presence in Mozambique has generated the most debate in the various segments of society. China is viewed as a 'strategic partner' in assisting Mozambique – one of the poorest countries in the world and heavily dependent on aid from the international community – and so the Mozambican government has attached great importance to cooperation with China. For example, the former prime minister of Mozambique, Aires Ali, made China his first official visit to a foreign country. Furthermore, the Mozambican government has gone to considerable efforts to build a positive image of the Chinese presence in Mozambique, which has been seriously called into question by several scandals concerning Chinese companies involved in various contraband resources, particularly timber.[1] For example, when Chinese doctors operated on the cataracts of 300 Mozambican patients, the president of Mozambique, Armando Guebuza, one of the major defenders of cooperation with China, stated that this action was further proof that those who criticised the cooperation between Mozambique and China 'didn't know what they were talking about and were raving' (*O País* 2011).[2]

Statistics from the Investment Promotion Centre (CPI)[3] for recent years show that the Chinese economic presence in Mozambique has been growing year after year, placing this 'emergent economy' among the ten largest investors in Mozambique from 2007 to the time of writing. Based on the data from the CPI, this chapter will analyse the weight, the distribution (geographical and by sector), the significance and the trends of Chinese investment in the Mozambican economy in the period 2000–2010. This is the period between the first China-Africa ministerial summit, held in October 2000 in

---
1 On this matter, see Mackenzie (2006).
2 This Chinese aid formed part of the project China-Africa Brightness Action, with the aim of curing patients with cataracts. It has been undertaken in other African countries, namely Zimbabwe and Malawi.
3 A state body subordinate to the Ministry of Planning and Development (MPD) and responsible for coordinating the promotion, analysis, follow-up and verification of the foreign investment made in Mozambique.

Beijing (which concluded with the creation of the Forum on China-Africa Cooperation – FOCAC) and the celebration, in 2010, of the tenth anniversary of this institution. Analysing the sector and regional distribution, based on the CPI information, of the Chinese investment projects authorised between 2000 and 2010, it is intended here to show the trend and the impact of Chinese direct investment on Mozambique during this period. It should be stressed that this deals only with investment projects submitted to the CPI for approval, and not all Chinese investment projects in Mozambique during the period under study. This is because submitting an investment project to the CPI for approval is optional, since opening and registering a company, and the subsequent obtaining of a licence to exercise the activity from the Ministry of Industry and Trade (MIC) or from the local state bodies and municipalities, is sufficient to do business in Mozambique (Conselho de Ministros 2004). The advantage of submitting the project to the CPI lies in obtaining the tax and customs incentives enshrined in Law no. 3/93 (Investments Law) and in the Fiscal Benefits Codes (Conselho de Ministros 2002).

This chapter is divided into two parts. The first is a brief survey of the various areas of cooperation between Mozambique and China, while the second maps the structure of the Chinese direct foreign investment (FDI) in Mozambique.

Short survey of China-Mozambique economic relations

The signing of an agreement on trade and on the Promotion and Reciprocal Protection of Investment, and the establishment of a Joint Economic and Trade Commission in 2001 may be regarded as the first two landmark events in relaunching the cooperation between Mozambique and China in the wake of FOCAC 2000. In the same year, and in the framework of the decisions emerging from FOCAC 2000, China announced that it was cancelling US$22 million of Mozambique's public foreign debt, which was 69% of Mozambique's total public debt with China (*People's Daily* 2001). In 2007, during Hu Jintao's visit to Mozambique, China pardoned a further US$20 million of Mozambique's public foreign debt. The amount cancelled now stood at 87.1% of the debt contracted by Mozambique between 1980 and 2005 (AIM 2007a). In 2008, Mozambique's foreign public debt to China was calculated at US$2.9 million (TA 2009).

Although it is difficult to quantify the total value of Chinese aid to Mozambique because of the scarcity of information, there are signs that the aid from China has been considerable. For example, during his visit to China, Aires Ali stated that China was willing to finance various projects in Mozambique to the tune of about US$172 million, in the form of grants, interest-free loans, and low interest loans (AIM 2010).

In terms of bilateral cooperation, China supports Mozambique in various areas, namely defence and security, health, education, agriculture, and infrastructures, among others. This support is provided in the shape of grants, technical assistance, and loans at no or low interest.[4]

Trade between the two countries has been undergoing accelerated growth. While, in 2002, the official data indicated that this trade was worth about US$48 million, in 2009 it was worth about US$517 million (MFAPRC 2006; China Tong Jian Investment Co Ltd 2010). Mozambique's main exports to China are timber, sesame, cashew nuts and other agricultural and mineral products (China Tong Jian Investment Co Ltd 2010). According to the Bank of Portugal (2011), between 2004 and 2010, China accounted for just 2.2% of Mozambique's total exports, and at this time was the fourth largest destination for Mozambican products. The first three positions were occupied by Holland (55.8%), South Africa (16.1%) and Zimbabwe (2.9%).

Among these goods, timber is the main product exported by Mozambique to China. It has been the subject of great controversy, with some segments of Mozambican society believing that the Chinese timber business in Mozambique is a real act of looting. In 2006, timber accounted for more than 90% of Mozambique's exports to China (Canby et al 2008). In 2009, China remained the main destination for Mozambican timber Government of Mozambique (GoM) (2011b).

As for Mozambique's main imports from China, these include manufactured goods, mainly vehicles and spare parts, electrical goods and iron and steel articles (Jansson & Kiala 2010). According to the Bank of Portugal (2011), between 2004 and 2010, 3.4% of Mozambique's imports came from China, which put it behind South Africa (35.2%) and Holland (14.8%).

The Chinese presence in Mozambique took on a new impetus with the visit to Mozambique of Chinese President Hu Jintao in February 2007. Just to give an idea of the importance of this, Chinese FDI in Mozambique rose from US$905 000 in 2006, to US$61.15 million in 2007, the year in which China came to figure among the ten largest investors in Mozambique. Hu Jintao visited, in addition to Mozambique, a further seven African countries, and through the China Exim Bank granted credits for various areas of around

---

4 According to Braütigam (2011, 2010, 2009), in general the Chinese aid programme is coordinated by the Foreign Aid Department of the Ministry of Trade, in collaboration with the Ministry of Foreign Affairs. The Foreign Aid Department deals with grants, loans with zero interest, programmes of young volunteers and technical assistance. Soft loans, with low or fixed interest rates, are provided by the China Exim Bank, under the management of the Ministry of Trade. Because the grants and the loans with zero interest are an instrument of diplomacy, they are granted to all countries that have diplomatic relations with China. The soft loans from the China Exim Bank have three goals, namely diplomacy, development and business.

US$177 million (GoM 2011a).[5] In Mozambique, among the various projects covered are the rehabilitation and modernisation of Maputo International Airport, the first phase of which has now ended (US$50 million); the project to expand the fixed telephone networks to all districts in the country (US$21.4 million); the construction of three buildings for the Attorney-General's Office (US$40 million); and support for agricultural development in Tete, Manica, Sofala and Zambézia provinces – that is, in the Zambezi valley ($US50 million). Of this fund, US$30 million dollars was used to build three agro-processing factories in the provinces of Tete (Angónia district), Zambézia (Namacurra district) and Manica (Guro district), and the remainder in the import of equipment (GoM 2011a).

Between 2007 and 2010, China made several grants to Mozambique – namely, support for flood victims (US$400 000); construction of four schools in Maputo, Gaza, Nampula and Niassa (CNY20 million, equivalent to about US$3 million, in January 2012); construction of an agricultural technology centre in Boane, Maputo province; and construction of a malaria prevention and treatment centre in Maputo (GoM 2011a). These two latter undertakings are part of the Chinese list of promises made to African countries during FOCAC 2006 (FOCAC 2010). Indeed, at this forum, China promised that it would set up 20 agricultural technology centres in the same number of African countries, in order to help develop African agriculture.[6] China also promised that it would set up 30 malaria prevention and treatment centres in various countries. Further Chinese grants included the donation of office equipment to the Mozambican parliament (CNY500 000, about US$80 000, in January 2012) and 72 buses for public transport, valued at US$8.7 million (FOCAC 2010). This was not the first time that China had supported the Mozambican parliament: the Mozambican parliament building was built in 1999 with Chinese aid. In 2008, there was also talk of likely Chinese funding to build a residential neighbourhood for Mozambican parliamentary deputies (*Notícias* 2008).

It is also important to note that Mozambique benefits from soft loans from the China Exim Bank to overcome its deficit in public infrastructures. Thus out of a list of 21 projects (valued at US$1.398 billion) regarded as priorities by Mozambique and submitted to the Chinese government for analysis and later funding, more than 60% are in the infrastructure sector, namely: the second phase of the rehabilitation and modernisation of Maputo International

---

5 In addition to Mozambique, Hu Jintao's African tour included Seychelles, Cameroon, Liberia, Sudan, Zambia, Namibia and South Africa.
6 Initially, China was willing to finance seven agricultural technology centres. The number was increased to 14 and is now up to 20.

Airport (US$64.4 million); 900 kilometres of electricity transmission line linking Zambézia and Nampula provinces (US$150 million); construction of a building for the Council of Ministers (US$48.7 million); construction of residences for officers of the State Security and Information Service (SISE) (valued at US$53 million); sports facilities (US$27.2 million); and various roads (US$544 million) (MINEC 2010; GoMa 2011).

Mozambique could also benefit from the construction of a railway linking Tete and Sofala provinces thanks to a partnership between the Mozambican state and the company China Qingho Group. The purpose of this line is to facilitate the movement of coal from Tete. Also as part of this partnership, the China Qingho Group could undertake the dredging of the port of Beira, which is severely affected by silting (MINEC 2010).

Looking at this list, one understands that apart from the various partnerships of a commercial nature, Mozambique is relying on China to finance some projects which, *a priori*, would be difficult for the so-called 'traditional' donors to fund. And this is why China is a country appreciated by the Mozambican political elite. As Mozambique's former prime minister, Luísa Diogo, said, China has supported Mozambique without 'pre-conditions' in various areas, unlike the countries which support the General State Budget (AIM 2007b). According to Diogo, unlike the 'traditional' donors, 'when we say that the Attorney-General's Office is a priority in Mozambique, they [the Chinese] agree with us' (AIM 2007b). In other words, China is seen as a partner who does not impose conditions on the way in which Mozambique should conduct its policies.

However, it should be stressed that, despite this positive vision, there is an awareness on the part of the Mozambican elite that, while China does not interfere in the internal affairs of Mozambique, it imposes certain conditions in matters of development aid. That is, when Luísa Diogo says that there are no 'pre-conditions' for China to grant aid, she is referring only to 'pre-conditions' of a political order, notably the question of good governance, because in fact, like any other donor, Beijing also has its 'pre-conditions'. But, unlike the so-called 'traditional' donors, in the Chinese case the pre-conditions are of an economic nature. Sustaining this argument, for example, is the statement by Luísa Diogo, according to which, in order for it to grant aid, 'China wants Mozambique to give some guarantees, such as natural resources' (Hanlon 2010; *Diário de Moçambique* 2010).

In this regard, one should cite the fact that the Chinese government is not financing the Mphanda Nkuwa and Moamba Major dams – projects proposed by the government of Armando Guebuza with the aim of transforming Mozambique into a regional leader in the generation and export of electricity –

because the guarantees were insufficient.[7] The Mphanda Nkuwa and Moamba Major dams, construction of which was estimated to cost US$2 billion and US$300 million, respectively, were part of an initial list of seven projects agreed between the Mozambican government and the China Exim Bank in 2006, which also included an agro-processing and seed production industry in the Zambezi valley, the rehabilitation of Maputo International Airport, and the construction of public buildings, of a technology development centre and of a national stadium (MPD 2006; MF 2006). Of this list of projects, only the two dams were not granted funding – Mphanda Nkuwa would have been financed in the form of Export Buyer's Credit and Moamba Major through a soft loan.

This means that, as much as Mozambique may recognise the 'strategic' importance of China, it does not neglect its 'traditional' partners, as can be seen in this statement by Luísa Diogo:

> We should not close our eyes and forget our traditional partners. But we need cooperation with China, and also with India. (Hanlon 2010; *Diário de Moçambique* 2010)

Despite the pre-conditions mentioned above, it must be recognised that Chinese openness towards funding projects that are not among the priorities of the 'traditional donors' can play a relevant role in the stability of African countries. It may be said, for example, that financing the construction of houses for high-ranking figures in the Mozambican army may certainly have contributed to boosting their morale. The same can also be said about the desire expressed by the Mozambican government for the granting of a loan to build houses for Mozambican secret service agents.

Weight and significance of Chinese investment in Mozambique

As mentioned above, various studies and Mozambican official sources indicate that China is one of the countries that is investing most heavily in Mozambique. What is most important here is to show the significance of this investment, since this analysis allows us to have a clear idea not only about the pattern of Chinese investment in Mozambique, but also about its trends. In the final analysis, this allows us to have a better understanding of the Chinese presence in Mozambique. In the 2000–2010 period, Chinese investment in the country amounted to about US$216.5 million, which is about 2% of the total foreign

---

7 One of the strategies of Armando Guebuza's government rested on building hydro-electric dams, the electricity from which would be exported. With this purpose in mind, in addition to Mphanda Nkuwa, hydro-electric power stations have been projected at Lúrio, Massingir and Moamba Major, and thermal power stations at Moatize and Temane.

Table 1.2 Total number of jobs generated

Country	Jobs		FDI	
	No.	%	No.	%
Others	207 860	95	10 612 290	98
China	9 914	4.5	216 524	2
Total	217 774	100	10 828 814	100

investment undertaken nationally, which, in the same period, was about US$10.6 billion. If all the investment projects authorised were implemented, they would have generated 9 914 jobs, the equivalent of 4.5% of the total number of jobs generated over the same period by the rest of the FDI (see Table 2.1).

In sector terms, much of Chinese investment in Mozambique is concentrated in manufacturing industry (77%), followed by aquaculture and fisheries (12%), and agriculture and agro-industry and construction (4%) (see Graph 2.1).

The manufacturing industry also accounts for the majority of the jobs created by Chinese investment (57%), followed by agriculture and agro-industry (26%), and construction (11%) (Graph 2.2).

In regional terms, 91% of Chinese investment is concentrated in Maputo, in southern Mozambique, followed by the central province of Sofala, with just 4% (Graph 2.3).

Likewise, most of the jobs created by Chinese investment are in Maputo, followed by Cabo Delgado and Sofala provinces (Graph 2.4).

During the period under analysis, four investment projects, three in the industrial sector and another in aquaculture and fisheries, represented about 80% of Chinese FDI. Of these four, two stand out also as examples of the alliance between Chinese capital and the new Mozambican bourgeoisie, formed by figures close to the Frelimo party.[8]

The four investments are:

(i) a cement factory (Africa Great Wall Cement Manufacturer), to be located in Marracuene, in Maputo province, with an investment of US$90 million (FDI = 45 million). This investment, approved in 2007, envisages the creation of 300 jobs;

(ii) the CIF-Moz Limitada cement factory, a joint-venture between

---

[8] Alliance with foreign capital has been one of the forms used by the new Mozambican bourgeoisie to implant itself in the world of business in Mozambique. The alliance between Chinese business people and the Mozambican political elites is no secret. The best known and most polemical example is the alliance in the timber sector. But there are signs of strong links in other sectors, particularly in mineral resources. Because of its importance, this matter deserves a deeper study which is not the subject of this chapter.

SPI – Gestão e Investimentos, SARL, the Frelimo Party holding company, and the China International Fund (CIF). This factory will be built in Matutuíne in Maputo province and the investment is estimated at US$72 million (FDI = 71.99 million). It was approved in 2008;

(iii) the Hong & Binga Development Fishery Company, which, among various activities, intends to undertake industrial fishing and naval construction. This company, with an investment of US$27 million (FDI = 26 million), and a plan to create 80 jobs, is an association between the Chinese company Poly Fuzhou Hongyong Pelagic Fishery Co. Ltd, and Monte Binga, SA, a Mozambican company owned 50% by the state. The other 50% is held by Mozambican generals on the reserve list belonging to Frelimo (Boletim da República 2009a). In addition to aquaculture and fisheries, Monte Binga, SA, is involved in other activities such as, for example, the exploitation of gold and other minerals in Niassa province (Boletim da República 2010); and

(iv) Henan Haode Mozambique Industrial Park, which seeks to set up a textile and clothing factory in Marracuene district, valued at US$26.5 million (FDI = 21.2 million). Corresponding to about 55% of all Chinese investment in this period, this was the largest Chinese investment project approved by the CPI in 2010.

Mineral resources: new focus of Chinese investment?

If the period 2000–2010, Chinese FDI was dominated by the manufacturing industry sector in 2011 and 2012, CPI data shows important changes oscillating between construction and tourism sectors. Equally, 2011 appears to be the most important year of Chinese FDI in Mozambique since 2007, the year in which China started to be part of the tenth most important investors in the country. In that year, Chinese FDI reached US$312.8 million, which is 32% of all FDI in Mozambique that year. Also in that year the construction sector represented almost 80% of all Chinese FDI. This was due to the construction of 5 000 houses between the Mozambican State represented by Fundo para o Fomento da Habitação (FFH), and the Chinese company Henan Guoji Industry and Development Co Ltd in Matola, on the outskirts of Maputo. This project intends to provide Mozambican youth and public servants with houses at affordable prices.

As stated above, in 2012 the tourism sector with 47% and the agriculture sector with 44% were the main targets of Chinese FDI in Mozambique. In that year, United Arab Emirates, South Africa and Mauritius respectively were

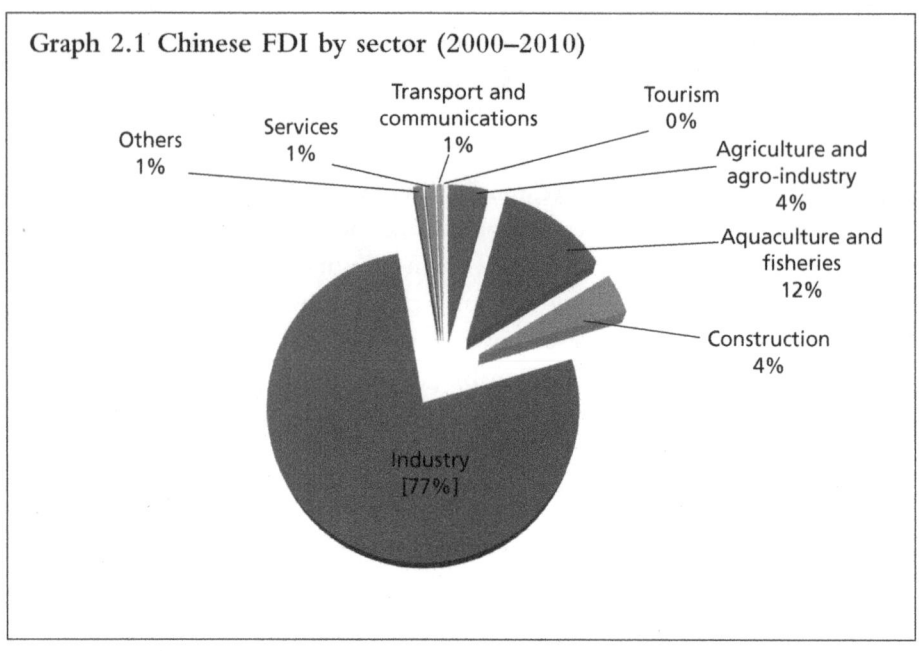

Graph 2.1 Chinese FDI by sector (2000–2010)

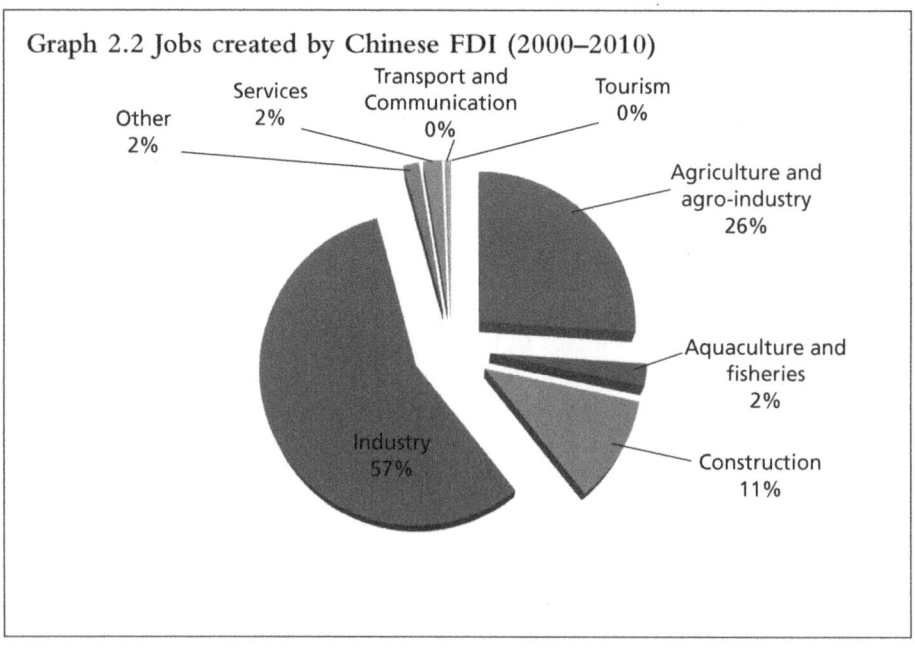

Graph 2.2 Jobs created by Chinese FDI (2000–2010)

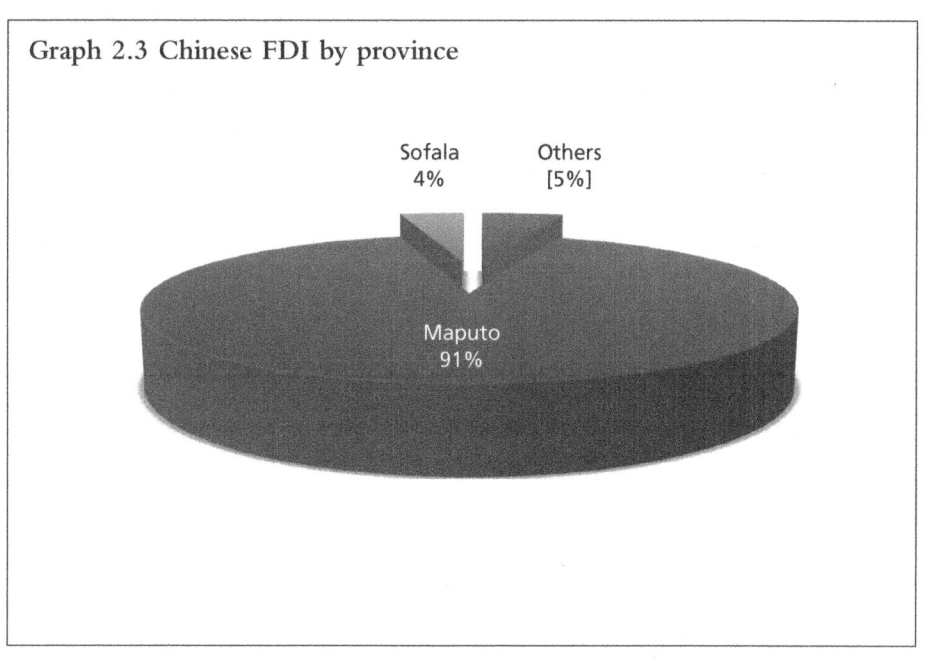

Graph 2.3 Chinese FDI by province

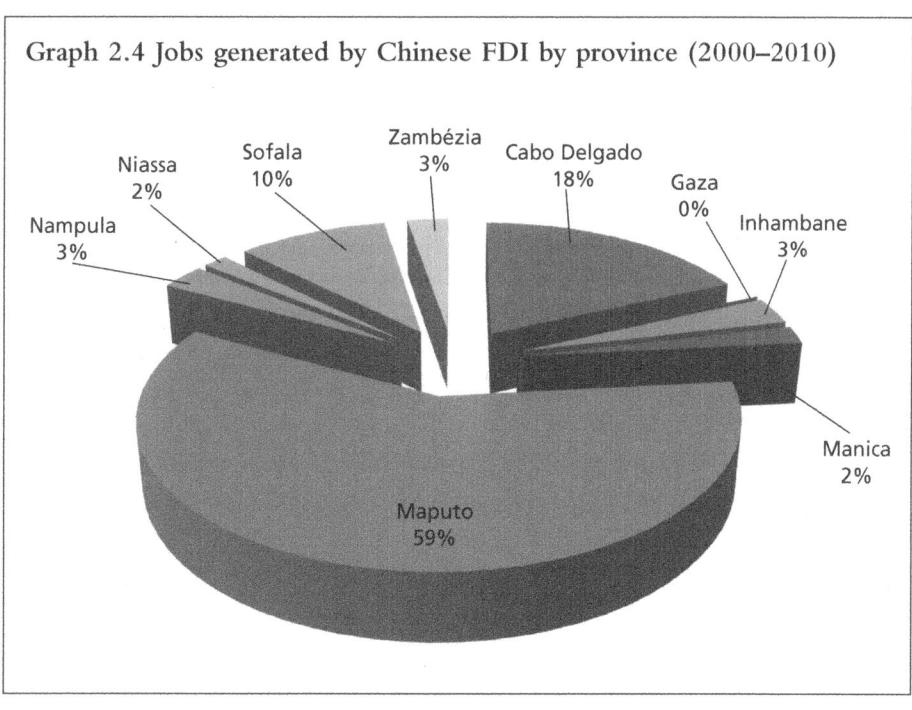

Graph 2.4 Jobs generated by Chinese FDI by province (2000–2010)

the main investor countries in Mozambique, while China occupied the fourth position. The Golden Peacock, one of the most luxurious hotels in Beira city, and perhaps in the country, was the main Chinese investment in the tourism sector.

Although it is not possible, based on the CPI data, to have a complete picture of the trends of Chinese investment in Mozambique, by cross-checking this data with other sources, it is possible to reach some conclusions. Proceeding in this way, the main conclusion is that recently the mineral resource sector seems to be the main target for Chinese investment in Mozambique.

The Chinese state company, the Wuhan Iron and Steel Corporation (WISCO), was in discussions with the Australian company Riversdale Mining Limited (RML), to acquire 40% of the Zambezi coal project belonging to this company, to a total of US$800 million.[9] If it was confirmed, which apparently is not the case, the WISCO investment would drastically change all the data advanced so far, both in terms of volume and in terms of the sector or geographical location of the Chinese FDI, since this sum is equivalent to about four times the total Chinese FDI invested in the period under analysis.

Chinese investment in the mineral resource sector, particularly in coal, could also undergo a gigantic leap with the investment of about US$5 billion announced by the private company, the China Qingho Group, in Maravia district, in the Tete province (*Net News Publisher* 2010). The China Qingho Group is also, in collaboration with the National Directorate of Geology (DNG), undertaking research in Tete and Niassa provinces in order to identify the areas where coal occurs (GoMb 2011). In addition to coal, the China Qingho Group is interested in exploring for oil, natural gas and other mineral resources.

Natural gas and other minerals (gold, iron, tantalite, diamonds and limestone, for example) also interest Chinese companies. In 2010, the Daqing Oilfield Drilling Engineering Company won an international tender to drill for natural gas in Mozambique, in an investment estimated at US$15 million. And in 2013, the China National Petroleum Corporation (CNPC) acquired from Italian ENI a 20% stake in Area 4 offshore, in Cabo Delgado province, north of Mozambique (ENI 2013). In February 2011, it was reported that Chinese companies had just requested licences from the Mozambican state to prospect for and then exploit various mineral resources in several parts of the country (Saúte 2011). This is the case, for example, with the Africa Great Wall Cement Manufacturer, a company which, in addition to its intention to produce cement, has received licences to exploit limestone in the districts of Magude (Maputo province) and Cheringoma (Sofala province) (Boletim da

---

9 This partnership would have allowed WISCO to hold 8% of the shares of Riversdale Mining, Limited.

República 2009b), and heavy sands in Angoche district (Nampula province) (Boletim da República 2011a); with CIF-Moz, Limitada, which wishes to exploit limestone and clay in Matutuíne (Maputo province) (Boletim da República 2011b, Boletim da República 2011c); and with Sogecoa, which in addition to being involved in hotels and construction (hiring of equipment and vehicles), recently obtained licences to prospect and exploit mineral resources, in particular gold in Gorongosa and Chifunde districts, in Sofala and Tete provinces, respectively. Right now, Sogecoa is prospecting for gold in Gorongosa district (*Notícias* 2011).

Finally, Chinese FDI in the industrial sector could also undergo an important leap with the confirmation by the Mozambican authorities of the investment by the China Tong Jian Investment Co Ltd, in an automobile assembly plant in Maluana, in Maputo province, valued at around US$200 million, the largest ever implemented in this sector in Mozambique (*Notícias* 2010; China Tong Jian Investment Co Ltd 2013). It is also estimated that this factory, foreseen to be finished by 2011 but was not yet by the beginning of 2014, will create about 3 000 jobs – which would be 53.6% of the total employment produced by Chinese FDI in the industrial sector between 2000 and 2010. Likewise, if the news given by the Ministry of Planning and Development (MPD) in August 2010 is confirmed, according to which Chinese businesses intend to invest US$13 billion in industry, tourism, mining, energy and technology in the 2011–2015 period, this could make China one of the largest investors in Mozambique (MPD 2010).

Conclusion

The central point of this study was to analyse the trends and impact of Chinese FDI in Mozambique over the 2000–2010 period, during which the Chinese presence in Mozambique was relaunched, particularly from 2007. Looking at its territorial and sector distribution, it was noted that Chinese FDI was concentrated (i) more in the industrial sector, in terms of the number of projects proposed to the CPI, the capital to be invested and the number of jobs to be created, and (ii) in the south of the country, particularly in Maputo (city and province).

However, although the industrial sector has attracted the greater part of investment and, driven by the automobile assembly industry, still shows signs of continuing to grow, the latest trends in Chinese investment in Mozambique show that, of the various sectors, it is mineral resources that are beginning to experience the greatest growth. If this happens, Mozambique would be no exception to much of Africa, since the bulk of Chinese investment on the continent is concentrated in this sector. This would also change the current trend for the concentration of Chinese investment in the south of the country. Nor would this be strange, because, while for many years the south, and Maputo in particular, has been the region that has attracted the most investment, the recent coal and gas investments in the centre and north of the country, particularly in Tete and Cabo Delgado provinces, are beginning to reverse this trend.

References

AIM. 2007a. 'China perdoa dívida moçambicana'. Mozambique News Agency, 7 February. Available from: www.portaldogoverno.gov.mz/noticias/ news_folder_politica/fevereiro2007/nots_po_125_fev_07/ [Accessed on 29 March 2011].

AIM. 2007b. 'Moçambique e China avaliam cooperação'. Mozambique News Agency, 9 February. Available from: www.portaldogoverno.gov.mz/ noticias/news_folder_politica/fevereiro2007/nots_po_124_jan_07/ [Accessed on 29 March 2011].

AIM. 2010. 'Primeiro-ministro considera a visita à China de êxito total'. Mozambique News Agency, 21 July. Available from: www.portaldogoverno.gov.mz/noticias/news_folder_politica/junho-2010/primeiro-ministro-considera-visita-a-china-de-exito-total/ [Accessed on 29 March].

Boletim da República. 2009a. *Hong & Binga Fishery Food Development Limitada*, III Série, nº 14, Suplemento, Maputo, 14 April.

Boletim da República. 2009b. *Aviso,* III Série, nº 31, 4º Suplemento, Maputo, 11 August.

Boletim da República. 2010. *Aviso,* III Série, nº 9, Suplemento, Maputo, 4 March.

Boletim da República. 2011a. *Aviso,* III Série, no 28, 2o Suplemento, Maputo, 15 July.

Boletim da República. 2011b. *Aviso,* III Série, no 19, Suplemento, Maputo, 12 May.

Boletim da República. 2011c. *Aviso,* III Série, no 43, Suplemento, Maputo, 27 October.

BP. 2011. *Evolução das economias dos PALOP e de Timor-Leste 2010/2011.* Lisbon: Bank of Portugal.

Bräutigam, D. 2009. *The Dragon's Gift: The real story of China in Africa.* New York: Oxford University Press.

Bräutigam, D. 2010. 'China, Africa and the International Aid Architecture'. Working Papers Series, 107. African Development Bank, Tunis, Tunisia.

Bräutigam, D. 2011. 'Aid "with Chinese characteristics": Chinese foreign aid and development finance meet the OECD-DAC Aid Regime'. *Journal of International Development,* 5(23), 752–764.

Canby et al. 2008. 'Forest Products Trade between China & Africa: An analysis of imports and exports'. *Forest Trends.* Available from: www.forest-trends.org/documents/publications/ChinaAfricaTrade.pdf [Accessed on 22 March 2011].

China Coal Resources. 2010. 'China Qingho wants to mine for coal in Niassa, Mozambique', 31 July. Available from: en.sxcoal.com/35021/NewsShow.html [Accessed on 12 March 2011].

China Tong Jian Investment Co Ltd. 2010. 'Seminar on investment opportunities in Mozambique'. Available from: www.chinatongjian.com/En/ yantaohuiDiv/Friendly_relations.html [Accessed on 12 March 2011].

China Tong Jian Investment Co Ltd. 2013. 'Chinese Investment Allows Mozambique to Become a Car Manufacturer'. Available from: http://www.chinatongjian.com/En/ news_show.asp?id=876 [Accessed on 22 January 2014].

Conselho de Ministros. 2002. *Decreto n.º 16/2002-Código dos benefícios fiscais,* Maputo, 27 June.

Conselho de Ministros. 2004. *Decreto n.º 49/2004-Regulamento do licenciamento da actividade*

comercial, Maputo, 17 November.
Diário de Moçambique. 2010. 'Luísa Diogo defende que China coopera de "maneira específica"', Maputo, 14 December.
Dyer, G & Anderlini, J. 2011. 'China's lending hits new heights', *Financial Times*, 17 January. Available from: www.ft.com/cms/s/0/488c60f4-2281-11e0-b6a2-00144 cfeab49a.html#axzz1GIebeVo4 [Accessed on 11 March 2011].
ENI. 2013. 'ENI sells a 20% share of Area 4 in Mozambique to CNPC and signs a Joint Study Agreement for cooperation for the development of the Rongchang shale gas block in China'. Available from: www.eni.com/en_IT/media/press-releases/2013/03/2013-03-14-eni-sells-20perc-share-in-mozambique.shtml [Accessed on 24 January 2014].
FOCAC. 2010. 'An Interpretation of New Measures on Economic and Trade Cooperation from 4th Ministerial Conference'. Available from: www.focac.org/eng/dsjbzjhy/t696509.htm [Accessed on 24 January 2011].
GoM. 2010. *Balanço do Plano Económico e Social de 2009*. Maputo: Government of Mozambique.
GoM. 2011a. *Balanço do Plano Económico e Social de 2010*. Maputo: Government of Mozambique.
GoM. 2011b. *Matriz dos projectos com a República Popular da China*. Maputo: Government of Mozambique.
Hanlon, J. 2010. 'Keeping options'. *Mozambique*, 174. Available from: www.gg.rhul.ac.uk/simon/GG3072/2010-64.pdf [Accessed on 31 March 2011].
Jansson, J & Kiala, C. 2010. *Patterns of Chinese Investment, Aid and Trade in Mozambique*. Stellenbosch: Centre for Chinese Studies.
Mackenzie, C. 2006. 'Forest Governance in Zambézia, Mozambique: Chinese takeaway!' Final report for Fongza.
MF. 2006. *Mozambican Priority Projects to be Financed*. Maputo: Ministry of Finance.
MFAPRC. 2006. 'Mozambique'. Ministry of Foreign Affairs of the People's Republic of China. Available from: www.china.org.cn/english/features/focac/183432.htm [Accessed on 22 March 2011].
MINEC. 2010. *Relatório da participação de Moçambique na III Conferência para a Cooperação Económica e Comercial entre a China e os Países de Língua Portuguesa e respectiva matriz de seguimento*. Maputo: Ministry of Foreign Affairs.
MPD. 2006. *Application for Financing of the Projects*. Maputo: Ministry of Planning and Development.
MPD. 2010. 'China vai investir 13 biliões de dólares nos próximos cinco anos'. Ministry of Planning and Development. Available from: www.mpd.gov.mz/index.php?option=comcontent&view=article&id=90%3Achina-vai-investir-13-bilioes-de-dolares-nos-proximoscinco-anos&catid=50%3Anoticias&Itemid=96&lang=pt [Accessed on 19 March 2011].
Net News Publisher. 2010. 'China Qingho to invest $5b in Coal Mining Projects in Mozambique'. 26 July. Available from: www.netnewspublisher.com/china-kingho-to-invest-5b-in-coal-mining-projects-in-mozambique/ [Accessed on 12 March 2011].
Notícias. 2008. 'China poderá construir futuro bairro para os deputados'. Maputo, 10 October.
Notícias. 2010. 'País passa a montar carros a partir de 2011'. Maputo, 18 December.
Notícias. 2011. 'Sogecoa pesquisa ouro'. Maputo, 1 September.
O País. 2011. 'Guebuza diz que quem critica cooperação com a china China está enganado'. Maputo, 27 September.
People's Daily. 2001. 'China Cancels Part of Mozambique's Debt', 12 July. Available from: english.peopledaily.com.cn/200107/12/eng20010712_74776.html [Accessed on 12 March 2011].
Portal of the Government of Mozambique. 2010. 'Em 2011: China concede três milhões de dólares às FADM', 29 December. Available from: www.portaldogoverno.gov.mz/noticias/

news_folder_politica/dezembro-2010/em-2011-china-concede-tres-milhoes-de-dolares-as-fadm/ [Accessed on 12 March 2011].

Saúte, C. 2011. 'Empresas chinesas vasculham minérios em Moçambique', *Canal de Moçambique*. Maputo, 7 February.

Secretariat of the Council of Ministers. 2010. *Aos Órgãos de Informação*. Maputo, 12 October.

TA. 2009. *Conta geral do Estado. Ano 2008*. Maputo: Administrative Tribunal.

WFP. 2006. 'China Emerges as World's Third Largest Food Aid Donor'. World Food Programme. Available from: www.wfp.org/node/534 [Accessed on 11 March 2011].

Chapter 3

Chinese Banking in Mozambique: The Macanese Connection

Ana Cristina Alves

From a historical perspective, China-Mozambique relations closely resemble China's footprint in most African countries. Beijing supported Frelimo in the 1960s during the liberation war, while diplomatic ties were established with Maputo soon after independence in 1975 and followed by a long hiatus (see Chapter 1). Bilateral relations were gradually revitalised in the 2000s, this time rooted on strong economic solidarity. Although Beijing's economic penetration in Mozambique has been relatively slow when compared with other resource-rich countries in Africa, it has gained pace in recent years. Two-way trade grew from US$70 million in 2004 to US$950 million by 2011 (interview, Chinese Economic Consulate 2012). Along with booming bilateral trade, the increased flow of Chinese investment into Mozambique in recent years has been one of the key traits of China-Mozambique relations. In 2008, China became the second largest investor in Mozambique after South Africa, up from the 26th position by 2000 (Macauhub 2009).

Chinese investment in Mozambique amounted to US$229 million in 2013 and it is expected to expand much further in coming years, especially as Chinese resources companies tap into Mozambique's vast mineral deposits, particularly natural gas. Mozambique's coal reserves in Tete province have attracted much interest, namely from Wuhan Iron and Steel, who signed an US$800 million Memorandum of Understanding (MoU) in 2010 with Riversdale to integrate the Australian-led consortium aimed at developing Benga mining concession (Ryan 2010), which, however, never came to fruition. Interestingly, despite the growing allure of Mozambique's untapped mineral resources (namely coal, natural gas and oil), Chinese investment has until very recently targeted mainly retail, services, manufacture, agriculture, logging, fisheries and the nascent banking sector.

Even though Chinese investment is in general well regarded in Mozambique, not all of the economic activity by the Chinese has met with local approval: the recorded involvement of Chinese (and Malaysian) companies in illegal logging and in the plundering of marine species (often in collusion with governmental authorities) has drawn much criticism in the Mozambican press, as has the periodic problems involving labourers working for the Chinese.

While Chinese investment in Mozambique follows in general the same pattern observed in other African countries, it is its engagement in the financial sector that stands out as distinctive and worthy of closer analysis. Unlike the pattern observed in other African countries, Chinese involvement in the Mozambican banking sector includes both state-owned banks (China Exim Bank and CDB) and private commercial interests, in the form of Geocapital, a Luso-Chinese joint venture. This diversity provides an insight into a dimension of Chinese financial engagement with Africa that is often overlooked, that is private capital and its strategic engagement with local elites.

A brief overview of the Mozambican Banking sector

The banking sector in Mozambique has gone through a significant expansion in recent years. While in 1997 there were only five banks operating in the domestic market, by the end of 2012 that figure had grown to 18 commercial banks. Despite the growing share of local capital in recent years, commercial banking in Mozambique remains dominated by foreign capital: 71% in 2012 (80% in 2005), the majority of which is Portuguese and South African capital. The largest bank in terms of assets is Millennium BIM, a joint venture between the largest private Portuguese bank, BCP, and a local partner. The second largest is Banco Comercial de Investimento (BCI), a venture between a Portuguese state-owned bank (Caixa Geral de Depositos), a Portuguese private bank (BPI) and a local financial group (Insitec) – a major Mozambican investment group in which President Guebuza is said to have direct interests), through which Portuguese credit lines are channelled to Mozambique. These are followed by Standard Bank (South Africa) and Barclays Bank Moçambique. Together these four banks represent 89% of total market assets. According to some sources (interviews, a Portuguese diplomat and independent researcher in 2010) the establishment of new banks as well as the entrance of foreign capital into the Mozambique banking sector is highly reliant on political connections at the top level. On the other hand, the entry of foreign capital and the fact that it dominates the sector seems to have reduced the promiscuity between the executive and the banking sector that led to the irregularities and even crimes associated with Banco Austral in the early 2000s.

Attracted by the opening up of the Mozambican financial sector and the myriad investment opportunities presented by the country's vast resources, Chinese public and private interests entered the sector in the early 2000s.

China's public arm: Exim Bank and China Development Bank (CDB)

As in most other African countries, Chinese policy banks (Exim Bank and CDB) entered Mozambique in the framework of intergovernmental cooperation agreements targeting mostly infrastructure development. Since 2001, China Exim Bank has provided a credit line of US$3.9 million for infrastructure projects in Mozambique, helping to finance an international conference centre, a new office building for the Ministry of Foreign Affairs, police equipment and 150 units of low-income housing in greater Maputo (AFRODAD 2010). As early as 2006 the Mozambican government applied to the China Exim Bank for loans of US$2 billion for the Mphanda Nkuwa dam project[1] on the Zambezi river, US$50 million to support agricultural investment in Zambézia province and another soft loan to rehabilitate the capital's international airport (AFRODAD 2010). This last loan, for US$115 million, was split into two phases: an initial loan for US$50 million, followed by US$65 million approved in 2010 to finance the reconstruction of the domestic terminal of Maputo's international airport by Anhui Foreign Economic Construction (Group) Co Ltd.

In 2007, the China Exim Bank and the World Bank established a widely publicised venture to jointly finance projects in Mozambique, Ghana and Uganda, but no concrete project financing agreements resulted. China Exim Bank does not yet have a branch in Mozambique, although the Mozambican prime minister's visit to China in late 2010 led to rumours that an operations office was going to be opened in Maputo, aimed at facilitating credit lines to Chinese investors (interview, a Portuguese diplomat 2010).

During that visit, two other concessional loans totalling US$100 million were signed with another Chinese state-run bank (CDB) to support the construction of a cement factory in Sofala province (US$80 million) and a cotton plant in Maputo province (US$20 million) (Mozambique News Agency 2010). In August 2011, a follow-up trip to China by President Armando Guebuza produced a framework agreement on financial cooperation that was signed with CDB. The agreement aims to introduce commercial loans to the private sector in Mozambique as well as channel funds to public investment (Macauhub 2011), which suggests greater involvement of CDB in the Mozambique financial sector in the near future.

The private arm: Geocapital

The investment group Geocapital is structured around a shared historical legacy rooted in Macau and a common key feature of Chinese and Lusophone business culture: the primacy of personal connections (*guanxi*). Headquartered

---

[1] The dam project was later awarded to a consortium of two national energy companies (60%) and a Brazilian construction firm, Camargo Corrêa (40%).

in the Chinese territory formerly under Portuguese administration, this group connects Chinese private capital to key political and business figureheads in the Lusophone world, in particular Mozambique.

The genesis of Geocapital

In the wake of Macau's handover to China (1999) a number of ideas germinated around the business opportunities presented by the territory's advantageous position as a potential bridge between China and the Lusophone world. Among the few that concretised the Macau Forum[2] and Geocapital stand out. The idea of the Macau Forum was pushed forward by the executive government of Macau as a means to retain its identity and value within the People's Republic of China (PRC) (interviews with the business community in Macau and Forum Macau Secretariat 2005–2009). The initiative pleased Beijing who perceived the Forum as a useful foreign policy instrument to expand its soft power and explore the business potential of Macau as an interface between China (as a funding source) and the Portuguese-speaking countries (as bastions of natural resources) (Alves 2008). The Forum was placed under the Ministry of Commerce of the PRC and formally established in Macau in 2003, where the Permanent Secretariat is based.

On the fringes of the Macau Forum, the idea of setting up a Sino-Lusophone private investment fund to channel investment into Lusophone countries gradually took shape in the inner circles of Macau's financial elite (interviews with business community in Macau 2005–2009). This private fund materialised in 2006 through a joint venture by a Hong Kong magnate (Stanley Ho) and a Lusophone financier (Jorge Ferro Ribeiro) under the name of Geocapital.

A close look at the key figureheads of Geocapital reveals the critical role played by personal connections linking capital and political influence in the setting up of this venture. The chairman of the board of directors is Stanley Ho,[3] who controls over 50% of Geocapital's shares and has large business interests in the gambling, hospitality, transport and financing sectors, including the Hang Seng Bank in Macau. Jorge Ferro Ribeiro is vice chairman and executive chair and the second-largest stakeholder in the venture. Acting as Stanley Ho's representative in Portugal, Ribeiro has accumulated interests in

---

2 Formal name: Forum for Economic and Commercial Cooperation between China and the Portuguese Speaking Countries.

3 Stanley Ho was granted exclusive rights for the gambling business in Macau during Portuguese rule. Although this came to an end (2002) shortly after the handover (1999), Stanley Ho still dominates the sector in Macau, having since expanded the gambling business to several Lusophone countries, including one casino in Maputo.

financing, telecom, tourism, and real estate in Portugal and Macau. The other key figures in this Sino-Lusophone investment fund have very useful political connections. Eminent member of the Portuguese Socialist Party, Almeida Santos, owns 5% of Geocapital and is president of the general assembly. He is a former president of the Portuguese Parliament (1995–2002) and has strong personal, political and economic connections to Frelimo in Mozambique.[4] Ribeiro is an old acquaintance who in 1974–1975 worked under Santos when he was the Portuguese Minister for International Cooperation. This puzzle is completed by Ambrose So, a Chinese entrepreneur with close links to Stanley Ho's business empire and the Chinese political nomenclature,[5] who serves as one of the three administrators of Geocapital (Geocapital 2010).

Geocapital was designed to capitalise on the growing synergies between China's dramatic economic growth and the opportunities and potential of the Portuguese-speaking countries, in particular Mozambique, Brazil and Angola. This Luso-Chinese investment society is structured around two core areas: finance and energy. Its strategy privileges joint ventures with local partners (more often than not governments or private entrepreneurs with close links to the executive) that can more efficiently direct their investments into the banking, agriculture (with emphasis on biofuels) and energy sectors.

While the Macau Forum has struggled to mobilise Chinese private capital to invest in the Lusophone world through an inter-governmental approach, Geocapital has been relatively successful in pursuing that same goal owing largely to its extensive network of personal connections.

Despite its short existence, the society has harnessed an impressive investment portfolio across the Lusophone world. In Mozambique Geocapital has ventured with local capital to start three companies: Zamcorp (agri-business), Moza Capital and Moza Bank (finance). In Guinea-Bissau the Luso-Chinese group has become the major shareholder of the country's largest bank, Banco da África Ocidental, and has a share in Geogolfo (agri-business and biofuels). In Cape Verde, the society has a share in Caixa Economica (the largest credit institution) in partnership with the local government and has entered another joint venture with the state for a research venture on biofuels. In Angola, it has forged a joint venture (Geopactum Oriente) with Global Pactum, a private financial group that controls one of the major Angolan Banks (Banco Privado Atlantico) with close links to Sonangol, the national oil company. In Brazil, Geocapital acquired VARILOG and VEM (among the largest aerospace

---

4 Santos had lived in colonial Mozambique between 1953 and 1974 where he opposed Portuguese rule alongside Frelimo.
5 Ambrose So is a member of the 11th National Committee of the Chinese People's Political Consultative Conference.

engineering and maintenance companies) in partnership with the Portuguese airline TAP. In Portugal, it holds a share in EDP-Energy (2.5%) and set up a strategic partnership with one of the largest shareholders of BCP, the country's largest private bank. In Timor Leste, Geocapital has plans to establish a local investment bank, Banco Timorense de Investimento (Geocapital 2010).

Although Geocapital has mounted on some of the synergies put in place by the Macau Forum, its track has been mostly independent and driven exclusively by private business interests.

Geocapital in Mozambique

Due to the personal connections highlighted above, the initial forays into business made by Geocapital happened in Mozambique. The idea of setting up the Luso-Chinese investment fund actually germinated around a specific business opportunity that emerged in Mozambique (interviews, the business community in Macau 2005–2009).

At the time (2005–2006), Maputo was looking for investors to kick-start the development of the Zambezi river valley, an area that covers 28% of the national territory with vast water and mineral resources and a huge agriculture potential. This created bright prospects for energy and agri-business investments which immediately captured the attention of the business community in Macau with connections to Mozambique.

Around this time the Portuguese government was preparing to hand over control of the Cahora Bassa hydro-power plant and it was rumoured that Lisbon was to sell its remaining shares (15%) in the project, attracting much interest from Geocapital entrepreneurs. Maputo bought 7.5% and Portugal and Mozambique struggled to reach an agreement regarding the selling of the remaining stake. In July 2012 the Portuguese state sold its remaining 7.5% in Cahora Bassa to REN (the national electricity grid company), in which a Chinese state-owned enterprise now holds a 25% stake.[6]

Cahora Bassa did not, however, exhaust Geocapital's interests in the Zambezi valley. In September 2005, Geocapital had signed an MoU with the Zambezi Valley Planning Office (GPZ, the governmental agency responsible for the development of the valley), headed by Sérgio Vieira, allegedly an old acquaintance of Almeida Santos (interview, and independent researcher 2010). The aim was to look into natural resources development opportunities, namely, hydro-electricity and thermal energy, coal, gas, agro-industry, rail transport, ports, minerals, real estate and tourism (Macauhub 2005). Three months later, Geocapital signed an agreement with two Mozambican companies to set up

---

6 China's State Grid Cor. acquired 25% of REN in February 2012.

a joint venture (Zamcorp) to promote the development of the Zambezi river valley through privileged access to Chinese capital. Zamcorp was formally established in June 2006 with an initial capital of US$500 000. The local partners include the corporate arm of GPZ (Sociedade de Gestao Integrada de Recursos, SOGIR) with a 55% stake, and Moza Capital (see below) with a 10% share. Geocapital retains the remaining 35%. The company established its headquarters in Tete province and opened a branch office (Zamcorp International) in Hong Kong.

Two other financial institutions have grown out of Geocapital's interests in Mozambique: Moza Capital (investment banking) and Moza Banco (universal licence). Founded in September 2005, Moza Capital aims to channel Chinese capital into the Zambezi valley. Moza Banco was established in late 2007 and started operations in June 2008. Both institutions are partnered with Capitais de Moçambique, a private Mozambican group of investors headed by Prakash Ratilal. Ratilal is a high-ranking official in Frelimo and former head of the Banco de Moçambique as well as an old acquaintance of Almeida Santos (interview, an independent researcher 2010). The two institutions have the same CEO in Prakash Ratilal and originally had the same ownership structure (51% Mozambique Capitais, 49% Geocapital) (Macauhub 2008).

Although Moza Banco holds a universal licence, its major interest lies in corporate banking (finance projects and enterprises) and investment banking (mainly agri-business) as a means to contribute to the development of Mozambique's natural resources (Ratilal 2008). With an initial capitalisation of US$15 million, the bank grew considerably during its first year, with revenues of US$2.2 million (Ratilal 2009).

Geocapital sold 25.1% of its stake in Moza Banco for US$9.5 million to the African branch of Portugal's second-largest private bank, Banco Espirito Santo (BES) in late 2010. The deal was concluded in January 2011, with the following ownership structure: Moza Capitais 50.4%, BES 25.1% and Geocapital 24.5%. According to one source in Moza Capital (interview, an official at Moza Capital 2010), this deal should not be seen as a divesting strategy but as a means to increase the bank's capital and to bring in a partner with more experience and know-how, which is critical to the bank's current expansion phase. As part of the deal, Moza Banco was to double its capital to US$30 million by mid-2011 with a view to expanding the bank's operations to other regions of the country (Macauhub 2011). As of late 2012, the Bank's capital had grown to US$45 million and 13 branches had been inaugurated across the country (MozManíacos Notícias 2012). However, despite the bank's plans to fund large projects in energy and agro-industry (Ratilal 2009), nothing ever came to fruition. In 2013, Geocapital sold its share to the other shareholders opting out of Moza Banco.

Assessing Geocapital's performance

Despite the high publicity and high expectations generated around the three ventures of Geocapital in Mozambique, their success in channelling investment into the development of the Zambezi valley is extremely limited. The sole exception was the US$50 million credit line from China Exim Bank to the corporate arm of the Ministry of Planning and Development, SOGIR, which was channelled through Moza Bank, following an agreement between Moza Bank and the Bank of China in early 2009 to facilitate the cash flow between the two countries (Ratilal 2009). This credit line was earmarked for agriculture equipment and machinery (US$20 million) and the setting up of three agro-processing plants (US$30 million – two cotton- and one-corn processing plant) in the Zambezi valley (interview, officials at GPZ 2010). Although these have been completed, the success of these plants has been constrained by poor planning namely relating to their integration in local producing and processing chains (interview, an IESE researcher 2013).

In the meantime, the institutional framework has changed – the GPZ was officially closed down in mid-2010 and Sérgio Vieira discharged. The general perception is that Vieira has done little for the development of the valley, something echoed in the public criticism levelled by President Guebuza at the GPZ in July 2008 (AIM 2008). In June 2010 a new agency was created under the Ministry of Planning and Development – Agência de Desenvolvimento do Vale do Zambeze (or Agência do Zambeze) to channel funds and coordinate the development of the valley (interview, officials at GPZ 2010). The new director, Roberto Albino (who headed the dismantling of GPZ), was nominated in April 2011. In early 2012, the agency announced plans to invest US$200 million in the development of the valley in the period 2012–2014. The projects (agriculture, fishing, agricultural mechanisation, agri-processing, agro-industries, land planning and infrastructure) are to be financed by the state budget and co-funded by Mozambican and foreign cooperation partners, namely China and India Export and Import Banks, the World Bank and the governments of Norway and the Netherlands (Macauhub 2012). Whether Geocapital's Mozambican financial institutions are to play any role in it remains, however, unclear. The fact that Geocapital was closely associated with Vieira might come at a cost for the company's interests in the Zambezi valley.

Conclusion

Political connections with the ruling party seem to be of paramount importance in all large investment projects in Mozambique and both public and private Chinese interests seemed to have perceived this at a very early stage. This particular feature, however, is not specific to Mozambique-China business as it replicates a formula that is common to all other investors.

Despite a decade-long involvement in infrastructure construction in Mozambique built on close intergovernmental relations, Chinese state banks have been struggling to get a foothold in mega-projects such as the development corridors (Nacala, Beira and Maputo). The largest infrastructure projects funded by China's policy banks so far are the Maputo Airport, and more recently the Maputo ring road and the Maputo-Catembe bridge (both under construction). Other large projects have either collapsed (Mphanda Nkuwa dam) or are struggling to meet expectations (agro-processing plants). As Mozambique's economic potential expands, both policy banks have shown interest in creating facilities to support Chinese wanting to invest in Mozambique. However, despite the many Chinese delegations of private investors that have visited the country in recent years, these financial instruments are yet to produce results.

Operating without the formal linkages to the Chinese state enjoyed by its public counterparts, Geocapital was built to seize investment opportunities in the Zambezi river valley through its strong personal connections within Mozambique. The bold initiative rested largely on the confidence that personal networks and local knowledge would be able to overcome local obstacles and deliver solid projects to the company. However, while these networks overcame regulatory obstacles that might have thwarted other investors seeking to enter the financial sector in Mozambique, they also failed to deliver.

Despite its financial muscle, close links with the business community in Macau, and its strong political capital in Mozambique, Geocapital has thus far failed to gain access to large development projects in the agriculture and energy sectors. This reality suggests that connections may facilitate entry into a market but do not necessarily guarantee results. It also implies that major obstacles exist in Mozambique, such as a lack of proper planning and local capacity at all levels, the loosely defined nature of projects on offer and inefficient internal coordination and management of investment opportunities.

With all the pre-requisites apparently in place, namely the growing attractiveness of the Mozambican economy and privileged platforms in place to channel investments into its market, Maputo is clearly in need of a more efficient strategy and coordination mechanism if it is to successfully attract big Chinese investment into the country. The Mozambican government will have to define a clear long-term strategy to attract Chinese public and private capital that is aligned to the country's development goals so as to ensure that new projects are in tune with the country's needs rather than the investors' interests. In this way, opportunities presented by Chinese public and private capital can be better coordinated, so that they complement rather than compete with each other.

References

AFRODAD. 2010. 'Factsheet, Chinese Development Assistance in Mozambique'. Available from: allafrica.com/stories/201011240038.html [Accessed on 18 June 2012].

AIM. 2008. 'Guebuza Calls for More Production from Zambezi Office', 30 July. Available from: allafrica.com/stories/200807300874.html [Accessed on 18 June 2012].

Alves, Ana Cristina. 2008. 'Chinese Economic Diplomacy in Africa: The Lusophone strategy'. In: Chris Alden, Dan Large & Ricardo Soares De Oliveira, eds. *China Returns to Africa: An emerging power and a continent embrace.* London: Hurst.

Geocapital. 2010. Geocapital website. Available from: www.geocapital.com.mo [Accessed on 18 June 2012].

KPMG Moçambique. 2011. Maputo. 'Sistema bancario em Moçambique continua concentrado em quatro instituicoes', 24 December. Available from: www.macauhub.com.mo/pt/2011/02/24/sistema-bancario-em-mocambique-concentrado-em-quatro-instituicoes/ [Accessed on 18 June 2012].

Macauhub. 2005. 'Macau company to develop Zambezi region in Mozambique', 9 December. Available from: www.macauhub.com.mo/en/2005/12/09/160/ [Accessed on 18 June 2012].

Macauhub. 2008. 'Mozambique: Moza Banco, with Macau Capital, Opens 16 June in Maputo', 13 June. Available from: http://www.macauhub.com.mo/en/2008/06/13/5212/ [Accessed on 18 June 2012].

Macauhub. 2009. 'Mozambique: China second largest investor in 2008 after South Africa', 27 March. Available from: www.macauhub.com.mo/en/2009/03/27/6795/ [Accessed on 18 June 2012].

Macauhub. 2011. 'Portugal's Espírito Santo Bank Concludes Process of Taking Stake in Moza Banco of Mozambique', 21 January. Available from: www.macauhub.com.mo/en/2011/01/21/portugal%E2%80%99s-espirito-santo-bank-concludes-process-of-taking-stake-in-moza-banco-of-mozambique/ [Accessed on 18 June 2012].

Macau Hub (2011b) 'China should diversify financial aid to Mozambique', 10 August. Available from: www.macauhub.com.mo/en/2011/08/10/china-should-diversify-financial-aid-to-mozambique//[Accessed 18 June 2012].

Macauhub. 2012. '200 milhões de dólares vão ser investidos no vale do Zambeze, em Moçambique', 27 January 2012. Available from: http://www.macauhub.com.mo/pt/2012/01/27/200-milhoes-de-dolares-vao-ser-investidos-no-vale-do-zambeze-em-mocambique/ [Accessed on 18 June 2012].

Mozambique News Agency AIM report. 2010. 'Prime Minister visits China', 22 June. Available from: www.poptel.org.uk/mozambique-news/newsletter/aim404.pdf [Accessed on 18 June 2012].

MozManíacos Notícias. 2012. 'Mozabanco responde ao crescimento de Manica', 9 November. Available from: www.noticias.mozmaniacos.com/2012/11/mozabanco-responde-ao-crescimento-de.html [Accessed on 5 December 2012].

Ratilal, Prakesh. 2008. Inaugural speech of Moza Banco SA, Maputo. 16 June.

Ratilal, Prakesh. 2009. Interview with *O País*: Olivia Massango, 'Nao temos ambicao de ser o numero um ou numero dois', in: *O País*, 18 June 2009. Avialable from: www.opais.co.mz/index.php/entrevistas/76-entrevistas/1714-nao-temos-ambicao-de-ser-o-numero-um-ou-numero-dois.html [Accessed on 18 June 2012]

Ryan, Brendan. 2010. 'Chinese back Mozambique coal project', Miningmx.com, 24 June. Available from: www.miningmx.com/page/news/energy/593886-Chinese-back-Mozambique-coal-project#.UueRwdJBtkg [Accessed 18 June 2012].

Interviews

Various interviews, business community in Macau and Forum Macau Secretariat, Macau, 2005–2009.

Instituto de Estudos Sociais e Económicos (IESE) researcher, Maputo, 26 September 2013.
Chinese Economic Consulate, Maputo, 17 February 2012.
Portuguese Embassy, Maputo, 3 November 2010.
Independent researcher, Maputo, 2 November 2010.
Official at Moza Capital, Maputo, 4 November 2010.
Officials at GPZ, Maputo, 4 November 2010.

Chapter 4

All Part of the Master Plan? Ethnographic Encounters with the Chinese in Mozambique

Mikkel Bunkenborg

Since the turn of the century, China's growing involvement in Africa has drawn countless headlines in Western media and much of the media coverage has tended to be highly critical of the Chinese interventions in Africa. Chinese activities in Africa are described as part of a global scramble for natural resources, and China has been depicted as an amoral political actor and vilified for supporting a number of unsavoury regimes. In contrast to the deep concern with good governance and long-term development which supposedly characterises Western interventions in African states, the Chinese offers of development projects with no strings attached are said to be motivated by narrow economic interests. The idea of China assuming a dominant position in African countries which former colonial powers have long regarded as their own backyard speaks directly to a growing Western anxiety about the rise of China and China in Africa has become a touchstone for gauging the intentions and moral fibre of China. In addition to alarmist media reports, there is a rapidly growing scholarly literature on the contemporary Chinese presence in Africa. This literature engages a broad variety of specific Chinese projects across the continent, yet descriptions of the haphazard practice of Chinese interventions in Africa cannot quite allay the suspicion that the West is witnessing the rise of a new superpower and that there is some sort of master plan behind the Chinese expansion in Africa.

Based on a collaborative ethnographic research project that seeks to explore and compare Chinese interventions in Mozambique and Mongolia,[1] this chapter takes issue with the idea of an underlying master plan and presents a series of ethnographic encounters with Chinese doctors, construction workers, entrepreneurs and traders. Chinese nationals in Mozambique are engaged in

---

1 The research project, entitled *Imperial Potentialities*, ran from 2009 through 2012 and was funded by the Danish Council for Independent Research in the Social Sciences (FSE). Involving three researchers, Morten Nielsen, Morten Axel Pedersen and Mikkel Bunkenborg, the project aimed to explore China's growing political-economic involvement in Central Asia and Sub-Saharan Africa via three tightly integrated ethnographic fieldworks on Chinese interventions in infrastructure and resource extraction in Mongolia and Mozambique.

a diverse range of projects and their activities in hospitals, walled construction sites, sawmills and shoe shops do not immediately lend credence to the idea of a planned and orchestrated Chinese expansion. But while the idea of a master plan behind the veil of practices seems questionable, the absence of such a plan does not preclude the possibility of systemic effects arising from disconnected Chinese activities. The disparate interactions between Chinese and Mozambicans may not proceed according to a plan, but it seems likely that the friction generated by Chinese projects of aid, construction, extraction and trade may eventually come to produce and codify ideas about differences between Chinese and Africans and thus contribute to shaping the contours of China as an emerging polity. For instance, security was a grave concern to most of the Chinese working in Mozambique, and illustrates how practical problems on the margins of an expansive Chinese polity may come to define the centre.

From plans to practice

Studying China's role in Africa was once a marginal specialisation, but the field has grown exponentially since the late 1990s as research funds became available and scholars poured in to uncover what the Chinese are really up to in Africa. As one might expect, researchers have not generally confirmed the alarmist image of ruthless Chinese grabbing land and resources, supporting dictators, ignoring human rights, wrecking local businesses and ruining the environment. Without ignoring the adverse effects of some Chinese initiatives, scholars have shed light on the complex history of China's engagement with Africa that goes back to the 1955 Bandung conference and offered more balanced accounts of the potentials and dangers inherent in China's embrace of the African continent (Alden 2007; Alden, Large & de Oliveira 2008; Taylor 2006).

One representative of a myth-busting political science approach to the theme of China in Africa, Deborah Bräutigam, provides a reassuring account of the Chinese presence in Africa: 'China is now a powerful force in Africa, and the Chinese are not going away. Their embrace of the continent is strategic, planned, long term, and still unfolding' (Bräutigam 2009:311). Echoing Joshua Ramo's (2004) upbeat description of the Beijing Consensus and the Chinese Model of Development, Bräutigam emphasises that China has managed to pull 200 million people out of poverty since 1978 and has a unique recent track record in spurring economic development that may well come to benefit African states. China thus comes across as a highly rational and pragmatic actor, a uniform super-subject, and what happens on the ground in Africa boils down to the intended and unintended effects of Beijing's master plan. The content of this master plan may leave us guessing – is it a rational plan for mutually beneficial economic cooperation and growth, as Bräutigam suggests? Or is it a sinister colonial scheme with no consideration for local populations? In any case, it is comforting to assume that there is a political centre that has a plan, knows what is going on, and can be relied upon to act in a rational and pragmatic manner.

While the political and economic rapprochement between China and Africa has often been framed in a political science perspective, there are relatively few ethnographic descriptions of the way Chinese entrepreneurs and workers interact with local populations. One notable exception is Ching Kwan Lee's description of the 'raw' encounters between Chinese bosses and local workers in a copper mine in Zambia and a textile factory in Tanzania. Describing the very different outcomes of labour conflicts in the two settings, Ching Kwan Lee criticises the idea of a Chinese master plan and emphasises that the Chinese presence is shaped through interactions with specific African states and societies. 'Preliminary findings from this comparative research on the labour politics of Chinese capitalism in southern Africa challenge the mistaken notion, prevalent in current debates and reports, that there is a singular "Chinese" interest always capable of imposing itself on a singular and vulnerable Africa which does not have any political leverage in encounters with the Chinese' (Lee 2009). Ching Kwan Lee's ethnographic take suggests that Chinese interventions in Africa are shaped in specific sites and cannot be understood merely as more or less successful expressions of a colonial blueprint. This constitutes a timely critique of the political science approach which assumes that there is a uniform subject and a master plan to be found behind the veils of political and economic practice, but surely this critique could be taken one step further: examining encounters between Chinese and Africans in their specificity without reducing them to enactments of underlying intentions is but the first step. The next step is surely to look forward to the systemic effects and the subjects these encounters might produce. If the encounters between Chinese and Africans are presently felt to be 'raw', how will they be cooked and processed and what sort of system will they feed into? Ching Kwan Lee notes the absence of a concerted colonial intention, but if the Chinese presence in Africa really is shaped by specific interactions rather than intentions, it does not seem entirely unlikely that colonial effects may arise incidentally.

This chapter takes issue with the idea that the Chinese engagement on the African continent should be understood in terms of a gradually unfolding strategy as Deborah Bräutigam suggests. Rather than the centrifugal unfolding of a preconceived plan originating in a well-defined and stable polity, we may be witnessing a process of centripetal enfolding where occurrences at the margins come to shape the nature of an emerging polity. As an academic field, China in Africa has been concerned with the way Chinese interventions in

Africa affected Africa, but perhaps it is time to turn the tables on that question and ask how 'The China Safari' (Michel et al 2009) may be changing China itself. One way of doing this would obviously be to ask questions about the role of Africans in China – as evident in the literature, there is no shortage of Africans in Southern China (Bodomo 2010; Mathews 2011) – but the Chinese enfolding of Africa is not necessarily that concrete. In this sense, Mei Zhan's description of the 'worlding' of Chinese medicine may offer an analogy to what is going on with China as such. Rather than seeing traditional Chinese medicine as an immutable medical system that has now become globalised, Mei Zhan sees Chinese medicine as a mutable set of discourses and practices that were remade through specific applications as a cheap preventive medicine suitable for the third world in the sixties and as an alternative, holistic medical practice suited to a cosmopolitan middle-class in the nineties (Zhan 2009). If Chinese medicine is not an essence but a mutable set of practices and discourses that change through specific instances of application, the same would apply to China as such. Mapping out how specific Chinese interventions in Africa may be changing China itself is obviously an overly ambitious project, but the material from Mozambique presented in the present chapter suggests that it would be worthwhile to start thinking of China as a polity in-the-making, an emerging effect of specific interactions, rather than a well-defined subject executing a master plan.

The socialist anachronism of medical aid

Dr Meng complained that they did not have proper facilities to receive visitors, but he rustled up some tea leaves and we sat down in his small room to drink tea and talk. Born during the Cultural Revolution, Dr Meng was a lively and opinionated interlocutor. He was assigned to work in a peripheral part of China after participating in the 1989 protests and he remained rather critical of the Chinese government. In particular, Dr Meng was sceptical of the way the Chinese government spent public money on aid projects such as the stadium in Zimpeto and the airport in Maputo. Surely the government should build aircraft carriers to protect Chinese interests in the South China Sea instead of giving away free buildings all over Africa.

Dr Meng was engaged in one of the classical development projects administered by the Chinese consulate in Mozambique, a medical team stationed at the central hospital in Maputo. Since 1976, when the project first started, the province of Sichuan has assembled medical teams, provided them with half a year of training in Portuguese, and sent them off to work in Maputo for two years until the next team took over. The present team, No. 18, consists of 12 doctors, an interpreter and a cook and, with the consulate's blessing, I was allowed to visit their quarters and speak to some of the doctors.

The doctors emphasised that their mission was to contribute to the good relations between the Chinese and Mozambican people and that the gratitude and respect of the patients was a great compensation for all the hard work. Even so, they were not entirely happy with their situation. Safety was a constant concern, partially because of the frequent robberies, but mainly because the proportion of HIV-positive patients was very high. In just one year, there were nine incidents where it was suspected that one of the Chinese doctor's might have been exposed to the HI-virus through surgical mishaps, and the necessary post-exposure prophylaxis was tough to get through because of the side effects. Apart from the dangers the doctors faced, they also felt that the Mozambican Ministry of Health did not really appreciate what they were doing. There was no one to greet them at the airport and they were expected to start work the day after they arrived. There were no local interpreters available and after just three or four days the doctors were asked to work shifts on their own even though their language skills were still inadequate. Their wages were paid from home but the Ministry provided the accommodation and this was also a source of some contention. As one member of the team pointed out, they were all experienced doctors with families, yet in Mozambique they were only provided with a single room each in communal apartments. Getting the Ministry to fix or replace things in these apartments was an interminable hassle, and so they had to put up with broken furniture and fixtures. All their colleagues in the hospital had their own apartments and made a pretty penny on the side in their private clinics. It was bad enough that the Chinese doctors were barred from making money outside the hospital, but the existence of these private clinics even hampered their efforts to improve services at the public hospital. As waiting lists at the public hospital were one of the things that might prompt the wealthier patients to choose a private clinic, the Chinese doctors felt that efficiency was frowned upon rather than encouraged by the other doctors at the public hospital.

The many construction projects funded by China across the African continent only became conspicuous in the 1990s, but the Chinese medical teams constitute a steady, low-profile aid effort that has been going on since 1963 and stationed more than 20 000 Chinese doctors for two-year periods abroad, most of them in Africa. The present popularity of Chinese doctors and medicines in some African countries – such as Tanzania (Hsu 2002; Langwick 2010) – is no doubt connected to this effort but the programme started in 1963 when Chairman Mao was preparing for the Cultural Revolution, and there was hardly any intention of opening up new markets back then. Even today, the efforts of these medical teams are framed as a disinterested gift from one people to another, but as health care is increasingly privatised in both China and the receiving countries, the socialist hue of the programme and the absence of a business angle seems increasingly odd to the people involved. The patients obviously stand to benefit from the scheme, but in view of the general commoditisation of health care, the Chinese doctors in Maputo felt that their efforts were insufficiently remunerated and their local counterparts seemed to regard their efforts to improve the public health care system as a threat to their opportunities for business.

In a blog post by Jian Hong (2011), a Chinese entrepreneur who has published a number of books on Mozambique,[2] it is suggested that the Chinese scheme for improving public health care is an unwelcome socialist anachronism in a world gone capitalist. Instead of continuing the scheme blindly, Jian Hong opines, the Chinese government should gradually eliminate the aid aspect and turn the scheme into an investment strategy with the goal of ensuring that African countries are opened up to Chinese pharmaceuticals and to Chinese doctors who want to establish private practices in Africa. The medical team is an old-school, public sector aid project and while there is no reason to assume that the practice of sending out medical aid teams will end anytime soon, Dr Meng's trenchant nationalism of and Jian Hong's concern with the wasted business opportunities suggest that this type of state-planned development intervention is rapidly becoming obsolete.

Zones of construction

Mr Yang was a wiry man in his late forties. He used to work as a foreman for a team of painters on the stadium in Zimpeto, but he was reassigned to work the night shift as a guard when the stadium was finished and thus he had time to chat in the afternoon. Dressed in the characteristic purple uniform of Sogecoa, he invited me into the fenced construction site on the outskirts of Maputo and we sat on the bunk beds in the dormitory room that he shared with a colleague, smoking Chinese cigarettes and drinking green tea. Mr Yang's two-year contract in Mozambique was drawing to an end, but having worked in Madagascar, Grenada and Zimbabwe he was confident that the company would send him off again after the Spring Festival. The pay was reasonably good, about US$800 a month paid out as a lump sum upon completion of the contract. The cost of food and everyday necessities supplied by the company

---

2 As suggested by the titles – *Chinese Businessmen in Africa* (2003), *The Last Gold Mine: The limitless business opportunities in Africa* (2007), *Across Southeast Africa* (2010), and *Mozambique Guidebook* (2010) – the books by Jian Hong offer an interesting combination of basic facts, amateur ethnography, and practical advice to Chinese businessmen in search of information about Mozambique. Jian Hong also runs a website about Mozambique in Chinese: http://www.mozjh.com.

was docked from a monthly allowance of US$100 but with a bit of frugality it was possible to save up half of the allowance. Many Chinese companies routinely hold on to the passports of their Chinese employees and this was also the case with Mr Yang and his colleagues, but they were not particularly concerned about that. There was a real risk of getting mugged in the streets of Maputo, and the fact that they might be accosted and fined as illegal aliens by the Mozambican police if they walked around without their passports was just another good reason to stay inside the construction site. The company would occasionally organise an outing to the Sogecoa supermarket or a visit to a Chinese restaurant, but Mr Yang and his colleagues generally worked, ate, and slept inside the fenced construction site for the duration of their contract without venturing out. This is probably not entirely unlike the situation of rural construction workers employed on construction sites in Chinese cities, and the fact that this particular site was located in Mozambique seemed little more than an inconvenient detail to Mr Yang and his colleagues.

While the Chinese state has offered aid to Mozambique in the fields of medicine, agriculture, and education for decades, recent years have also seen massive investments in public buildings and infrastructure. Starting in 1999 with the Parliament, the Joaquim Chissano International Conference Centre, the Ministry of Foreign Affairs, and other public buildings were financed through donations and concessional loans from the Chinese state and built by Sogecoa (Mozambique), the Mozambican branch of AFECC (Anhui Foreign Economic Construction Co). The same company was also contracted to build the national stadium in Zimpeto and Maputo International Airport. The bulk of Sogecoa's business in Mozambique consists of contracts for the Chinese state, but the company now wins a variety of tenders and deals in real estate on its own. As noted in studies of Chinese construction projects in southern Africa (Bosten 2006; Burke 2007), the projects financed by the Chinese state seem to serve as stepping stones for Chinese companies and having established themselves locally, they start to bid for public tenders or contract projects for private investors of their own accord. Contracting for the Chinese state is considered to be quite attractive; the company may be certain that the money is there, and as the technical supervision is usually done by another Chinese company, there is a good chance that the projects may be completed without costly disputes. Sogecoa seems to have very good relations with government officials in both China and Mozambique, and the company has won the majority of the contracts in Mozambique, but other Chinese construction companies, such as CCM and the China Henan International Cooperation Group, Co Ltd (CHICO), have likewise carried out contracts for the Chinese state and then moved on to operate independently.³

While Chinese workers do not really leave their construction sites, the compounds are not entirely self-contained and the Chinese employees often supervise groups of local workers. Mozambican laws stipulate that a certain proportion of workers must be local and in most cases it would not only be expensive but also illegal for Chinese companies to rely entirely on Chinese labour. Few of the Chinese workers claim to speak Portuguese, but quite a few of them note that the interaction with local workers produces a kind of language that is neither Chinese nor Portuguese. It is a language of single words, technical terms and simple expressions such as 'good morning', 'good evening', and 'faster', but the Chinese say that it works as a means of communication within the compounds even if people outside do not understand. A number of Chinese foremen have pointed out that the Mozambican workers address them as '*amigo*' whereas white people are addressed as 'boss' or '*patrao*' and they present this as an indication of the amicable relations between Chinese and Mozambicans. The Chinese generally seem to think the Mozambican workers appreciate the Chinese work ethic, especially the fact that Chinese bosses do not disdain manual labour, but while the Chinese have the impression that they are making themselves understood as '*amigos*', the Mozambican workers generally say that they do not understand the Chinese and there seems to be a great deal of resentment and confusion among the Mozambican workers. Dissatisfaction about wages and working conditions occasionally results in strikes and violence and as segregated as these construction sites are, they cannot fail to generate tensions and conflicts.

Take-away timber

Mr Nie was the managing director of a Chinese timber company in Cabo Delgado. He was only 26 years old, but the way he issued rapid and precise orders in Chinese and Portuguese on his cellphone suggested the sort of ruthless efficiency one might have expected from a businessman twice his age. Mr Nie grew up in Guangxi and, having graduated from college, he went straight to Mozambique and worked for a timber company in Beira with his uncle, who was skilled in woodcutting. He managed to learn some Portuguese and when his contract was due to expire he happened to land a job with another Chinese timber company and relocated to Montepuez. The new boss groomed him for a management position, sending him from one end of the

---

3 Morten Nielsen's chapter in this volume describes how CHICO won the international tender to build a section of EN1 for World Bank money. In the event, that project was subcontracted to another company, the seventh division of China Railways Engineering Corporation.

company to the other, taking him out for meetings and dinners with the local elite, and ensuring that he could communicate in Portuguese. After a year of training, the boss went home to China and left Mr Nie in charge of the whole company, which had a sawmill in Pemba with 50 local employees, a concession area of some 40 000 hectares, and four logging teams with heavy equipment and a total of 100 workers. In the beginning, Mr Nie was constantly on the phone to China, but after a year on his own, he felt confident that he had tried and solved all the various problems that might arise in the normal course of work. Every so often, he would drive the 300 odd kilometres to the concession areas and back in one day in order to resolve disputes between the Chinese foremen and the local workers, to pay out wages, or check on faulty equipment. It is usually just a question of money, he said, and noted how he had learnt to hand out tips for everyone, including officials, during his time in Mozambique. Mr Nie seemed genuinely proud of his job as a manager; he was making US$2 000 a month, and he was probably right in claiming that it would have taken at least ten years of hard work in China to get the kind of salary and responsibility that he had reached in just three years in Mozambique. Mr Nie had no intentions of leaving Mozambique any time soon; even if the country ran out of timber, there were plenty of business opportunities in real estate and tourism, and Mr Nie was actually thinking about settling down permanently with his Mozambican fiancée, a girl from a wealthy local family.

In terms of natural resources, the mining industry has yet to take off in Mozambique and hardwood is the single most important export item that goes from Mozambique to China (Jansson & Kiala 2009:5), constituting 69% of total export value in 2008 (Ilheu 2010: 22). The first Chinese logging companies in Mozambique were established in the 1990s in order to bypass South African logging companies who were then acting as intermediaries, but the sector is now dominated by Chinese companies and the timber goes to China where it is made into furniture and floor boards. Originally, only Mozambican nationals could apply for the logging licences, which allowed them to cut and sell 500 cubic metres of timber in areas where they could reach an agreement with the locals. Since 2002, it has also been possible for foreign companies to apply for larger concession areas, and the Chinese companies now use a variety of strategies for obtaining timber: purchasing some of the timber, cooperating with licence holders by providing trucks and chainsaws in return for timber, or operating larger concession areas where the Chinese companies retain full operative control over equipment and man power.

Despite the emerging regulatory frameworks, Catherine Mackenzie's (2006) provocative description of Mozambican forestry as a 'Chinese takeaway' seems to resonate with local views of the industry. In the concession areas, the locals are not compensated for the hardwood extracted, and even in the case of individual licences where the locals should actually have a say, the offer of wages for a number of local men and the promise of a school building is usually enough to induce communities to part with their ebony and rosewood. Paying minimum wages – and sometimes less – for manual labour and little compensation to the community for the loss of hardwood, the Chinese companies generally seem to be exacerbating rather than alleviating rural poverty while the profits end up in the pockets of local elites and Chinese businessmen. The logging quotas and the ban on export of unprocessed wood are intended to make forestry a sustainable industry and increase the number of jobs in timber processing in Mozambique, but there is a very considerable illegal export of unprocessed logs as they are exempt from import duty in China and fetch a higher price. The Chinese companies with concession areas have been obliged to install some basic processing equipment and some of them make a simple rough cut of the logs, which reduces the value but makes the timber legal. In other cases, however, the inspectors from the Agricultural Department and the customs officers are persuaded to describe containers full of trunks as containers full of planks.

Writing from the perspective of an environmental non-governmental organisation, Daniel Ribeiro (2010) suggests that there is a massive illegal export of unprocessed, above-quota logs despite occasional seizures of ships and containers. Simple bribes are no doubt part of the picture, but illegalities on such a scale would hardly be possible without the collusion of high-level Mozambican officials and in this respect, the Shanghainese woman managing the largest timber company in Pemba offered an interesting story. Ten years earlier, her boss was buying timber in Beira and struck up a conversation with a Mozambican man in a restaurant. The man turned out to be the governor of Cabo Delgado and he invited the Chinese entrepreneur to start up a business in Pemba. From other sources, we learnt that the governor sat on the company board and placed a trusted official from the Agricultural Department in the company, thus promoting smooth cooperation between the company and the supervising administrative unit. It was never entirely clear how this intimate relation between the local state and the Chinese entrepreneur worked, but there seemed to be a general understanding that this particular company was protected and some of the workers remarked that the inspectors never entered the sawmills of that particular company. The Shanghainese manager had started up a business association for the Chinese companies in Pemba, and while some of their activities were purely social, she also tried to help her compatriots with the various problems they encountered in Mozambique. Interestingly, she had recently contacted the Chinese ambassador in Maputo and complained that the embassy had forgotten all the Chinese in Northern Mozambique. As a consequence, she was now regularly in contact with the Chinese embassy as a representative of the Chinese community in the area. As this case illustrates, private Chinese businessmen are fully capable of forging alliances with local elites without any political backing from home but acquiring such backing is highly desirable and the Chinese embassy is consequently drawn into new and potentially quite contentious fields of interest.

Shoes and security
A young Mozambican man with a big stick and a shot-gun slung over his shoulder was posted at the entrance to the small crowded Chinese shoe shop in downtown Maputo. The middle-aged Chinese couple who owned the business didn't really believe that the guard would contribute much to improving their security but, having been robbed at gunpoint a week earlier, they felt that something had to be done. Mr Jia and his wife had spent some years trading in Eastern Europe before they moved to South Africa. South Africa proved to be a profitable place to do business, but they found the country far too dangerous and quickly moved on to Mozambique. Having spent most of his youth in Maputo, their 24-year-old son was fluent in Portuguese and he was currently working as an interpreter in Angola, earning an extravagant USD$3 000 a month. Their daughter was about to graduate from high school and they were debating whether they should follow their daughter when she started university in some developed country – Mozambique, they felt, had become less profitable and more dangerous over the past years. Yet business seemed pretty brisk in the shoe shop, a new container full of shoes had come in, and the customers were lining up on the street outside the shop. Whenever the shop became too crowded, Mr Jia said, thieves would take off with the shoes on display, and so the guard was instructed that only six customers were allowed inside. Mozambican street vendors were the most frequent customers, and some of them had set up shop on the pavement right outside the store. In China they obviously would not have tolerated that, Mr Jia said, but Mozambique was so disorganised that there was nothing that could be done about it, and while the street vendors were making profits that might have gone into Mr Jia's pockets, they were also saving him the trouble of retail sales.

Only a couple of the stores in the neighbourhood had signs indicating Chinese ownership, but it turned out that Mr Jia's shop was but one among a score of Chinese shops, most of them specialising in shoes. Though some of the shop owners claimed to have made quite a bit of money before the influx of Chinese competitors and the fluctuation of exchange rates curtailed their profits, the shops were unassuming affairs conducted on run-down premises rented from owners of Indian or Pakistani descent. The Chinese shops were thus quite inconspicuous, but nonetheless almost half of them were hit by a gang of armed robbers in the summer of 2011. One of the shop owners had fired a gun into the air when the robbers took off, but the round in the chamber proved to be too old and the strangled sound from the dud bullet was a source of a great deal of mirth among the bystanders. Another Chinese shop owner remarked that this was probably the extent of the resistance the robbers would encounter – the police was inefficient and even if the culprits were apprehended, the laws of the country seemed to favour local robbers over foreign victims.

In response to the recent spree of robberies, some of the Chinese shop owners had sent a letter to the Chinese embassy in Mozambique and asked the embassy to convey their concern over the lack of security in Maputo to the relevant Mozambican authorities. The shop owners seemed fairly sure that nothing would come of this petition as the embassy was generally reluctant to flex its muscle on behalf of Chinese nationals, but there were other initiatives on the drawing board. Representatives from the various Chinese associations in Maputo had met with personnel from the embassy to discuss the possibility of setting up something they called the Centre for Police Civic Cooperation 警民合作中心. This centre was intended to facilitate cooperation between local police and Chinese nationals in different ways, and one of the proponents was hoping that the centre would not only cultivate relations to police officers in Maputo, but also provide a 24-hour response service to Chinese nationals. As part of this service, the centre would send a bilingual Chinese to ensure smooth communication between the Chinese national and the police. In June 2011, there were intense discussions on what form such a centre should take and which of the competing Chinese associations would be in charge.

Surprisingly, the embassy responded to the worries of the shop owners in a fairly forceful manner and on 26 July, the Chinese ambassador met with the Mozambican chief of police and commanders of the Rapid Intervention Force, the Maputo City Police, and the Maputo Province Police. As one might expect, the official Chinese communiqué on this meeting is couched in rhetoric on the amicable relations between the two countries, but the ambassador actually states the problem quite explicitly, stating that 'it is necessary to establish an efficient working mechanism to ensure that the legal rights of Chinese nationals in Mozambique are fully and effectively protected' (MFAPRC 2011). The outcome of the meeting was that 'the two sides formally announced the establishment of the Police and Citizen Joint Defense Mechanism involving the Mozambican Police, the Chinese Embassy, and representatives from Chinese companies and residents in Mozambique' (MFAPRC 2011). Some of the

Chinese nationals selling shoes in downtown Maputo had hoped for an actual centre operating round the clock, but a framework for consultations between Chinese businessmen and Mozambican police on issues of security was more than most of them expected, and the new Chinese ambassador has apparently continued the regular consultations. According to a news item posted on the website run by Jian Hong (2013), the Chinese ambassador and representatives from various Chinese associations and companies met eight representatives from the Mozambican police, including the Deputy Police Commander, at the Sogecoa Hotel in Maputo on 11 October 2013. All told, around 60 people participated in this meeting and some of the Chinese businessmen expressed their wish for increased police patrolling around construction sites and called for swifter police response to robberies. Clearly, the security concerns of Chinese companies in Mozambique have not been resolved overnight through the intervention of the Chinese embassy, but the case illustrates quite nicely that the Chinese embassy in Mozambique is not just a vehicle for policies from Beijing and it makes one wonder whether Chinese embassies may increasingly be forced to respond to local pressures from Chinese business and civil society organisations.

Conclusion

> Today the imminence of the "Chinese century" may appear more real than ever, just as the American empire once seemed the inevitable end of history. Many of us hold our breaths in anticipation and anxiety. It would be useful, however, to remind ourselves that the "global" is not always a very reliable map for locating the future, and that the problems with metaphors of the yellow peril, the communist takeover, or an emerging global economic giant is not that they are too wild but rather not imaginative enough. (Zhan 2009:201)

The four ethnographic encounters described above suggest that the Chinese presence in Mozambique cannot really be understood as the enactment of a master plan made in Beijing, and the Chinese engagement in Africa seems to be working out in ways that were not anticipated in any plan. The importance of private initiative beyond the plan was forcefully illustrated when I met a group of young Chinese en route from Dar es Salaam to Maputo. They boarded the aeroplane in Pemba with a large assemblage of flashy carry-on luggage. I was seated next to one of them, a 20-year-old man who became visibly nervous when I struck up a conversation in Chinese. He insisted that they were going to Maputo to have fun for a couple of days, but it was obvious that they were not really enjoying the trip. He found the aeroplane food inedible so he had not eaten since Hong Kong, and he was struggling to understand the announcements in English. Someone had spilt sugar in the overhead luggage compartment and ants were constantly dropping down on him from above. At one point, he tried to change seats, but the other passengers laughed at his incomprehensible English and he was obliged to return. He pulled his black jacket of imitation leather over his head to avoid the ants and the questions, but after half an hour of silence he asked me apprehensively whether I thought it was permissable to go 'poo-poo' on an aeroplane toilet. The young man was clearly not a seasoned traveller on his way to have fun in Maputo, and being somewhat frustrated with all the evasive answers, I ended up assuring him that I was not going to denounce him and asked directly if he was a migrant worker. He seemed almost relieved at the question and explained that his family in Fujian province had sent him off to make his way in the world. He had a return ticket but he was going for an interview with a potential employer and if things worked out he was planning to stay and work as a cook. When we landed in Maputo, it turned out that the young Chinese passengers had no checked luggage and they were taken directly to a mini bus that was waiting outside the airport. I never saw the young man again, and he never responded to my emails.

When I told this story to a Chinese friend residing in Mozambique, he suggested that the youngsters were probably on their way to South Africa. The fact that they had very little luggage indicated that they were going to walk across an unguarded section of the border. This was a regular industry, my friend claimed, and he explained that as many as 30 Chinese enter South Africa illegally through Mozambique every week. Some are caught as illegal aliens and deported back to Mozambique, others get shot when they set up shop in dangerous neighbourhoods, but most of them disappear into jobs in Chinese businesses and gradually acquire the papers, forged or real, that enable them to live in South Africa. This sort of migration is neither controlled nor condoned by the Chinese state; it happens outside the framework of any master plan. The fact that there is a great deal of private entrepreneurial activity involved in the Chinese presence in Africa may not come as a great surprise, but what does seem rather surprising in the ethnographic encounters described above is the extent to which private Chinese entrepreneurs and local Chinese associations have started to appeal to the Chinese embassy and, by implication, the Chinese state, to protect their legal interests in foreign countries. 'The Chinese embassy just tells you to be good and adhere to the local laws. Even when you're treated unjustly by the local authorities, they never intervene,' one Chinese businessman complained and went on to express his admiration for the hawkish style of the Portuguese. One of his Chinese friends held a Portuguese passport, and when he got into trouble with the Mozambican police, the Portuguese embassy had spared no expense to defend the interests of a Portuguese national. There seemed to be general consensus among the small-time Chinese businessmen that the Chinese government has poured aid into Africa with little to show for it, and that it is high time to take a much more forceful stance to protect the property and safety of Chinese nationals.

In a recent article, David A Robinson (2012) provides an overview of the Chinese engagement in Mozambique and discusses how this particular case may contribute to more general arguments about China's aims and impacts in Africa. Robinson concludes that China's engagement is economic and diplomatic rather than military and strategic, and that the drive to acquire natural resources does not preclude a sincere commitment to promoting economic development and social stability. On a certain level of generality, this is all very true but the aims of the political centre are probably not a very reliable indicator for what is going on and what will happen in the future. It seems fairly evident in the ethnographic material presented here that the Chinese in Mozambique are not only conducting business and forging local political alliances in ways that were not anticipated in any plan, they are also speaking back to the political centre in Beijing, demanding that the Chinese state start flexing its muscles and step in to protect their rights and interests. The deployment of a frigate to combat piracy in the bay of Aden and the spectacular evacuation of almost 40 000 Chinese nationals during the initial stages of the civil war in Libya in 2011 suggests that the Chinese government is only now coming to realise that decisive interventions abroad are not just possible but also supported with great enthusiasm by public opinion at home. On 28 February 2011, the US version of the *China Daily* carried an editorial stating that 'This is the first time the Chinese navy has participated in such a mission. It once again proves the People's Liberation Army is a reliable force safeguarding the safety of all Chinese people, be they at home or overseas.'

Judging by the surprising rescue mission in Libya, it is contingencies on the margins rather than pre-existing, central blueprints that will decide how the expansive Chinese polity develops. As the number of Chinese nationals abroad and the value of their private and corporate investments continue to grow, it will be increasingly difficult to 'safeguard the safety of all Chinese people at home and overseas' and surely it is merely a matter of time before some contingency on the margins comes to undermine the present policy of non-intervention in the internal affairs of other countries. Exactly how China will adapt to challenges on the margins seems very much up in the air and that, I would argue, is the reason why it is important to study how Chinese doctors, construction workers, timber merchants and small-time traders interact with locals in places like Mozambique. Not because these ethnographic sites and moments elucidate how a pre-existing master plan is being executed, but rather because the run-down housing of Chinese doctors, the construction sites run in broken Portuguese, the decrepit sawmills and rented shoe shops are the kinds of places where China is fitfully hammered into new and surprising shapes.

References

Alden, Chris. 2007. *China in Africa*. London: Zed Books.
Alden, Chris, Large, Daniel & de Oliveira, Ricardo Soares. 2008. *China Returns to Africa: A rising power and a continent embrace*. London: Hurst.
Bodomo, Adams. 2010. 'The African Trading Community in Guangzhou: An emerging bridge for Africa-China Relations'. *The China Quarterly*, 203:693–707.
Bosten, Emmy. 2006. 'China's Engagement in the Construction Industry of Southern Africa: The case of Mozambique'. Paper read at 'Asian and Other Drivers of Global Change', 19–21 January, St Petersburg.
Bräutigam, Deborah. 2009. *The Dragon's Gift: The real story of China in Africa*. New York: Oxford University Press.
Burke, Christopher. 2007. 'China's Entry into Construction Industries in Africa: Tanzania and Zambia as Case Studies'. *China Report*, 43(3):323–336.
China Daily. 2011. 'Timely Evacuation'. China Daily Editorial 28 February 2011. Available from: usa.chinadaily.com.cn/opinion/2011-02/28/content_12087127.htm [Accessed on 23 January 2014]
Hsu, Elisabeth. 2002. '"The medicine from China has rapid effects": Chinese medicine patients in Tanzania', *Anthropology and Medicine*, 9(3):291–312.
Ilheu, Fernanda. 2010. 'The Role of China in the Portuguese Speaking African Countries: The case of Mozambique (Part II)'. Centre of African and Development Studies, Technical University of Lisbon.
Jansson, Johanna & Kiala, Carine. 2009. *Patterns of Chinese Investment, Aid and Trade in Mozambique*. Stellenbosch: Centre for Chinese Studies, Stellenbosch University.
Jian, Hong 剑虹. 2003. 中国商人在非洲：商情，风情，人情. 北京：中国经济出版社.
Jian, Hong 剑虹. 2007. 最后的金矿：无限商机在非洲 *The Last Gold Mine*. 北京：中国时代经济出版社.
Jian, Hong 剑虹. 2010. 东南非洲之旅：穿越东南非洲 *Across Southeast Africa*. 北京：中国科学文化音像出版社.
Jian, Hong 剑虹. 2010. 东南非洲之旅：莫桑比克指南 *Mozambique Guidebook*. 北京：中国科学文化音像出版社.
Jian, Hong 剑虹. 2011. 中国援非医生能走多远. Blog post 6 August 2011. Available from: bbs.tianya.cn/post-5033-1714-1.shtml [Accessed on 23 January 2014].
Jian, Hong 剑虹. 2013. 2013年中莫警民联谊会议在马普托华安九点举办. Available from: www.mozjh.com/xinwen-nr.asp?divaction1=yes&divaction=yes&id=7595938 [Accessed on 26 January 2014].
Langwick, Stacey. 2010. 'From Non-Aligned Medicines to Market-Based Herbals: China's relationship to the shifting politics of traditional medicine in Tanzania'. *Medical Anthropology: Cross-Cultural Studies in Health and Illness*, 29(1):15–43.
Lee, Ching Kwan. 2009. 'Raw Encounters: Chinese managers, African workers and the pPolitics of casualization in Africa's Chinese enclaves'. *The China Quarterly*, 199(-1):647–666.
Mackenzie, Catherine. 2006. 'Forest Governance in Zambézia, Mozambique: Chinese Take Away!' Final report for Fongza. Available from: coastalforests.tfcg.org/pubs/GovernanceZambézia-MZQ.pdf [Accessed on 26 January 2014].

Mathews, Gordon. 2011. *Ghetto at the Center of the World: Chungking Mansions, Hong Kong*. Chicago: University of Chicago Press.

MFAPRC, 中华人民共和国外交部 Chinese Ministry of Foreign Affairs. 2011. 驻莫桑比克大使黄松甫与莫警察部队负责人举行工作会晤 2011. Available from: cs.mfa.gov.cn/lsbh/lsxw/t842919.htm [Accessed on 15 February 2012].

Michel, Serge, Beuret, Michel, Woods, Paolo & Valley, Raymond. 2009. *China Safari: On the trail of China's expansion in Africa*. New York: Nation Books.

Ramo, Joshua Cooper. 2004. *The Beijing Consensus: Notes on the new physics of Chinese power*. London: Foreign Policy Centre.

Ribeiro, Daniel. 2010. 'Disappearing Forests, Disappearing Hope: Mozambique'. In: A Harneit-Sievers, S Marks & S Naidu, eds. *Chinese and African Perspectives on China in Africa*. Cape Town: Pambazuka Press.

Robinson, David A. 2012. 'Chinese Engagment with Africa: The case of Mozambique'. *Portuguese Journal of International Affairs*, 6:3–15.

Taylor, Ian. 2006. *China and Africa. Engagement and compromise*. London: Routledge.

Zhan, Mei. 2009. *Other-worldly: Making Chinese medicine through transnational frames*. Durham: Duke University Press.

Chapter 5

How *Not* to Build a Road: An Analysis of the Socio-economic Effects of a Chinese Infrastructure Project in Mozambique

Morten Nielsen[1]

What do infrastructure projects amount to beyond the physical concreteness of construction materials? Is it possible that the mixing of sand, gravel and cement does *not* result in the construction of a road despite the apparent material existence of the latter? By examining the socio-economic effects of a particular Chinese infrastructure project in the southern part of Mozambique, this chapter will be guided by these seemingly paradoxical questions. Based on my ethnographic fieldwork among local road workers employed by CHICO,[2] a Chinese construction consortium, to upgrade and rehabilitate the EN1 highway between the towns of Xai-Xai and Chissibuca, I focus on the everyday encounters between these young Mozambicans and their Chinese superiors. As we shall see, according to the Mozambican workers, given the unacceptable working conditions, the poor salaries and the assumed unintelligibility and hostile behaviour of their Chinese counterparts, their labour cannot be considered as proper work and so, consequently, the mixing of sand, gravel and cement does not result in the building of a road.

During the last decade, the Chinese expansion in sub-Saharan Africa in general and in Mozambique in particular has increased its pace at a staggering rate. Currently, Chinese companies (both private and public) are involved not only in natural resource extraction but, equally, in infrastructure projects, the development of IT technologies and agricultural farming. According to a high-level Mozambican official at (ANE – the National Road Administration) Administração Nacional de Estradas,[3] nearly all public tenders are currently won by Chinese companies and not least so because of their highly competitive prices. 'Despite the often poor quality, we need to accept the Chinese companies,'

---
1 This chapter is based on ethnographic fieldwork carried out as part of the collective research project 'Imperial Potentialities'. Besides the author, the project team is composed of Morten A Pedersen and Mikkel Bunkenborg, University of Copenhagen. The research project is fully funded by the Danish Council for Independent Research, Social Sciences (Forskningsrådet for Samfund og Erhverv).
2 CHICO is an acronym for China Henan International Cooperation Group Co Ltd.
3 The National Road Administration.

he told me. 'They are always the cheapest and we don't have a lot of money'. As we shall see below, this comment succinctly sums up one of the primary factors in explaining the ease with which Chinese companies operate and expand in Mozambique while also implicitly suggesting possible tensions in the relationship. As such, this chapter might be taken as an attempt at unfolding some of the unexpected effects from an increased Chinese presence in a fragile nation-state in sub-Saharan Africa.

The material traces of an emerging empire

With the Mozambican peace agreement in 1992, the destructive civil war between the ruling Frelimo party and the Renamo movement that had lasted since shortly after independence in 1975 was finally brought to an end. Faced with the overwhelming challenge of reviving a paralysed state administration and rebuilding an infrastructural system in ruins, the Frelimo government turned to international lending institutions and political allies for support (Abrahamsson & Nilsson 1995; Hanlon 1991, 1996). During the protracted struggle against the Portuguese colonisers, Frelimo established a collaborative relationship with China that involved military support and guerrilla training (Dinerman 2006:21). Although the friendship cooled down somewhat in the mid-1980s when Mozambique made its 'turn toward the West' by adopting a series of International Monetary Fund-sponsored economic adjustment programmes, China remained a potential political ally (Roque 2009; cf. Hanlon 1996:16). From the early 1990s onwards, the relationship has been massively reinvigorated through a series of inter-governmental agreements and memoranda preparing the way for China's intensified presence in Mozambique. And judging from recent statements by the political elite in Mozambique, their Chinese counterparts will be confronted by few hindrances (if any at all) on the road towards further economic involvement in the country. In a response to the increased Chinese presence in sub-Saharan Africa, Armando Guebuza, Mozambique's president, stated that '*China é muito bem vinda em Mozambique*' (China is very welcome in Mozambique) (*Revistamacau* 2006). The cordial openness towards China might be read from the seemingly unlimited economic room for manoeuvre allocated to the latter. From an insignificant position in 2003 as the 260th 'biggest' investor, China is now among the ten biggest investors in Mozambique alongside countries such as Portugal, Italy and France (Macauhub 2009). The same gigantic leap can be read from the bilateral trade between the two countries which reached US$284.11 million in 2007, eight times more than in 2001 (Chichava 2008:9). If we narrow in on the most recent period, China's increasing economic presence is even more pronounced.

According to the CPI,[4] in the third quarter of 2011 China was the second largest foreign investor in Mozambique only surpassed by the USA (Club of Mozambique Lda 2012).[5] Hence, although relatively modest in comparison with other African states, such as Angola and Sudan, Mozambique's economic collaboration with its Asian counterpart is worth noticing simply because of the current pace which has one of the fastest growing rates for any single nation trading with China (Horta 2007).

According to the Ministry of Planning and Development, the Chinese government is currently financing 12 major infrastructure projects in Mozambique totalling nearly US$1 billion,[6] the most visible being perhaps the high-profile construction of a new national stadium on the outskirts of Maputo inaugurated in April 2011. Not all construction projects are realised through inter-government agreements, however, and the more than 30 Chinese companies active in Mozambique also work for municipalities, international donor organisations and private enterprises (Jansson & Kiala 2009). Of particular importance is CHICO, which has proven to be a remarkably competitive actor during tenders for infrastructural projects, not least when pertaining to the rebuilding of national roads. Since 2007, CHICO has constructed a 154-km road between Muxungwe and Inchope, 200-kilometre tarred road between Chitima and Mágoé in the Tete province and concluded a 300-metre bridge over the Incomati river in the Maputo province (Macauhub 2007; 2008a; 2008b).

In December 2008, CHICO was awarded the contract of rehabilitating and upgrading 96 kilometres of the EN1 highway between Xai-Xai and Chissibuca. Funded by the International Development Association (IDA), the project is undertaken as part of the Government of Mozambique's Integrated Road Sector Programme with an agreed contract sum of MZM1 269 447 739 (US$40 557 400). In January 2009, work began on the highway between Xai-Xai and Chissibuca and with only minor setbacks the construction project was completed in March 2011 with a final delivery to ANE the following month (Club of Mozambique Lda 2011). In its final phase, the construction team was composed of 56 Chinese on site and 261 local Mozambicans hired directly by CHICO (Scott Wilson Ltd 2010). As an important third party, ANE assigned Scott Wilson Ltd, an international construction consultancy, to supervise the project and, throughout the process, 21 full-time staff members

---

4 The Centre for Investment Promotion.
5 Apparently, this rise followed the approval of four investment projects worth a total of US$45.1 million.
6 '*Projectos submetidos para o financiamento externo do Exim Bank da China do Governo da China*', 6 August 2009 (Projects submitted for external financing through the China Exim Bank, Government of China). Document from the Ministry of Planning and Development.

headed by Samuel Nhemachena have accompanied the construction team while working on the road.[7] Since the beginning of the construction process, a group of 'checkers' have monitored all work activities and written daily reports to Samuel Nhemachena.[8] In those many instances when a checker estimated that immediate action was required, say, when the milling machine had cut too deep, an engineer was called from Scott Wilson to decide whether or not to make the layers of sand, gravel and cement anew.

Everyday bewilderment
Towards the end of the construction process, lines had to be painted on the new asphalt road. According to Samuel Nhemachena, in January 2011, Mr Wu Jinhou Sheng, the CHICO site agent, declared that the Chinese work crew was ready to commence with the road-marking process and that a spraying machine had been imported from China in September 2010. Somewhat surprised to learn that a spraying machine had been at the construction site for several months, Nhemachena requested an inspection of the machinery and an initial test to be carried out on a small country road near the EN1 highway before allowing the Chinese work team to proceed with the actual marking. As he was soon to realise, the Chinese technicians were not at all equipped to handle the spraying machine and they were therefore ordered to continue honing their painting skills on the country road until they could make at least 200 metres of perfect road marking (see Figure 5.1). Each month, Scott Wilson has drawn up a 'Works Progress Report' to be distributed to all stakeholders and in the report from February 2011, it is stated that,

> The trials [with the spraying machine] were not successful as there were a number of problems with the machine and personnel... The Contractor [i.e. CHICO] however maintained that he could do the work using the same machine and he tried and rectified most [but not all] of the problems... The Engineer [i.e. Scott Wilson] was of the opinion that the Contractor's machine was not good enough to carry out work of such magnitude. The Contractor's personnel also looked like they were not experienced enough to carry out the work. The Engineer therefore advised the Contractor to replace his machine or hire another machine or better still sub contract the entire road marking activity. Up to the end of February 2011, the activity of road marking

---

7 The Scott Wilson team was composed of four engineers, two technicians and 15 'checkers'.
8 In accordance with the initial contract, although operating as part of the Scott Wilson team, salaries for the checkers were paid by CHICO.

Figure 5.1 The 'trial section' where Chinese personnel were honing their painting skills

had not yet commenced and the Contractor had not clearly informed the Engineer what plans he was making to be able to achieve good and acceptable quality of work on this activity (Scott Wilson Ltd 2011:19).

As Samuel Nhemachena later told me, he allowed the Chinese crew to experiment with the spraying machine during the first weeks of January only to realise that they were incapable of making the road markings by themselves. In order to complete the construction process, CHICO therefore sent for a technician from the Chinese company that initially sold them the spraying machine and, finally, in late February 2011 the first tests were made on the EN1 highway. While sitting at a roadside café near the Chissibuca construction site in April 2011, Samuel described the difficulties associated with the painting process. 'When they were finally ready, I told them that I'd give them 200 metres on the road. The first day they didn't even complete 100 metres... Something on the spraying machine apparently broke and I immediately told them to get off the road. They eventually got it working. Not the first day though! It was only in March that the actual marking could begin. But it's not the CHICO crew painting the lines. The technician is doing all the work... Apparently, he hangs around until the process is completed'. I asked Samuel whether the technician had been able to actually carry out the road marking. 'Well, only a few days ago I got a call from one of my checkers telling me that the line was not straight. He had told them [the Chinese team] to stop but they refused. It was only when I called their guy and ordered them to stop that they actually did that... They really don't have a clue of what they are doing!' Samuel shook his head and roared with laughter.

Still, it was not only the lack of technical skills that caused the marking process to be continuously postponed. In the 'Works Progress Report' from February 2011, it is stated that '(o)n the trials for the road marking carried out, the reflective beads are not holding onto the paint. It is necessary to check on the quality of the paint. This should have been tested previously, to avoid delays now waiting for results to enable decisions to be made' (Scott Wilson Ltd 2011:14). According to Samuel, the checkers soon discovered that the quality of the paint was below the acceptable standard and he therefore instructed the CHICO foreman to make sure that proper materials were, in fact, being used. Not long after, Samuel was contacted by a Mozambican worker complaining about the poor work conditions while reorganising stored road paint at the CHICO compound. Wondering about why the materials engineer at CHICO had not informed him that they had a stored quantity of road paint while also being puzzled about the 'reorganisation' carried out by the road workers, Samuel and Taurai Mutanguro, the senior inspector of works, made an unannounced visit to the CHICO compound and demanded to inspect the storage room. The Chinese materials inspector took them to a small wooden shed at the back of the compound that was apparently locked and only 30 minutes later did he manage to locate the key so Samuel and Taurai could be let inside the storage room. 'When we finally got in there, some people (Mozambican workers) were still busy cleaning up'. Samuel took a sip of his beer before continuing. 'They had been working all day behind a locked door without the Chinese letting them outside. All the tins were neatly closed but there was still fresh paint on the ground'. From subsequent conversations with the Mozambican workers doing the reorganisation in the wooden shed and the materials inspector from CHICO, Samuel learnt that the paint had been stored outside for more than two months, exposed to the intense midday heat. Not only had many of the containers dried out; it was nearly impossible to use the remaining paint (as was documented in the 'Works Progress Report'). 'That's why it took so long for them to open the door'. Samuel thumped on the table with his index finger to emphasise his point. 'They didn't want us to find out that they were using the dried-out paint. So the workers were ordered to open all the tins and if the paint was dry, they removed the crust and poured what was at the bottom into a new container… But what I simply don't understand is why they didn't tell us about the paint in the first place. Why did they want to conceal that they had acquired the paint and the spraying machine? I really don't get that…'

The day after my conversation with Samuel Nhemachena, I had planned to meet some of the young Mozambicans who were still working on the road. At the time of my visit, road marking was the only major project to be completed and with only one spraying machine, the need for local personnel was minimal. I found the remaining road crew approximately 25 kilometres from the Chissibuca camp moving forward at a slow but stable pace (see Figure 5.2). Besides the technician who was operating the spraying machine, two CHICO engineers were constantly adjusting spraying speed and pressure. Three Mozambican workers were responsible for redirecting the traffic and two others were cleaning the asphalt on each side of the newly painted lines. I knew two of the Mozambican workers from my previous visits to the construction site and every time the spraying machine had to be adjusted, we had a few moments to catch up. Whereas Nelson had been working with CHICO since the beginning of the project period, Sérgio was hired during the most intense phase when several construction teams were operating simultaneously on various different sites. While sitting under a shady *nkanhú* tree, I asked them about the incident with the dried-up paint at the CHICO storage and, surprisingly, Nelson had been in the small wooden shed pouring paint from one container to another when Samuel and Taurai made their unannounced visit. 'Yeah… it was pretty hot in there.' Nelson looked past me and smiled. 'The entire day we were working without masks and without gloves pouring old paint into a huge container. It was almost like clay. And you know, they never told us anything… They just pointed towards the containers and locked the door'. Having been silently listening to Nelson's account, Sérgio slowly got up and put on his cap while casting a quick glance at the Chinese foreman coordinating the work on the spraying machine. 'Ah! The Chinese… they are not really human…'

How *not* to build a road

Similar to other infrastructure projects carried out by Chinese companies, a fenced compound has been built to accommodate the Chinese workers from CHICO during the construction phase. Every morning, the Mozambican workers arrived outside the compound in Chidenguele and, depending on the

Figure 5.2 The remaining road crew and the spraying machine

planned activities for the day, were transported to different sites where they worked in teams headed by Chinese foremen. At the outset, the stretch of the EN1 highway to be rehabilitated was divided into smaller segments with each work team operating from the outer end-points towards the centre. Broadly speaking, the construction process was constituted of three consecutive phases: (i) preparation; (ii) milling; and (iii) surfacing. The process began by preparing the roadbed and securing the pavement layers (the three layers of sand, cement and gravel underneath the surfacing asphalt). After a meticulous milling process where the top layer (the 'stabilised base') was mixed with cement, water was poured on for hardening the mixture and sprayed with tack coat before asphalt was put on as the final surface. Although some Mozambicans were assigned to particular tasks, for example, truck drivers or guards, the majority worked on all three phases of the project with the two first (preparation and milling) being the most time-consuming.

In the 'Works Monthly Progress Report' from September 2010, it is stated that the contractor's (CHICO) ability to complete the work within the contracted period depends on '[p]roper execution of the work to required standards. If work is not properly executed, the Contractor has been advised to re-work. This is a waste of time and resources on the part of the Contractor and should be avoided' (2010:7). According to Samuel Nhemachena, this small quotation aptly sums up a predominant difficulty regarding the collaboration with CHICO. After having accompanied the Chinese engineers for more than two years, Samuel was completely convinced that his Asian counterparts had little or no knowledge about actually building roads and this was the primary cause for the innumerable difficulties and frequent re-workings of the highway. Surprisingly, even among senior staff at ANE, I heard similar accounts. During a prolonged conversation with Clóvis Wate, a road engineer, I asked him about his collaboration with CHICO.

> Wate: The group of (Chinese) workers involved in this project really don't know how to do their job; the inspector (*fiscal*) has to teach them. Basically, the Chinese are still learning to do their job.
> Morten: So the Chinese don't have sufficient technical skills required to execute this project?
> Wate: No, they don't.
> Morten: How is it then possible for the Chinese to be working here?
> Wate: Well, that's because of the inspectors… even though it's not really their responsibility. They teach the Chinese how to do their job.

During the milling process, checkers from Scott Wilson walked a few metres behind the imposing milling machine and continuously tested the thickness of pavement layers. As was frequently the case, the blade cut too deep so that the cement from the stabilised base was mixed with the two bottom layers. If the blade was immediately adjusted, the milling continued without further delays. Numerous times, however, the attempted corrections did not have the desired effect and after inspection from the materials engineer at Scott Wilson, the stretch of road under construction had to be remade. According to Samuel, problems like these occurred almost on a daily basis. When making the stabilised base, the proportion between sand and cement would be incorrect or the density and compaction of the pavement layers unsatisfactory. Not surprisingly, Samuel was quite puzzled by the whole set-up. Even when instructed about proper construction techniques, the young engineers did not seem to be particularly interested in improving the quality. Still, as Samuel and his team tried to remain adamant regarding the quality of the construction work, CHICO was forced to spend huge amounts of money remaking their own previous work. 'I don't think that they generate any money here at all!' We were having dinner after a long day at the construction site when Samuel voiced his overt bewilderment about the Chinese and their peculiar comportment. 'The way I see it,' Samuel continued, 'they must be getting capital injections from the company in China'.

I asked why CHICO would possibly want to keep funding a project carried out by seemingly inexperienced and incapable engineers and thereby enduring continuous financial losses. 'That's also what I don't understand,' Samuel said before bursting into roaring laughter. 'The road might be there but it's already crumbling. Only a few years down the line, there won't be any road.'

To be sure, the Mozambican workers were as puzzled about their Chinese superiors as were Samuel and his colleagues from Scott Wilson. I was sitting by the roadside with a group of workers waiting for the materials engineer to decide whether the improper mixture of sand and cement recently detected by the checkers was sufficient cause for a reworking of the road. Inâncio nodded towards the young Chinese foreman engaged in an intense discussion with the engineer. 'They have to use more cement.' He looked the other way while shaking his head. 'Ah! I don't know why they work like this. There are already cracks (*rachas*) in the road.' Throughout the course of the project, many local workers had, indeed, considerable difficulties deciphering the peculiar actions of the Chinese. The particular tasks to be executed during the day were indicated by the foremen through the use of physical signs and monosyllabic exclamations as most of the Chinese spoke little or no Portuguese. According to the Mozambicans, the minimal degree of verbal communication often gave rise to unmanageable problems and particularly so when working with short-tempered superiors. While describing the quotidian and violent assaults, Inâncio introduced me to a colleague a bit further down the road. The right side of his face was visibly swollen with several scratches running from the hairline towards the chin. As Inâncio told me, the young Mozambican worker had been severely beaten by his Chinese foreman who was apparently upset by the former's inability to decipher how to carry out a particular task.

The mysteries of Chinese payment policies

Although the frequent attacks were considered both completely unacceptable and extremely stressful, their significance waned when compared to the complete lack of dialogue regarding the incomprehensible wage policies and the still missing contracts for most of the workers. According to the 'Work Progress Report' from February 2011:

> The Contractor [CHICO] has, from the beginning of the works, been encouraged to make sure that all of his workers have signed contracts before they start to work and that they were being paid salaries in line with the Government gazetted ranges of wages. In June, the Contractor submitted some copies of employment contracts for about 100 workers. Despite further requests, the Contractor has not submitted to the

Engineer any more signed employment contracts for his workers.' (Scott Wilson Ltd 2011)

During the final phase of the project, out of a total of 261 Mozambicans working for CHICO, only 103 (39.5%) had signed contracts and very few of these were formulated according to Mozambican labour laws. Hence, without contractual agreements, demands for improved rights were accompanied by uncertainty and fear of losing jobs. At the construction site, the only outside agent was the Scott Wilson unit and being contracted by ANE purely to carry out the overall audit of the project, Samuel and his colleagues were essentially incapable of anything other than reporting to their Mozambican counterparts the untenable labour situation. The overt risks notwithstanding, three times during the project period a group of workers did initiate a walkout to protest against the unfair wage policies and, particularly, against the refusal of the Chinese to pay holiday allowances and overtime. Although the initiatives did seem to have positive effects, as the Chinese agreed to pay one holiday per month, it was still quite difficult to decipher how and if the days were in fact registered. I asked Alex, a skinny Mozambican worker from Chidenguele, whether he thought the strikes had been successful. 'The result of the strike was that we made demands for holiday allowances and they accepted that… only… it's very little money. And I don't know whether I am actually getting the correct salary. You see, it's impossible to tell whether I get my holiday allowance or not.' As Alex and his colleagues explained to me, the main problem was the incomprehensible manner in which their wages were paid out. Monthly salaries were handed out as wads of money to the Mozambicans, who were required to stand in line and wait to be called forth one after the other. Besides the general discomfort about exposing to one's peers the amount of money earned (Pedersen & Nielsen 2013), this procedure made it virtually impossible to verify whether the received amount was correct or not. If pay slips accompanied salaries at all, they were written in Chinese, which made it somewhat difficult to figure out how the money had been calculated (see Figure 5.3). When the Mozambicans questioned their salaries, Chinese superiors monitoring the process immediately pushed them forward. Inâncio, the young worker mentioned earlier, expressed his frustrations about the situation while sitting at the roadside with a group of colleagues. 'They don't even put the money in an envelope. They just count the money and hand it to us as if they were offering it to us… it doesn't even seem like they are paying us at all' (*nem parece que estão a pagar*). One of Inâncio's colleagues intervened. 'He is right, you know. The Chinese is no good (*O chinês não é bom*). The money he is giving us is money without value'.

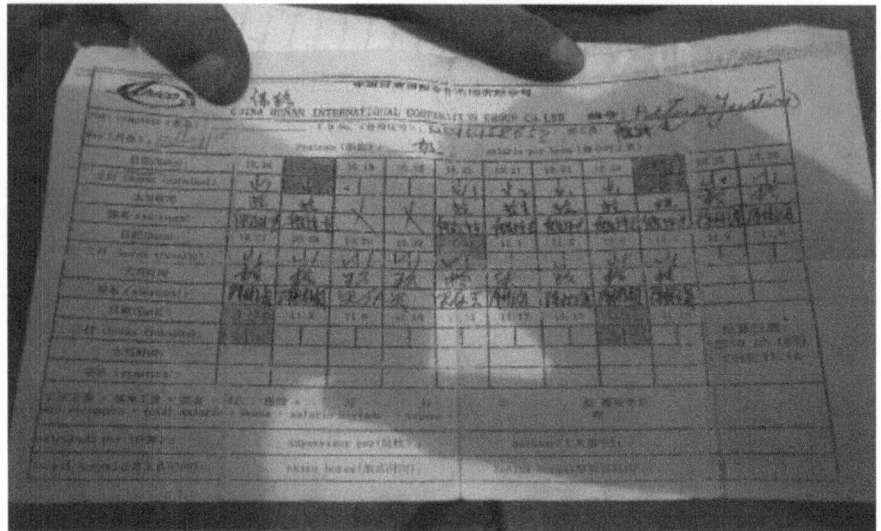

Figure 3 Example of a pay slip received by a Mozambican worker. As can be seen from the picture, all text is written in Chinese.

'If there are no memories, there are no dreams'

It is of course no startling realisation that salaries were of primary importance to the local workers. Even when employed by national companies the large majority of the young Mozambicans received meagre salaries that rarely reached the nationally agreed minimum wage.[9] Still, from my conversations with the road workers it seemed that working for the Chinese construction company was unlike conventional employment situations and particularly so regarding its long-term effects. As I was told numerous times, the work carried out at the construction site did not create proper memories (*lembrança*). Towards the end of my stay in Chidenguele in November 2010, I had a long conversation with Alex about the long-term effects of having worked for CHICO.

> The work doesn't make us remember anything at all [*não fica lembrança de nada*]. The pay is really bad and it doesn't allow us to start our own construction projects. If the money sufficed for buying construction materials for building our own houses, then it would come to constitute a proper memory. If we actually did receive proper salaries that allowed us to build houses and buy furniture [*mobília*], buy a bed and that kind of stuff… Then, after having completed the construction project, I would

---

9 The minimum wage for construction work in Mozambique is currently MZM2 435 (US$79) per month.

be thinking that "I worked for this company and I managed to buy these things".

As Alex poignantly describes, an important temporal relationship has been established between the hardships endured at the construction site and its future effects where the meaning of the former seems to be predicated on the productive realisation of the latter (see also Nielsen 2013). In other words, only when salaries received from his Chinese employers sufficed for buying something of lasting value, such as furniture or construction materials for a cement house, did the work carried out at the road between Xai-Xai and Chissibuca convey meaningful value. 'As workers, we have to continue imagining that we are going to buy things... a bed, a bike...' Nelson explained. 'But if the pay is really bad, then it's not even possible to buy five sacks of rice.' I asked Nelson if it was possible to imagine buying stuff when the pay was bad. 'No! Not when the pay is as bad as this. We have this mentality that we do what we have to do and then build houses for our families. But when the salary is really bad then we don't even have enough money to buy food (*alimentação*)... If there are no memories, there are no dreams.'

Although the amount of money received from the Chinese superiors was undoubtedly of primary importance, other factors affected the memories of having worked at the construction site. As I gradually found out, it was of crucial importance that the relationship between employer and employee was acknowledged by both as being of significant value. Through the exchange of labour and salaries, each party ideally gives something of themselves. At an interactional, everyday level, we might define this 'something' as the recognition of the other as a social person with whom interaction is not only possible but also desirable. Acts of mutual recognition might consequently occur in numerous ways, such as when employers allow employees a day off due to family bereavement or, equally likely, by advancing a smaller amount of the monthly pay and, conversely, when employees accept difficult working conditions and poor salaries based on oral agreements (rather than written contracts) with their employer. According to the young Mozambican, the situation was somewhat different at the road construction site, however, as their Chinese superiors were apparently incapable of engaging in meaningful social relationships. Even minor mistakes ignited the short-tempered Chinese and more than once it resulted in serious beatings. Indeed, as Samuel Nhemachena later told us, three 'checkers' had been physically assaulted by Chinese foremen when trying to interrupt their work.[10] Moreover, in contrast to standard, albeit

---

10 On one occasion, the assailant was taken to the local police station but no charges were pressed.

informal, work ethics in Mozambique, CHICO did not make advances on salaries. Those fortunate workers who had signed contracts with CHICO received monthly payments of roughly MZM3 000 (US$92). For the large majority without a contractual agreement, however, salaries varied and rarely exceeded MZM2 000 (US$61). Hence, halfway through the month, many Mozambican workers were short of money and thus in need of immediate advances of their salaries. Without this opportunity, a widespread tendency was to take a few (unpaid) days off while searching for other possible income-generating activities. 'This job deprives us of a lot of things,' Alex sighed. 'It doesn't provide any kind of security. They don't allow us to do anything else even when we have stuff to do at home. And if I have been away for only one day, they will probably fire me when I get back the next day.'

These various aspects of the social relationship between employer and employee were crystallised by the contested salaries. In a sense, the money *as such* seemed to manifest the problematic character of the Chinese superiors. 'It's not sufficient for buying construction materials,' Sérgio told me. 'In fact, you can't even buy proper meals (*ranchos*) for 30 days. Ah! The Chinese salary is complicated (*o salário dos chineses é complicado*).' Without any physical proof to document that they had, in fact, worked at the construction site, it was almost like the road in itself lost its significance. 'This money doesn't give me any memories of having built a road,' Alex sneered. 'The work that we did doesn't deserve this salary. This is a project of great magnitude (*envergadura*) It covers a lot of kilometres… From where we are right now, there is at least 95 kilometres to Chissibuca. This project has lasted more for than 18 month and even so we don't manage to commence building our own houses from the salaries we receive… This is not a proper road, you know.' Hence, in a peculiar reversal of conventional causality, the road seemed to acquire its particular qualities (its 'roadness', as it were) based on the subsequent conversion of salaries into something durable, such as construction materials for a cement house. Due to the problematic character of the Chinese counterparts, it was clearly not possible to make such conversions and so the sand, gravel and cement which the road workers meticulously mixed together did not constitute a road but merely an aggravation of what was already a problematic situation.

Conclusion

As I was about to return home after my last fieldwork in Mozambique, I arrived at the new airport built by a Chinese construction consortium.[11] Before entering the car park, all cars stop at an automatic bar where the driver pushes

---

11 The airport is being built by the Anhui Foreign Economic Construction Corporation (AFECC).

a button to receive a slip of paper with the time of arrival. Although the airport had been inaugurated only a few days earlier, the machine did not function. Instead, a young Mozambican airport official was sitting on a plastic chair next to the defunct bar writing out small notes with the approximate time of arrival. I rolled down the car window and although I did not say anything, I must have looked quite puzzled. The official nodded towards the impressive new airport behind him, shook his head and with an almost overbearing smile he said, 'China!'

In order to outline some of the unexpected socio-economic effects of Chinese interventions in Mozambique, I have focused on the everyday encounters between young Mozambican workers and their Chinese superiors. Hence, as is hopefully clear by now, rather than presenting a general account of China's presence in Mozambique, this ethnographic analysis serves primarily to indicate particular sites of contestation and tension arising with (but not entirely caused by) the increased activities of the former. In doing so, my reading of the socio-economic situation has emerged through the perspectives of the Mozambican workers precisely in order to flesh out the confusion and bewilderment of interacting with a counterpart that is radically different. Although this could lead to the conclusion that Chinese engineers are *ipso facto* unintelligible 'others', this is of course a far too easy and reductionist conclusion. Rather, from this narrowly focused ethnographic account, the challenge is to examine the broader political and socio-economic factors that give rise to such seemingly untenable situations. According to the anthropologist Anna Tsing (2005), we need to understand in greater detail processes of 'global friction' where different actors are brought together in 'productive moments of misunderstanding'. Whereas an initial analysis of the 'moment of misunderstanding' at the road construction site might suggest that we read backwards, as it were, from the situation in order to decipher individual strategies of all interacting agents and thereby examine the origin of these conflicts, Tsing guides our attention towards the socio-cultural 'stuff' that is actually being produced through these encounters, such as the reconfiguration of social relationships and the flexible imageries of particular future scenarios far away from the hardships endured while mixing cement, sand and gravel. Since I first started exploring different local socio-economic effects of Chinese interventions in Mozambique in 2009, the situation has changed dramatically, with increased economic investments, large-scale infrastructure projects and, equally important, transfer of personnel. The massive presence of Chinese companies has undoubtedly had numerous productive outcomes and made thousands of jobs available for Mozambican citizens. Still, as I have described above, in fragile situations, such as that which currently characterises Mozambique, the 'global friction' between interacting agents might, over time, create massive crises. Currently, there seems to be an increasing awareness among many Mozambicans, such as the young airport official writing out paper-slips for visitors at the new airport in Maputo, that massive foreign investments is a double-edged sword that needs to be critically examined. The next couple of years will show whether this increased awareness will also lead to improvements for the Mozambican population.

References

Abrahamsson, H & Nilsson, A. 1995. *Mozambique: The troubled transition*. London: Zed Press.
Chichava, S. 2008. *Mozambique and China: From politics to business?* Discussion paper no. 05/2008. Maputo, Instituto de Estudos Sociais e Económicos.
Club of Mozambique Lda. 2011. 'Chinese Construction Group CHICO Due to Deliver Road in Mozambique in May'. Available from: www.clubofmozambique.com/solutions1/ sectionnews.php?secao=business&id=21391&tipo=one [Accessed on 14 April 2011].
Club of Mozambique Lda. 2012. 'US is Biggest Foreign Investor in Mozambique between January and September'. Available from: www.clubofmozambique.com/solutions1/ sectionnews.php?secao=investment&id=23707&tipo=one [Accessed on 18 January 2012].
Dinerman, A. 2006. *Revolution, Counter-Revolution and Revisionism in Postcolonial Africa: The case of Mozambique, 1975–1994*. Oxon: Routledge.
Hanlon, J. 1991. *Mozambique: Who calls the shots?* Bloomington: Indiana University Press.
Hanlon, J. 1996. *Peace Without Profit: How the IMF blocks rebuilding in Mozambique*. Oxford: James Currey.
Horta, L. 2007. 'China, Mozambique: Old friends, new business'. Available from: farmlandgrab. org/2322 [Accessed 10 July 2009].
Jansson, J & Kiala, C. 2009. *Patterns of Chinese Investment, Aid and Trade in Mozambique*. Stellenbosch, Centre for Chinese Studies, Stellenbosch University.
Macauhub. 2007. 'Chinese Company Builds Moamba Bridge in Mozambique'. Available from www.macauhub.com.mo/en/news.php?ID=2683 [Accessed on 11 April 2011].
Macauhub. 2008a. 'Chinese Company to Build Road in Tete Province'. Available from: www. macauhub.com.mo/en/news.php?ID=6312 [Accessed on 10 April 2011].
Macauhub. 2008b. 'Chinese Contractor Finishes Work on Bridge over Incomáti River at the End of the Month'. Available from: www.macauhub.com.mo/en/2008/06/03/5147/ [Accessed on 10 April 2011].
Macauhub. 2009. 'China and Macau amongst 10 Biggest Investors in 2008'. Available from: www.macauhub.com.mo/en/2009/02/19/6582/ [Accessed on 19 February 2010].
Nielsen, M. 2013. 'Analogic Asphalt: Suspended value conversions among young road workers in southern Mozambique'. *HAU: Journal of Ethnographic Theory*, 3(2):79–96.
Pedersen, MA & M Nielsen. 2013. 'Trans-temporal Hinges: Reflections on an Ethnographic study of Chinese infrastructural projects in Mozambique and Mongolia'. *Social Analysis*, 57(1):122–142.
Revistamacau. 2006. 'O regresso dos chineses. Available from: www.revistamacau. com/2006/06/30/mocambique-o-regresso-dos-chineses/ [Accessed on 10 April 2011].
Roque, PC. 2009. *China in Mozambique: A Cautious Approach. Country Case Study*. South African Institute of International Affairs.
Scott Wilson Ltd. 2010. *Works Monthly Progress Report No. 18 September 2010*. Maputo, Administracão Nacional de Estradas.

Scott Wilson Ltd. 2011. *Works Monthly Progress Report No. 23 February 2011*. Maputo, Administracão Nacional de Estradas.

Tsing, AL. 2005. *Friction: An ethnography of global connection*. Princeton: Princeton University Press.

Chapter 6

Myth and Reality: Chinese Involvement in Mozambique's Agricultural Sector

Sigrid-Marianella Stensrud Ekman

When Lester Brown published his book *Who Will Feed China* in 1997, it generated a heated debate over the future of China's food security and its effect on global food markets. Concerns were raised over the capacity of the global food supply to meet future demand, in particular with the rise of China which has a fifth of the world's population yet has limited natural resources for food production.

In recent years this debate has once again come to life as shortages in food caused prices to hit a new all-time high in 2008 and spiked again in 2010 and early 2011, sparking riots and social unrest across the world (Hanson 2008:10). With the increased awareness of global warming, ever more land is being used for non-food agricultural production, such as biofuels and expanding urban areas, the competition causing a rise in the price of food produce as supplies drop and input costs increase. In an attempt to curb the price increases and national shortages, food producing countries such as Argentina, Thailand and Ethiopia (among several others) imposed export restrictions and bans on food produce with the consequence of further exacerbating the situation on the global market and for food-importing countries as supplies available to the international market dropped.

From the apparent volatility of the global market, a new concept has been born: 'land grabbing'. The main argument is that in order to guarantee food security, nations that are limited in their capacity to produce food domestically will lease farm land overseas and produce food for their home markets, thereby vertically integrating food production in order to ensure a stable supply of the essential products. In essence, a country vertically integrating food supplies through overseas farming is 'adding land', a resource normally regarded by economic theory to be a fixed input, thus expanding production potential without exposing themselves to the volatile international market.

China is known for its lack of land and abundance of people and since 2004 has been a net-food importer. Vast numbers of media articles have reported that China has begun to lease land abroad, notably in Mozambique (Groenewald, 2009; Macauhub 2008, 2009a; Horta 2007, 2008, 2009; Chiakwelu 2009; Smith

& Talbot 2009; GRAIN 2008). Concerns have been raised regarding the neo-colonialist nature of these land leases and agricultural investments.

But how pressing are food security matters in China really? And what are the nature and underlying drivers of Chinese involvement in the Mozambican agricultural sector? Is vertically integrating food production in Mozambique really a viable solution to address China's domestic needs? And more importantly, to what extent is China really involved in the Mozambican agricultural sector? Field research for this chapter revealed that the reports regarding Chinese agricultural investments in Mozambique are greatly exaggerated, and that the underlying drivers for Chinese interest in the Mozambican agricultural sector are not a direct concern for domestic food security. China's involvement is much more complex than just a drive for natural resources.

This chapter will attempt to provide an overview of Chinese projects and investments into Mozambique's agricultural sector, and analyse China's domestic food situation and the viability of vertically integrating food supply. Through understanding the nature of Chinese agricultural projects in Mozambique and China's domestic food security situation we can detangle the real underlying drivers for the Chinese interest in agriculture. It will be proposed that the argument presented for vertically integrating food production as a security measure is too simplistic and does not take into account other drivers for agricultural investments such as the search for profit, the internationalisation of Chinese firms, and agricultural expertise as a tool for aid. Furthermore, China's domestic food prospects are perhaps not as dire as one might think.

The drive for self-sufficiency by investing abroad

Why would the Chinese government feel such a drive to secure land for 'domestically produced' food abroad? After all, economic trade theory demonstrates that trading on the international market can lead to efficiency gains, enabling countries to consume beyond their production possibility function. One argument is that economic trade theory assumes that such trading relationships are always possible and steadily available. In reality such supply linkages may be broken or disrupted since economics and commerce do not operate in a vacuum separate from politics, culture and societal forces (Vyas 2000:4403). One example of political and societal interference is when food-producing countries impose an export ban, such as was the case in 2008 when countries like Vietnam and Argentina restricted supply to the international market (Freeman et al 2008:10).

Markets are driven by two forces, supply and demand. Demand is defined as the willingness and the *ability* to pay for a good; it is these things combined that stimulate supply (Sen 1981:433; Sen & Sen 1982:456). Yet we know that people are very capable of physically demanding food even when they are *not able* to pay for it, to the extent that they can be pushed to mass upheaval, social unrest and even revolution (Freeman et al 2008:3; Erlich et al 1993:26). It is for this reason that countries can find themselves in a situation where demand and supply in the economic sense reach equilibrium and markets clear, while society is still experiencing a shortage in a social sense (starvation), causing much aggravation and frustrations that can disrupt social harmony (Weng 2008).

The food crisis in 2008 did not escape China, and agflation (food inflation) has continued to worry Chinese policy makers in the ensuing years. While core inflation in China was at a mere 1.7%, agflation lay at double digits in 2008. In the fall of 2013 non-food inflation stood at 1.6% while the consumer price index rose by 3.1%, indicating that inflation is still driven mainly by the rising cost of food (Bloomberg 2013), exerting pressure on the 70 million urban workers. Vulnerable to rises in food prices, the increasingly large urban population continues to feel their budgets pressed (Davies 2008:3; Wen, et al 2008:9).

The argument has therefore been presented that China would lease land abroad to set up Chinese state-operated or government-backed farms overseas producing crops for export to the home country. If, as in this view, China is not buying crops from another country, but buying the rights to use of the land and all crops produced on it (Smaller & Mann 2009:7), they can extract and plant as domestically needed, thereby circumventing the international market. As opposed to traditional foreign direct investment (FDI), these types of investments would be resource seeking rather than market seeking (FAO 2009). The ventures would be driven by a search for resource security rather than profit.

In short, vertically integrating using overseas land is a substitute to domestic production, which would give similar security benefits to that of producing domestically, in that it avoids the uncertainties of the volatile global market (GTZ 2009:13). In essence the usage rights of the land would become 'Chinese' if usage rights are purchased. Hence the parallels drawn to neo-colonialism.

Coloniser, competitor or comrade?

Chris Alden, one of the most prominent experts on Sino-African relations, writes that Chinese engagement in Africa is usually viewed through one of three lenses. These perspectives of China in Africa are: China as an economic competitor; China as a coloniser; and China as a development partner (Alden 2007:5–6).

The first perspective on China in Africa views China as a competitor in markets, and is often used when discussing trade relations such as that of textile markets both in Africa and third markets, where China has a definite advantage over African manufacturers.

The second view of China as a coloniser often emerges in the media as a result of China's interest in natural resources and land. The extraction of these natural resources is compared to that of the imperial powers in the 19th century who simply extracted and exported raw materials without any value being added to the African countries, halting the development of local economies (Freeman et al 2008:3).

The third view of China, as a development partner, takes a positive-sum approach and attempts to explain how Sino-African relations is an advantage for both Africa and China. This view is compatible with the ambitions of Chinese foreign policy in which the principle of mutual benefit is a central guiding principle, and this is also the position proclaimed by many African governments.

While the Chinese government wishes to promote China abroad as a development partner, as an older brother for the developing country community, the media is increasingly hostile to China's engagement in Africa, often referring to China's activities in Mozambique as neo-colonialist. However, taking a closer look at the dynamic of China's agricultural investments it appears that China in this case more closely fits the description of a comrade, and perhaps competitor, than the often portrayed coloniser.

Mozambique's agricultural potential
The Zambezi river runs through what is called the Zambezi valley in central Mozambique, creating a geographical environment regarded as highly suitable for agricultural production. The fertile Zambezi valley stretches out 22 500 000 hectares, covering four provinces: the Tete province, nine districts of the Zambézia province, four districts of the Manica province, and four districts of the Sofala province (interview, former GPZ representative, Maputo 2010). In total Mozambique offers 30–36 million hectares of arable land with only about 15% of it under current cultivation according to official estimates (Roque 2009:9; Arndt et al 2008:1).

Mozambique also has a strategic position as a port nation (Roque 2009:13), facilitating transportation links between the Indian Ocean and inland countries such as Zambia, Swaziland, Zimbabwe and the north-eastern parts of South Africa. Food produced in Mozambique can thus easily be used for exports both overseas and to the regional southern African market.

Although often described as virgin land, much of the land is already under traditional usage by local populations. Yet productivity lies far below potential levels due to lack of infrastructure and inputs, such as modern farming

Table 6.1 Mozambique's food security ranking

Mozambique's Food Security Ranking	
Global Hunger Index (GHI)	21.5 (alarming hunger)
GHI ranking (out of 84)	64
Share of undernourished population	39.2%
Share of underweight children under five years	14.9%
Under five mortality rate	10.3%
Vulnerability and exposure to shocks	High
Country in crisis	No

Source: *Global Hunger Index, IFPRI, 2013*

techniques, improved seeds or fertilisers. As such the land can be described as immensely underutilised albeit not unused.

The Gabinete de Promoção do Zambezi Vale (GPZ)[1] was a governmental body set up to promote investments in the Zambezi valley, which was seen as key to initiate Mozambique's green revolution due to its vast potential (interview, former GPZ representative, Maputo 2010). Despite the tremendous potential held by Mozambique's fertile lands, Mozambique is nonetheless a nation with an unstable food supply of its own due to chronic underinvestment in the region's agricultural sector.

Table 6.1 describes Mozambique's current food security situation based on data from 'The Global Hunger Index' (GHI), published by the International Food Policy Research Institute. The GHI indicates the level of food security and hunger problems in various countries, and is measured on a scale from 0 to 100, 0 being full food security. Values exceeding 20 are defined as alarming hunger.

One of the arguments presented for land leases as a new form of colonisation is that these land leases take place in countries with poor food security of their own. The extraction of food from hungering countries is thus not a win–win situation and is morally opposable.

However, these arguments fail to take into account that the reason Mozambique does not enjoy food security is because Mozambique lacks the capital and technology necessary to fully take advantage of its abundant natural resources (GTZ 2009:13). China, by providing such inputs, could contribute to productivity growth which in turn could improve Mozambique's food security situation. It is plausible to assume that the Mozambican government's interest in leasing land to foreign investors arose precisely because Mozambique's food

---

[1] The GPZ was dissolved in 2010.

security is vulnerable, and a desire to improve Mozambique's agricultural productivity and food supply stability. FDI into land is thus not viewed as incompatible with host-country food security but mutually supporting. This view of mutual benefits is held by both the Chinese and the Mozambican government regarding investments between the two nations (Roque 2009:10).

Agricultural trade between China and Mozambique is currently very limited. Looking at Mozambique's exports to China we find that they currently consist mainly of wood and only a limited amount of food products. Duty-free arrangements for Mozambican products to enter China have had only a limited impact on exports to China since Mozambique currently has a low supply capacity (but still holds great potential for a larger capacity) (Jansson & Kiala 2009:3). Studies have found that China is not a major destination for Mozambican agricultural exports, and that Mozambican agricultural production currently does not overlap to a great extent with Chinese food demand (Villoria et al 2009:4–5). The rapid increase in trade volume between the two countries is for the most part due to imports of Chinese manufactured goods, such as cheap electronics and steel/iron products and has very little to do with food produce (Jansson & Kiala 2009:5).

China's agricultural engagement in Mozambique: myths and reality

China's relationship with Mozambique has intensified over the years, particularly with regards to agriculture. In the decades after Mozambique's independence from Portuguese rule, China provided training and technical expertise to Mozambique's agricultural sector through three projects. The first agricultural technical cooperation started as early as 1976, lasting until 1998, the second technical cooperation project for agriculture began in 1983 and lasted for two years, and the third project ran between 1986 and 1989 (Chinese Embassy in Maputo 2002). None of these historical projects involved leasing land for commercial or strategic use.

However, in the aftermath of the 2008 global food crisis many news articles have reported that China is investing US$800 million into developing agriculture in Mozambique, often insinuating that this is done through land leases with plans to establish large-scale farms and relocate thousands of Chinese settlers in order to stabilise China's food security (IPIM 2009; Macauhub 2009a; Horta 2009:11; GRAIN 2008). Most of the reports rely on information that is not based on actual field research despite the fact that the lack of data calls for such investigation. Within agriculture (excluding forestry) there are three main contentious issues in which China is said to be involved: (i) land leases and farming investments in the Zambezi valley, (ii) the construction of the Mphanda Nkuwa Dam, and (iii) the agricultural technology centres.

Investments into the Zambezi valley

In the media, China has been reported as leasing large tracts of land in Mozambique with the aim of satisfying its food security issues. In conjunction with this, it is claimed that thousands of Chinese settlers would immigrate to Mozambique for farming purposes. Some also claim that a Memorandum of Understanding was signed between Mozambique and China in 2006 regarding this mass-settlement of Chinese farmers and acquisition of farmland (Groenewald, 2009; Macauhub 2008, 2007; Horta 2007, 2008, 2009; IPIM 2009; Chiakwelu 2009; Smith & Talbot 2009; GRAIN 2008; GTZ 2009).

This study's field research in Mozambique revealed no evidence supporting these claims, however. At the time of the media hype surrounding the Chinese land grab, the Mozambican National Directorate for Land had not heard of any such land leases by China or Chinese companies in the Zambézia province (interview, Directorate for Land and Forestry, Ministry of Agriculture, Maputo 2010). In 2006, the Chinese government pledged to offer Mozambique monetary assistance. The Mozambican government were themselves allowed to determine what projects this money would finance (interview, former GPZ representative, Maputo 2010). Most of the money is dedicated to infrastructure projects such as construction of the new airport, the national stadium and other buildings of symbolic value in Maputo. Only a small fraction went towards agricultural investments in the Zambezi valley.

Through extensive lobbying the GPZ obtained US$50 million of the soft loan given to Mozambique by China Exim Bank in order to fund agricultural development projects in the Zambezi valley (interview, GPZ representative, Maputo 2010; interview, former finance minister; Maputo 2010). Of this US$50 million, US$19 million is being used to import agricultural tools and machinery, and the remaining US$31 million was allocated towards setting up three processing plants, one of which is for cotton, a non-edible agricultural product:

(i) one rice-processing factory in Gogodane, Zambézia province: capacity 150 tonnes per day (AllAfrica 2011)
(ii) one maize-processing factory in Ulongué, Tete province: capacity 25 000 tonnes of cereals per year
(iii) one cotton-processing factory in Guru, Manica province (African Agriculture 2009)

These projects were chosen, and will be run, by the Mozambican government (interview, former GPZ representative, Maputo 1 February 2010; interview, former finance minister, Maputo 2010). The extensive lobbying that the GPZ had to perform to obtain these funds for developing the agricultural sector in the Zambezi valley indicates that this is not investment directed by the Chinese government as part of a food security strategy.

Despite representing an increase in Mozambique's processing capacity, it will still lie well below meeting Mozambique's domestic demand (interview, former GPZ representative, Maputo 2010; African Agriculture 2009). It is therefore unreasonable to argue that these would buffer Chinese food security. Furthermore, these factories are set up to process existing cultivation of grain. These are not investments into expanding grain cultivation, but to increase the processing capacity of grain in Mozambique to obtain higher value added on the grain produced (interview, former GPZ representative, Maputo 2010).

What is more interesting is that despite the keen media interest in 'Chinese neo-colonialism' in Mozambique, other foreign investments into land leases by investors from countries such as South Africa, the United Kingdom, Sweden, Vietnam and Finland (interview, former GPZ representative, Maputo 2010; interview, former finance minister, Maputo 2010) have received less media attention. China's public image is that of a threat, and this could pose real difficulties for future deals (interview, former governor of the Central Bank, Maputo 2010). Media reports on China's 'land grabbing' could create obstacles for further agricultural cooperation of any kind between China and Mozambique.

The Mphanda Nkuwa dam

In 2006 the Mozambican government requested a US$2.3 billion loan from China Exim Bank to construct the controversial Mphanda Nkuwa dam on the Zambezi river (AIM 2006; AFRODAD 2008; Roque 2009:5). It has been suggested that this was done in exchange for land in the region of the Zambezi valley (Horta 2008). The Mozambican government has also called for assistance to finance the construction of two other dams in Cabo Delgado (Chipembe and Nguri) in order to improve the agricultural production of the region. However, these requests had not yet been approved at the time of writing. The new dam would vastly increase Mozambique's capacity to produce electricity. However, it is now known that Mphanda Nkuwa Hydroelectric Company (HMNK), a consortium consisting of the Brazilian company Camargo Corrêa, Mozambican Insitec and the publicly owned Mozambican electricity company, EDM, has been awarded a concessional contract giving HMNK the right to build and operate the dam (AllAfrica 2010).

Agricultural technology centre

During Hu Jintao's visit to Mozambique in 2007, a technical cooperation agreement was signed with Mozambican president Armando Guebuza. The agreement covers agriculture, albeit not exclusively (china.org.cn 2007). As a follow up, at the 2006 Forum on China-Africa Cooperation (FOCAC) summit, China announced that they wished to establish ten agricultural technology centres across Africa (later expanded to 14 centres, then 20), to promote technology transfers and scientific research in order to raise agricultural productivity on the continent (Jansson & Kiala 2009:7). Mozambique received one of the first centres, which is located in Umbeluzi, the Boane district, covering 55 hectares of land for research and training (Jansson et al 2009:72; Makoni 2009). The centre is run by Lianfeng Farm from Hubei province and the Mozambican Ministry of Science and Technology (Bräutigam 2009; Jansson et al 2009:73).

It was expected that the centre's research on seeds and training local farmers in modern cultivation techniques would significantly improve productivity and transform the Mozambican agricultural sector (Jansson et al 2009:73–74). Some estimates state that rice production will increase from 100 000 tonnes to 500 000 tonnes as a result of improved seeds and new planting techniques (IPIM 2009; Macauhub 2009b; Chiakwelu 2009; Makoni 2009).

The article argues that:

> Mozambique's increased rice production is clearly destined for export to the Chinese market, since rice accounts for just a tiny fraction of the Mozambican diet... (Macauhub 2009b)

However, as Deborah Bräutigam (2009) points out, Mozambique itself has a supply-demand deficit in rice; increased rice output could be used to satisfy this shortage in the Mozambican market, and so it is not clear that increases in rice production would be destined for export. In 2008 Mozambique imported 380 000 tonnes of rice from the global market, an amount that is higher than China's own rice imports of 330 000 tonnes (USDA database 2008). According to Alveranga (2008:66), Mozambique turned to China first to cover its rice shortages during the 2008 food crisis. This runs counter to the argument that rice production in Mozambique by Chinese firms 'clearly' must be destined for export back to China (Horta 2008). Media reports give the impression that the Chinese government selects a country in which they would like to establish an agricultural demonstration centre, but this is not strictly the case. African countries first request an agricultural demonstration centre, after which the Chinese authorities send a team to investigate the viability and decide whether or not such a centre should be established. The centres are established on the basis of the African countries' demand rather than Chinese desires (email correspondence, Bräutigam 2010). It is therefore not unreasonable to assume that Mozambique requested an agricultural demonstration centre to promote increases in rice production to satisfy domestic consumption. Without any actual deals on rice earmarked for Chinese export claims to the contary are rendered nothing more than speculation.

Despite this, the boost in agricultural productivity could still benefit China overall. A green revolution in Mozambique will have a positive, albeit indirect, effect on Chinese food security (email correspondence, Alden 2010). The potential for productivity expansion in Africa is great, which has been nearly exhausted in other parts of the world. Currently, however, Africa is a net-food importer from the global market. Initiating a green revolution on the continent would release supplies on the global market, making them available for other countries (email correspondence, Bräutigam 2010). This could help stabilise global markets and buffer against future food crises.

A second (general, not agriculture-specific) research centre is now planned to be constructed in the Moamba Technology Park. The Mozambican government has requested funds, but these had not yet been approved by the Chinese government at the time of writing. Various media reports state that the combined value of these two research centres lies at US$700 million (email correspondence, Bräutigam 2009; Macauhub 2009). However, only CNY55 million is being invested in the Umbeluzi centre (email correspondence, Bräutigam 2010; interview, GPZ representative, Maputo 2010). This figure is sometimes reported to be in US dollars, but it is worth noting that the correct currency is Chinese Yuan, as stated on the contract signed between the Mozambican and Chinese authorities (email correspondence, Bräutigam 2010; *China Monitor* 2009:71; Chiakwelu 2009; Makoni 2009). Bräutigam believes that it is the figure of US$700 million that has given rise to the bogus figure of $800 million often reported in the media (email correspondence, Bräutigam 2009).

Zamcorp

On 15 April 2006 the Mozambican government and the GPZ, through the publicly owned company Sogir, together with Geocapital and Mozcapital, established a company called Zamcorp, worth US$500 000. Geocapital, a Macau-based firm owned by Stanley Ho, will hold a 35% share in Zamcorp. The role of Zamcorp is to promote the Zambezi valley region and identify opportunities for investment, agriculture being one of the top priority areas, and will use Macau as a platform for reaching Chinese investors (GPZ 2006:2–

3). The Chinese side of Zamcorp is a private investor, not from mainland China. Zamcorp can therefore not be viewed as a vehicle steered by the government in Beijing as part of a greater grand strategy to secure food supplies. At the time of writing, Zamcorp has applied for 21 000 hectares of land for jatropha cultivation and biodiesel production, but is still awaiting approval.

Existing Chinese agro-investments

Despite not living up to the media hype on land grabbing for food security, there nonetheless exists some Chinese interests in Mozambican agriculture.

In 2007, thanks to an agreement between Hubei and Gaza provinces, a rice production project was set up in Xai-Xai, capital of Gaza by the Chinese state-owned company Hubei Liafeng.

Apart from rice production, the aim of the project was to provide technical training for local farmers. The project has been awarded 20 hectares of land with the possibility to rent land from a public irrigation company of up to 20 000 hectares expanding gradually. To date US$250 million has been committed to the project.

A team of Chinese agronomists from the Chinese Academy of Agricultural Sciences funded by the Bill & Melinda Gates Foundation was sent to the farm in Xai-Xai to experiment with various types of hybrid rice. The resulting yields were promising (see Table 6.2), but the project did not manage to expand as projected due to a lack of equipment and managerial issues (Chichava 2013:11).[2]

Due to the failure of Hubei Lianfeng to expand the project as planned, a private company, Wanbao Oil and Grain Co Ltd has taken over ownership. The plan is to eventually supply one-fifth of Mozambique's rice deficit needs (Chichava 2013:12). In 2013, RBL and Wanbao signed an agreement through which it granted 20 000 hectares of the public company lands to the Chinese company in exchange for developing irrigation infrastructure and technology transfers. As of 2014, however, Wanbao was only cultivating rice on 1 000 hectares due to floods and natural disasters. With 380 employees, Wanbao is one of the largest agricultural employers in Gaza, but with 320 of the employees being Chinese and only 60 Mozambicans the local impact of job creation is limited. Concerns regarding the planned size of Wanbao and disputes with local communities who have been evicted are raising tensions that could lead to conflict between the public company and Wanbao, on the one hand, and

---

2 For a more in-depth analysis of the technical cooperation between Mozambican farmers and Hubei Lianfeng, please see Chichava's (2012) occasional paper 'Xai-Xai Chinese rice farm and Mozambican internal political dynamics: A complex relation'.

Table 6.2 Output of Hubei Lianfeng farm from 2007 to 2010

Year	Area under cultivation (hectares)	Tonnes / ha	Production (tonnes)
2007–2008	20	9	180
2008–2009	30	9	270
2009–2010	40	9.5	380

Source: Chichava 2010; data from the provincial Directorate of Agriculture in Gaza 2010

Table 6.3 Chinese companies' agro-investments in Mozambique

Year	Project	Location	Ha	Investment (US$)	Product	Approved
2010	Sunway	Nampula	500	500 000	Peanuts and sesame products	Approved
2011	Chamei Agricola	Zambézia	1000	750 000	Rice	Approved
2012	China-Africa Agriculture Zambézia	Zambézia	3 000	1 000 000	Cotton	Not approved
2012	Agricola CCM	Manica	5 000	50 000 000	Rice	Not approved

Source: CEPAGRI data 2002–2013

the local communities on the other. The Wanbao project is the closest Chinese project akin to what is popularly dubbed 'land grabbing' in Mozambique, but as the company only aims to sell on the local market it still does not fit into the 'Chinese hunt for land to stabilise food security' argument.

An additional four requests have been registered at the Centre for Agricultural Investment Promotion in Mozambique (CEPAGRI) since 2009 for Chinese-funded projects: two of these proposals were rejected, two were approved, (see Table 6.3).

Only Sunway and Chamei were approved but neither of these projects is currently operating. Chamei never started up due to conflicts with the local community and Sunway ran into financial difficulties.

China's agricultural cooperation programmes in Mozambique

In addition to the agricultural investments made by a handful of Chinese companies, the Chinese government has made agriculture a top area for cooperation with African countries. As with much of China's engagement in Africa, this is nothing new. China has had agricultural cooperation programmes

Table 6.4 China's agricultural projects and development cooperation in Mozambique

1976–1998	Agricultural technical cooperation agreement (I)		
1983–1985	Agricultural technical cooperation agreement (II)		
1986–1989	Agricultural technical cooperation agreement (III)		
2002	MoU Agricultural Scientific and Technical agreement		
2004	Technical Cooperation Agreement (not exclusively agriculture)		
2006–	US$50 million soft loan for setting up three processing plants and import agricultural machinery and technology	Import of agricultural machinery	US$19 million
		Rice (Gogodane, Zambezi)	150 tonnes/day
		Maize (Ulongué, Tete)	25 000 tonnes/year
		Cotton (Guro, Manica)	
2006–	Agricultural Technology Center (Umbeluzi, Boane)	Operated by Lianfeng farm (Hubei Province) and Mozambican Ministry of Science and Technology	52 hectares CNY55 million (approximately US$8.4 million)

Sources: Ministério da Agricultura e Desenvolvimento Rural; email correspondence Deborah Bräutigam, 2009; interviews with Mozambican officials, 2010; AllAfrica, 2011, Chichava, 2010; Chinese Embassy in Maputo, 2002.

in Mozambique dating back as early as the mid-1970s. Table 6.4 gives an overview of past and current agricultural development cooperation and official agro-projects provided by China in Mozambique.

Getting the facts and figures straight

China has shown interest in Mozambican agriculture through various measures such as soft loans, financing of huge projects (Mphanda Nkuwa dam) and technological assistance. In addition, a handful of Chinese investors see opportunities in Mozambique's agricultural sector. Yet, despite numerous media reports on 'China's aggressive hunt for land' in order to secure food supply, there is very little evidence to support this view of China in Mozambique as neo-colonial.

China's engagement in Africa usually occurs in a cloud of non-transparency leaving much to be guessed by spectators and thereby giving rise to confusion (GTZ 2009:27; Kaplinsky & Morris 2009:3). The mix up between money devoted to technology centres and money invested into agricultural developments in the Zambezi valley gives the impression that China is investing hundreds of millions into setting up farms.

Double counting also seems to be common. Possibly, this is due to the time lag that follows announcement of aid or a loan until it is disbursed, and it is often disbursed in several packages rather than all at once. One example is the US$18 million reported to be invested by China in agricultural projects in the Zambezi valley (Jansson & Kiala 2009; AIM 2008). The news reporting gives the impression that this is additional money, when it is actually part of the US$50 million soft-loan dedicated to the Zambezi valley, provided to Mozambique by China. The lack of clarity thus lays the foundation for misinterpretations. Confusion regarding the currency can also cause the reported amount invested to be inflated.

It is important to make a distinction between Chinese investments into agriculture, such as leasing land, and Chinese aid and assistance programmes, such as constructing the technology demonstration centres. This differentiation can be hard since Chinese aid and business is often coupled. The picture that emerges from Chinese agricultural investments in upgrading Mozambique's agricultural technology is an image of China as a development partner rather than a coloniser.

There is indeed interest by Chinese companies in investing in Mozambique's agriculture, but these are limited to a handful of actors. Much of the investment is, however, directed at forestry, not food production. The single largest food-producing Chinese funded farm, Hubei Lianfeng in Xai-Xai, has stated that Mozambique is the target market. Therefore it is difficult to support the claims that China is on a 'shopping-spree' for land driven by food security concerns.

Even though agricultural investments, such as land leases by China, could bring tremendous benefits, by transferring technology and much-needed capital to Mozambique (interview, former finance minister, Maputo 2010; GTZ 2009:21, Jansson et al 2009:74; IRRI 2009:4), it is important to remember that land and food is intrinsically linked with national security in China. The same is true for the Mozambican government and caution is to be expected before any agreements can be made. It is also important to keep in mind that the Mozambican government is not a unified actor, but consists of different layers, parties and factions. Thus we should not be surprised if some shifting between enthusiasm and caution is observed.

China's domestic production capabilities: a state of desperation?

Notwithstanding the lack of evidence in Mozambique supporting the claim of a strategic Chinese land hunt, it is worthwhile to further explore this claim by looking at China's food security situation.

China experienced a rapid increase in agricultural production after reform in 1978, which can, to a large degree, be ascribed to structural changes and improved incentives for farmers (Jin et al 2002:917). Now that this structural induced once-off increase in productivity is starting to level out, further growth in the sector must come from technology (new seeds, fertilisers, farming techniques, irrigation and so on) or increased inputs of land and water (FAO 1999; Erlich et al 1993:14; Freeman et al 2008:5).

About 20% of the world's population resides in China, yet China only possesses approximately 7% of the world's arable land. This is less than 40% of the world average land per capita ratio, some reporting it to be as low as 9% of the world average (email correspondence, Bräutigam 2010; Liu 2006; Freeman et al 2008:5). Agriculture only accounts for 15% of China's gross domestic product, and although one would expect a diminishing share of agriculture in the economy as a country industrialises, agriculture still employs 40% of the Chinese workforce (Sandrey 2006:4).

For the greater part of PRC history, self-reliance was an important principle. However, there is a slight shift away from this strategy as China becomes more and more integrated into the international community. China's agricultural imports have been steadily increasing since 1998. In 2004, China became a food net-importer, and China now ranks among the top ten largest importers of agricultural products (Villoria et al 2009:3). It is, however, worth noting that China's domestic suppliers still meet over 90% of the demand (*China Monitor* 2006; Freeman et al 2009:5) and self-reliance still forms the cornerstone of China's food security policy (Freeman, et al 2008:8).

Nonetheless, demand for food produce is increasing while domestic resources such as land are decreasing. With rising incomes the demand for meat, a product that is extremely land intensive to produce has increased rapidly (FAO 1999; Shen 1998:33). Urbanisation increases the pool of people vulnerable to food price shocks as rural farmers leave their land and find paid jobs in the cities. It is estimated that 300–400 million Chinese will move from the rural areas to the urban centres in the next three decades. The share of urbanites will increase from 47% to 75% according to government expert Han Jun, thereby creating a larger mass of people potentially frustrated with the volatility of food prices (*Guardian* 2010).

Estimates predict that China's agricultural imports will grow at double-digit rates over the next decades (Freeman et al 2008:7). By 2020 China will need 700 million tonnes of grain for direct food consumption, and an additional 608 million tonnes of milled grain (part of which is used as feed grain to produce meat) (*China Monitor* 2006:6). According to Zhang Xiaoqiang, deputy director of the National Development and Reform Commission, China's food security challenges are 'daunting' but not impossible (Xinhuanet 2008a).

The official aim for 2020 is to produce 540 million tonnes of grain domestically (Xinhua 2008b; BBC News 2008), and the outlook seems relatively

Graph 6.1 Average yields for rice, soybean and maize, 2012

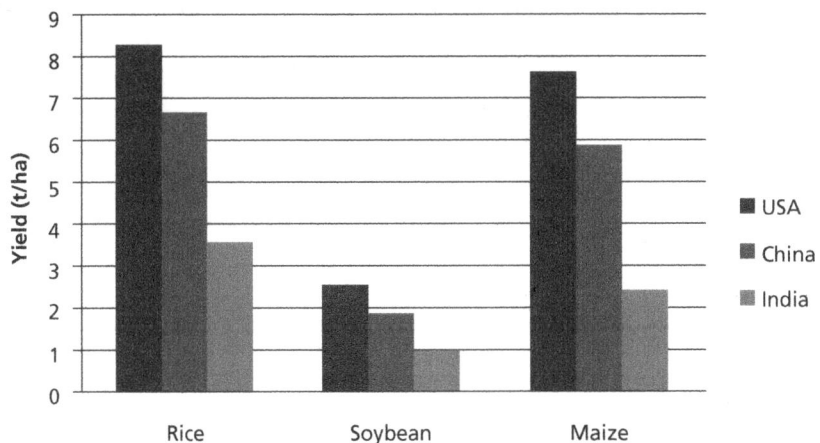

Source: FAO

optimistic; 2008 was a bumper year for grain production in China, with 512 million tonnes of grain being produced, largely through the help of governmental subsidies which doubled between 2007 and 2008 to CNY103 billion (Xinhua 2008). This was well ahead of meeting the predicted needed grain supplies of 500 million tonnes in 2010 (Liu 2006) and despite enduring the worst drought in 50 years, China's grain production grew by 2.9% year on year to 2010, to 546.41 million tonnes, exceeding the 2020 target ten years ahead of schedule (National Bureau of Statistics, China).

There are still productivity gains that can be made in China. Being at the forefront of agricultural technology, for example with hybrid rice, China is doing comparably well in expanding its agricultural productivity when measured against the rest of the world. Growth in global cereal production lies at -1.6% if China, India and Brazil are excluded, but when including these three countries the fall in cereal production is reduced to 0.9% (Braun 2008:7). Deepening land-reform in China can also further push up productivity levels (Lohmar 2013:18). While Chinese yields are relatively high, China's efficiency in producing some key crops still lies well below what is attained in other countries, such as the USA (see Graph 6.1). There is therefore still room to improve production.

According to Huang, director of the Center for Chinese Agricultural Policy at the Chinese Academy of Sciences, fears of China's food security being under dire pressures are therefore exaggerated. Development of domestic agriculture and self-sufficiency remain high on the policymakers' agenda in Beijing, and public spending in the sector has steadily increased (Huang 2013:21). Since the opening up and reform in 1978, China's agricultural sector has grown 5% annually on average, whereas population growth during the same time period only grew by 1.25%. Currently population growth lies at a mere 0.5% (Huang 2013:20). The centre predicts that China will be able to maintain an average annual growth above 3% in the agricultural sector, which would enable domestic production to satisfy China's target of 90% self-sufficiency in 2030, after which food demand is expected to stabilise (Huang 2013:22).

Presently China's domestic producers are doing relatively well to meet the demands of the Chinese market. It has to be expected that China will eventually have to procure increasing amounts of food from other sources, particularly with regards to grain for animal feed as the dietary preferences of the increasingly wealthy Chinese populace change (Huang 2013:20). It is therefore in China's interest to participate in ensuring global stability of food supply. However, it would be misleading to believe that China is currently on a hunt for land driven by desperation. Rather, we see that China possesses expertise within agriculture, such as in hybrid rice technology, which could be exported to areas of the world where the green revolution has yet to take place, such as Mozambique.

China's official stance on overseas farming as a strategy for food security
In 2008, *The Financial Times* published an article reporting that the central government in China was about to pass a proposal by the Ministry of Agriculture giving official strategic support for leasing land overseas with the purpose of producing food due to looming constraints on domestic production (Anderlini 2008). This has subsequently been denied by Chinese authorities.

No doubt food security is a national concern, and the Chinese government sees it as their task to 'ensure stable production and prices of vegetable basket products for urban and rural consumers' (*China Daily* 2008). But this will not be done through an official strategy of vertically integrating farming through overseas land leases, according to Zhang Xiaoqiang at the National Development and Reform Commission (Xinhuanet 2008). In the 'National Food Security and Long-term Planning Framework (2008–2020)' the government states that China will aim at maintaining a food self-sufficiency rate of at least 90% (Xinhua 2008).

Government expert Han Jun denies any official government involvement in overseas expansion of Chinese farming, stating that the government views such a policy as not reliable enough to be trusted for food security (*Guardian* 2010). Vertically integrating food supply does not isolate a country from dependence on the host country. It is unlikely that a government pushed by its local population and facing domestic instability caused by lack of food would allow free export of food produce. Rather than reducing reliance, overseas farming increases dependence on the host country. The logic of overseas land leases therefore fails. Although vertically integrating food supply could positively contribute to food supply, it is by no means a substitute for domestic production. 'Ultimately China will have to rely on domestic production,' says Xie Guoli from the Ministry of Agriculture (*Guardian* 2008).

Drivers for Chinese interest in overseas agriculture

A research paper composed by the Brussels Institute of Contemporary China Studies on China's policy on foreign farming (Freeman et al 2008:10) argues that China uses aid in order to boost agricultural productivity abroad. The paper found that there is indeed a policy encouraging outward investment into agriculture, but that this falls under China's general 'Go Global' strategy, rather than forming part of a national food security plan (Freeman et al:11). The 'Go Global' strategy for agriculture gives incentives in terms of diplomatic support, export credits and subsidies for pre-investment expenses. Agricultural projects are, however, not eligible to receive subsidies for operating costs (Freeman et al 2008:14; Cotula et al 2009:55). Freeman et al argue that the recent discussions on further official support for outbound agricultural investments might stem from the fact that the incentives under the 'Go Global' strategy have been unsuccessful with regards to promoting Chinese agricultural firms abroad. In 2006, Chinese outbound agricultural investments represented only 0.9% of total outbound investment (Freeman et al 2008:9, 15).

Looking at Africa in particular, between 1988 and 2010, a mere 4.2% of Chinese outbound direct investment was directed to agriculture (including forestry and fisheries) (Huang & Wilkes 2011:3). By 2010, only 35 investments into agriculture in Africa were recorded by the Chinese Ministry of Commerce (MOFCOM) (Huang & Wilkes:5). Although there likely exists a number of smaller agro-investments made by individual Chinese entrepreneurs who fall under the radar and are not officially recorded, one would expect that any strategic agro-investments directed from Beijing would be captured in MOFCOM's registry.

These investments are better viewed as driven by the general globalising trend of Chinese companies and investments than as forming part of a grand political strategy. They can also be viewed as part of the wider renewed business interest in agriculture, sparked by higher food prices (Cotula et al 2009:55). Since the financial crisis in 2008, investors have been looking for alternative sectors to divert money to (GTZ 2009:12, 15). As such, the heightened interest for 'virgin land' can be explained as a result of market forces rather than by geopolitical strategies.

Conclusion

Although there certainly exists an interest in Mozambican agriculture on the part of both Chinese business and China's government, this does not amount to vast land grabbing for the sake of securing food supplies for China's growing consumerism. China has a history of agricultural cooperation with Mozambique that is still ongoing, which is complimented by a handful of Chinese agro-investments existing at the time of writing. Approximately half of the land awarded to Chinese investors is focused on the biofuels industry and is not aimed at cultivating food crops, and the main Chinese investor engaged in food production is targeting the domestic Mozambican market. There is no sign of China searching for agricultural resources in Mozambique as part of a grand strategy to ensure domestic food security.

A closer look at China's food security situation and the condition of the Chinese agricultural sector further dispels the myth that China is on a hunt for foreign land to secure food supplies. China's official policy is to maintain a self-sufficiency ratio of 90% and the performance of the agricultural sector gives credibility to this policy aim.

Through its current role in Mozambican agriculture, China can be perceived as a partner in the development process, rather than as a neo-colonial 'land grabber', as portrayed by the media. Through the establishment of agricultural technology and research centres, China is exploring how to use an area of expertise as aid. A few Chinese investors also see potential in the Mozambican agricultural sector.

Media reports often mention that China has only 7% of the world's arable land, but 20% of the world's population, thereafter arguing that China needs to explore land overseas in order to secure food supplies. But perhaps instead of viewing China's agricultural expansion outwards as an act of desperation, we should view it the other way around: that despite the fact that China operates under such grave land constraints it is still able to provide for 90% of all its domestic food demands, and that this is a remarkable achievement. We ought to view China's outward agricultural expansion as a result of its agricultural success, rather than driven by the looming limitations, whereby Chinese actors (both public and private) see an opportunity and niche in a relatively unexploited market for both aid and profit.

References

ADB. 2008. *Soaring Food Prices: Response to the Crisis*, May. Available from: www.adb.org/Documents/Papers/soaring-food-prices/soaring-food-prices.pdf [Accessed on 8 December 2009].

AFRODAD. 2008. *China-Mozambique Fact Sheet*. Available from: www.afrodad.org [Accessed on 18 January 2010].

AIM. 2006. *President Guebuza Defends Cooperation with China*, 31 January. Available from: www.poptel.org.uk/mozambique-news/newsletter/aim313.html#story2 [Accessed on 29 February 2010].

AIM. 2006. *China Exim Bank to Finance Mphanda Nkuwa*, 2 May. Available from: www.poptel.org.uk/mozambique- news/newsletter/aim319.html#story8 [Accessed on 28 February 2010].

AIM. 2008. 'Agreements signed with China', 8 December. Available from: www.poptel.org.uk/mozambique- news/newsletter/aim369.html#story7 [Accessed on 28 February 2008].

Alden, C. 2007. *China in Africa*. London: Zed Books.

AllAfrica. 2010. 'Concession Contract for New Zambezi Dam Signed'. Available from: allafrica.com/stories/201012240181.html [Accessed on 30 December 2010].

AllAfrica. 2011. 'First Stone Laid for Namacurra Rice Processing Factory'. Available from: allafrica.com/stories/201105040162.html [Accessed on 24 May 2011].

Alveranga, D. 2008. *China's Economic Involvement in Mozambique and Prospects for Development: An analysis of the process and impacts of recent major investments*. Stellenbosch University: Master's thesis.

Anderlini, J. 2008. 'China eyes overseas land in food push'. *The Financial Times*, 8 May. Available from: www.ft.com/cms/s/0cb8a989a-1d2a-11dd-82ae-000077b07658.html [Accessed on 14 March 2010].

Arndt, C, Benefica, R, Tarp, F, Thurlow, J & Uaiene, R. 2008. *Biofuels, Poverty, and Growth: A Computable General Equilibrium Analysis of Mozambique*. IFPRI Discussion Paper 00803.

BBC News. 2008. 'China to Increase Grain Output', 3 July. Available from: news.bbc.co.uk/2/hi/business/7487157.stm [Accessed on 6 December 2009].

Bloomberg. 2013. 'China Export Drop Limits Recovery; Food Stokes Inflation' October 14.

Braun, J. 2008. *Food and Financial Crises: Implications for agriculture and the poor*. IFPRI Food Policy Report.

Braun, J & Meinzen-Dick, R. 2009. '*Land Grabbing' by Foreign Investors in Developing Countries: Risks and opportunities*. IFPRI Policy Brief.

Bräutigam, D & Tang, X. 2009. 'China's Engagement in African Agriculture: "Down to the Countryside"'. In: D Bräutigam, ed. *The Dragon's Gift: The real story of China in Africa*. New York: Oxford University Press.

Bräutigam, D. 2009. Comments on *'Land Grabbing' by Foreign Investors in Developing Countries*. IFPRI Policy Brief, 1 May 2009. Available from:www.ifpri.org/blog/land-grabbing-foreign-investors-developing-countries [Accessed on 19 December 2009].

Brown, L. 1995. *Who Will Feed China?: Wake-Up Call for a Small Planet*, New York, W.W. Norton & Company.

Chiakwelu, E. 2009. 'China's innovative agricultural investment in Mozambique'. *Africa Political and Economic Strategic Centre*. [Available from: groundreport.com/chinas-innovative-agricultural-investment-in-mozambique/].

Chichava, S. 2008. *Mozambique and China: From politics to business? Discussion Paper 5*, Maputo: IESE.

Chichava, S. 2010. *China in Mozambique's Agriculture Sector: Implications and challenges*. Maputo: IESE. Available from: http://www.iese.ac.mz/lib/noticias/2010/China%20in%20Mozambique_09.2010_SC.pdf [Accessed on 29 April 2009]

China Daily. 2008. 'President Hu Stresses Stable Food Prices, Supply of Farm Produce', 10 March.

China Monitor The. 2006. 'China's Agricultural Developments'. Centre for Chinese Studies, Stellenbosch University, 11.

China Monitor The. 2009. 'Chinese Agricultural Technology Development in an African Context'. Centre for Chinese Studies, Stellenbosch University, 40.

China.org.cn. 2013. 'Hu Unveils Demonstration Center of Chinese Agricultural Technology in Mozambique'. Available from: www.china.org.cn/english/infernational/199602.htm [Accessed on 12 December 2013].

Chinese Embassy in Mozambique. 2002. *China, Mozambique Cooperation Project Profiles*, 26 July. Available from: mz.mofcom.gov.cn/aarticle/zxhz/sbmy/200207/20020700033969.html [Accessed on 4 April 2010].

Cotula, L, Vermeulen, S, Leonard, R & Keeley, J. 2009. *Land Grab or Development Opportunity? Agricultural investment and international land deals in Africa*. FAO, IIED & IFAD: London.

Davies, M. 2008. 'China, Africa and the Global Food Crisis'. *The China Monitor*, 30 June. Centre for Chinese Studies, Stellenbosch University.

Erlich, P, Erlich, A & Daily, G. 1993. 'Food Security, Population and Environment'. *Population and Development Review*, 19(1), Population Council.

Food and Agriculture Organisation (FAO). 1999. 'Poverty Alleviation and Food Security in Asia: Lessons and Challenges'. Available from: www.fao.org/docrep/004/ab981e/ab981e0c.htm [Accessed on 25 September 2009].

FAO. 2009. 'Foreign Direct Investment: Win-win or land grab?' Available from: www.fao.org/fileadmin/templates/wsfs/Summit/WSFS_Issues_papers/WSFS_F DI_E.pdf [Accessed on 19 November 2009].

Freeman, D, Holslag, J & Weil, S. 2008. 'China's Foreign Farming Policy'. *(BICCS) Asia*, 3(9).

Governo de Moçambique (GdM). 2011. 'Matriz dos projectos com a República Popular da China'. Maputo.

GRAIN. 2008. *Seized* (annex), October. Available from: www.grain.org/briefings/?id=212 [Accessed on 24 October 2009].

Groenewald, Y. 2009. 'Made in China, in Africa'. *Mail & Guardian*, 30 May. Available from: mg.co.za/article/2009-05-30-made-in-china-africa [Accessed on 22 September 2009].

GPZ. 2006. 'Nasceu a Zamcorp: Zambeze Corporation, Sarl'. *Boletim Informativo do GPZ*, 1(4).

GTZ. 2009. *Foreign Direct Investment (FDI) in Land in Developing Countries*. Deutsche Gesellschaft für Technische Zusammenarbeit on the behalf of Federal Ministry for Economic Cooperation and Development. Eschborn.

Guardian, The. 2008. 'Chinese debate pros and cons of overseas farming investments', 11 May. Available from: africanagriculture.blogspot.com/2008/05/chinese-debate-pros-and-cons-of.html [Accessed on 20 October 2009].

Guardian, The. 2010. 'China's soil deterioration may become growing food crisis, adviser claims', 23 February. Available from: www.guardian.co.uk/environment/2010/feb/23/china-soil-deterioration-food-supply [Accessed on 26 February 2010].

Hanson, S. 2008. 'China, Africa and the Global Food Crisis'. *The China Monitor*, 30 June. Centre for Chinese Studies, Stellenbosch University.

Horta, L. 2007. 'China, Mozambique: Old friends, new business', 13 August. Available from: www.isn.ethz.ch/isn/Current-Affairs/Security-Watch/Detail/?id=53470&lng=en [Accessed on 18 October 2009].

Horta, L. 2008. 'The Zambezi Valley: China's first agricultural colony?' Available from: csis.org/blog/zambezi-valley-china%E2%80%99s-first-agricultural-colony [Accessed on 18 October 2009].

Horta, L. 2009. 'Food Security in Africa: China's new rice bowl'. *China Brief* (The Jamestown Foundation), IX(11).

Huang Wenbin, Andreas Wilkes. 2011. Analysis of China's overseas investment policies, *CIFOR Working Paper 79*, available from: http://www.cifor.org/online-library/browse/view-publication/publication/3697.html, Bogor.

IPIM. 2009. 'Angola and Mozambique within China's food security network', 8 June. Available from: www.ipim.gov.mo/worldwide_partner_detail.php?tid=11388&type_id=1293 [Accessed on 15 January 2010].

IRRI. 2009. 'International land acquisition for rice production', 10 November. Available from: beta.irri.org/publications/index.php?option=com_wrapper&Itemid=18 [Accessed on 7 March 2010].

Jansson, J & Kiala, C. 2009. *Patterns of Chinese aid and trade in Mozambique*. Centre for Chinese Studies, Stellenbosch University.

Jansson, J, Kiala, C, Liu, H, Hon, T & Burke, C. 2009. *Evaluating China's FOCAC Commitments to Africa and Mapping the Way Ahead*. Report. Centre for Chinese Studies, Stellenbosch University & Rockefeller Foundation. Stellenbosch.

Jin, S, Huang, J, Hu, R & Rozelle, S. 2002. 'The Creation and Spread of Technology and Total Factor Productivity in China's Agriculture'. *American Journal of Agricultural Economics*, 84(4).

Kaplinsky, R & Morris, M. 2009. 'Chinese FDI in Sub-Saharan Africa: Engaging with large dragons'. *European Journal of Development Research*, 24(1).

Keidel, A. 2005. 'The Economic Basis for Social Unrest in China'. Conference paper. Carnegie Endowment for International Peace.

Klein, B, Crawford, R & Alchian, A. 1978. 'Vertical Integration, Appropriable Rents, and the Competitive Contracting Process'. *Journal of Law and Economics*, 21(2).

Li, P, Wei, L, Zhang, J & Rui, B. 2008. 'China Afflicted by Global Food Price Surges', 27 February. *Economic Observer Online*. Available from: www.eeo.com.cn/ens/Industry/2008/02/27/92921.html [Accessed on 26 September 2009].

Li, P & Rui, B. 2008. 'Food Security: Moving towards the precipice?' 28 February. *Economic Observer Online*. Available from: www.eeo.com.cn/ens/Observer/2008/02/28/92948.html [Accessed on 26 September 2009].

Liu, Y. 2006. 'Shrinking Arable Lands Jeopardizing China's Food Security'. *World Watch*, 18 April. Available from: www.worldwatch.org/node/3912 [Accessed on 22 September 2009].

Macauhub. 2008. 'China and Mozambique Invest in the Zambezi Valley to Make Chinese "Grain-Store" Says Researcher', 21 July. Available from: www.macauhub.com.mo/en/news.php?ID=5748 [Accessed on 14 November 2009].

Macauhub. 2009. 'China Builds Agricultural Technology Research Centre in Mozambique', 26 August. Available from: www.macauhub.com.mo/en/news.php?ID=7994 [Accessed on 16 December 2009].

Macauhub. 2009a. 'China's Centre for Agricultural Technology in Mozambique Opens at Start of 2010 to Boost Productivity', 30 November. Available from: www.macauhub.com.mo/en/news.php?ID=8521 [Accessed on 12 December 2009].

Macauhub. 2009b. 'Chinese Agricultural Investment in Mozambique to Feed China', 14 December. Available from www.macauhub.com.mo/en/news.php?ID=8605 [Accessed on 16 December 2009].

Makoni, M. 2009. 'Mozambique: China's Farming Ambitions Take Shape'. AllAfrica, 11 November. Available from: http://allafrica.com/stories/200911120929.html [Accessed on 20 November 2009].

Menete, Z. 2004. *System of Rice Intensification Dissertation Research Preliminary Results*. CIIFAD (Cornell International Institute for Food, Agriculture and Development). Available from: http://ciifad.cornell.edu/sri/countries/mozambique/index.html [Accessed on 16 February 2010].

Pehnelt, G & Abel, M. 2007. *China's Development Policy in Africa*. South African Institute for International Affairs.

Roque, P. 2009. *China in Mozambique: A cautious approach country case study*. (SAIIA).

Sen, A. 1981. 'Ingredients of Famine: Analysis and entitlements'. *The Quarterly Journal of Economics*, 96(3). MIT Press.

Sen, A & Sen, AK. 1982. 'The Food Problem: Theory and policy'. *Third World Quarterly*, 4(3).

Shen, J. 1998. 'China's Future Population and Development Challenges'. *The Geographical*

Journal, 164(1).

Smaller, C & Mann, H. 2009. *A Thirst for Distant Lands: Foreign investments in agricultural land and water*. Occasional paper. International Institute for Sustainable Development. Winnipeg.

Smith, B & Talbot, A. 2009. 'China Continues its Aggressive Pursuit of Africa's Resources', 16 November. Available from: http://wsws.org/articles/2009/nov2009/afch-n16.shtml [Accessed on 6 January 2010].

USDA database. 2008. Available from: http://www.usda.gov/wps/portal/usda/usdahome?navid=DATA_STATISTICS [Accessed January 2010].

Villoria, N, Hertel, T & Nin-Pratt, A. 2009. *China's Growth and the Agricultural Exports of Southern Africa*. Occasional paper. International Food Policy Research Institute.

Vyas, V. 2000. 'Ensuring Food Security: The state, market and civil society'. *Economic and Political Weekly*, 35(50).

Wen, T, Liu, H & Li, C. 2008. 'Grain Issues and Inflation in Modern China'. *The China Monitor: China, Africa and the Global Food Crisis*, 30, June 2008. Centre for Chinese Studies, Stellenbosch University.

Weng, S. 2008. 'Central Dossier Adds to Agriculture Reform Crescendo', 26 February 2008. *Economic Observer Online*. Available from: www.eeo.com.cn/ens/Observer/2008/02/26/92884.html [Accessed on 26 September 2009].

Xinhuanet. 2008a. 'Chinese grain output expected to rise for 5th consecutive year', 11 October. Available from: news.xinhuanet.com/english/2008-10/11/content_10180886.htm [Accessed on 4 January 2010].

Xinhuanet. 2008b. '发改委:无海外屯田计划今后食用油加工领域中方控股', 13 November. Available from: www.news.xinhuanet.com/fortune/2008-11/13/content_10351772.html [Accessed on 20 December 2009].

Correspondence and interviews

Six interviews with Mozambican government officials, 2010.

Two interviews with DNTF, 2010.

Four interviews with Civil society, 2010.

Three interviews with CPI and CEPARGI, 2010–2013.

Email correspondence with Chris Alden, Oxford University, 2010.

Email correspondence with Deborah Bräutigam, 2009–2010.

Email correspondence with GPZ Office for Development of Zambezi valley, 2009.

Chapter 7
The Chinese Agricultural Technology Demonstration Centre in Mozambique: A Story of a Gift

Sérgio Chichava, Jimena Durán and Lu Jiang

This story officially started on 4 November 2006 at the Beijing Summit of the Forum on China-Africa Cooperation (FOCAC), when former Chinese president Hu Jintao presented eight steps for the consolidation of the Africa-China strategic partnership. Regarding agriculture, one of the principal promises was the establishment of ten agricultural demonstration centres in Africa (FOCAC 2006). At the 4th Ministerial Conference FOCAC in November 2009, the number was increased to 20 agricultural technology demonstration centres. This action was included along with other Chinese measures aiming at boosting the African agricultural sector, considered by both sides as important in fighting poverty and food insecurity in Africa (MOFCOM 2011).

China's agricultural engagement in Africa takes many forms in the wide range of economic cooperation and aid instruments. Chinese agricultural aid projects in Africa seem to evolve towards business-oriented logic, in order to guarantee the sustainability of the projects after decades of failure of almost all of them in Africa. The agricultural demonstration centres have to be understood in this context and they are examples of combining aid with business. These centres could be understood in the broader framework of China's National Development and Reform Commission plan for investment in Africa, where agricultural technology and seed cultivation were designed as two major sectors that could be useful and profitable (Bräutigam & Xiaoyang 2009; Bräutigam 2009).

The first countries to benefit from these agriculture demonstration centres were Mozambique, Zambia, Zimbabwe, Uganda and Cameroon. The construction of the centres and the first three years' management were to be funded by the Chinese government. Thereafter, the management of the centres is expected to be conducted by the Chinese enterprises or research institutes designated by the Chinese government. Table 7.1 shows the status of the first group of 14 demonstration centres in Africa and the institution concerned with the management of each centre.

Table 7.1 Chinese agricultural demonstration centres in Africa (2006–2013)

Country	Status	Units
Benin	Construction started in March 2009 Inaugurated in January 2011	China National Agricultural Development Group Co Ltd
Cameroon	Construction started in July 2009 Handed over in July 2013	Shaanxi Land-Reclamation Agriculture & Industry and Commerce Cooperation
Congo (Brazzaville)	Contract signed in March 2008 Handed over in September 2012	Chinese Academy of Tropical Agricultural Sciences
Ethiopia	Contract signed in April 2008 Handed over in 2012	Guangxi Bagui Agricultural Science and Technology Co Ltd
Liberia	Construction started in April 2009 Handed over in July 2010	Hunan Yuan Longping High-tech Agriculture Co Ltd
Mozambique	Construction started in August 2009 Handed over in July 2011	Hubei Lianfeng Agricultural Development Corporation
Rwanda	Construction commenced in 2009 Handed over in 2011	Fujian Agriculture and Forestry University
South Africa	Contract signed in 2008 Construction finished in 2011	China National Agricultural Development Group Co Ltd
Sudan	Construction started in September 2009 Handed over in 2011	Shandong International Economic & Technical Cooperation Group Ltd
Tanzania	Construction started in October 2009 Handed over in April 2011	Chongqing Seed Group
Togo	Construction commenced in October 2008 Handed over in 2011	Jiangxi Huachang International Economic and Technical Corporation-
Uganda	Construction commenced in October 2009 Handed over in 2010	Sichuan Huaqiao Fenghuang Group Co Ltd
Zambia	Construction started in November 2009 Handed over in June 2011	Jilin Grain Group
Zimbabwe	Construction started in October 2009 Handed over in February 2011	MAE Northern Co Ltd

Source: Compiled by authors, from various media reports

According to our findings, Liberia was the first African country to host a Chinese agricultural demonstration centre (CADC) as part of this policy process. Furthermore, it is possible to see that to date 14 CADCs were set up and formally handed over to the African governments by the Chinese. During the first phase of activity, which experience suggests can vary from three to eight or more years, CADCs are mainly managed by Chinese enterprises or research institutes seconded by African partners. The second phase, which commences when the CADC is assessed to be sustainable, involves the transfer of responsibility to the African host government.

It is important to say that, even if the centres were offered within a multilateral framework, the negotiation of each centre was developed on a bilateral base, each country deciding which sub-sector within agriculture must be prioritised. For example, in the case of South Africa and Uganda, the agricultural technology demonstration centre is more focused on fish farming or aquaculture than is the case in CADCs found in other countries.

Taking the case of the CADC in Mozambique, locally known as Centro de Investigação e Transferência de Tecnologias Agrárias do Umbéluzi (CITTAU), and through ethnographic and neo-institutional approaches, the principal aim of this chapter is to show how a lack of coordination, ambiguities, and unclear mandates and responsibilities among the Mozambican and Chinese institutions are undermining the functioning of CITTAU since it was handed over in 2011.

First, the process of CITTAU's implementation in Mozambique will be described. Second, the institutional dynamics of CITTAU's day-to-day management among different actors involved – namely the Ministry of Agriculture (MINAG) through the Instituto de Investigação Agronómica de Moçambique (IIAM), the Ministry of Science and Technology (MCT), and the Chinese Lianfeng company – are to be analysed.

A steady start: from promise to reality

When Hu Jintao visited Mozambique in February 2007, it was announced that Mozambique would be the first African country to benefit from one of the Chinese agro-technology centres. The study of feasibility by a Chinese mission of experts was organised between 30 May and 6 June 2007 with technical and logistic support from the MINAG and the MCT (MCT 2007). During this Chinese mission to Mozambique several issues related to the setting up and the management of the centre, the type of agricultural technology to be transferred by the centre, and the responsibilities of each side were discussed.

For the siting of the centre, the initial idea was to establish the centre in the northern province of Nampula. However, this idea was discarded and two other potential locations in the south of the country were proposed by the

Mozambican side: the district of Moamba (north-east of Maputo, the capital) or the district of Boane (south-west of Maputo). Boane was chosen in the end due to several practical factors. The existence of an agricultural research station, the Umbeluzi agricultural station of the IIAM, was the main reason for the choice of Boane (MTC 2007). Created in 1909 under Portuguese colonial rule, the Umbeluzi Agricultural Station occupies an estimated 700 hectares (Boletim do IIAM 2009). Moreover, the district of Boane is about 20 kilometres from Maputo and near Matola, the most important industrial centre of Mozambique. Matola shelters the most important aluminium production project in Mozambique by Mozal – a key export product and foreign exchange earner – and it is a booming district as a result of Maputo's expansion (MAE 2005). An engineer from MCT working on the coordination of Boane's centre states:

> The localisation of the centre is advantageous because of the proximity to Maputo (capital city) and the availability of the Umbeluzi Agricultural Station. Likewise, Umbeluzi River has running water all year long. The irrigation system present in the zone since the colonial times was rehabilitated by the Chinese to have water in the centre. (Interview, MCT Engineer, Maputo, 8 February 2012)

As part of the Mozambican government's contribution to the project, it was agreed that the IIAM would donate 52 hectares along with a tax-free grant on all Chinese materials related to the building construction (MCT 2007). The Chinese side, for its part, was in charge of the conception and construction of the building as well as assigning Chinese specialists and supplying equipment (MCT 2007).

Experts from both sides – Mozambique and China – decided to prioritise the cultivation of maize, rice, cassava and vegetables in the compound. The crop types chosen to be tested corresponded to the dietary habits of the local people. The cooperation was based on a negotiation of each country's priorities, and the projects had to adapt to the demands and conditions of each African country.

The process moved quite rapidly from the project's approval in 2008 through its construction phase in 2009 through to its handover in 2011. The construction was entirely carried out by a Chinese company, though some Mozambican workers were employed in the process. The demonstration centre in Boane has two buildings. The first hosts one meeting room, six administration offices, one library, two classrooms, and two laboratories – one seed laboratory and one soil laboratory. The second building hosts the residencies for Chinese researchers and workers (12 bedrooms), one kitchen and a common dining room (MTC 2012).

CITTAU is defined as an institution for research, technological development, technology transfer, innovation, human capital formation and agricultural and livestock production, and is seen by Mozambican authorities, in the words of President Armando Guebuza, as an important instrument in the struggle against poverty and food insecurity. It is also seen as a concrete symbol of Chinese commitment to Mozambique, one which does not get the recognition that it deserves (AIM 2011). Moreover, thanks to Chinese technology, Mozambicans will learn how to increase their productivity without needing large land concessions:

> The goal is not to only increase production, because this can be done in several ways. Production is not only increased by increasing the production area. We must bear in mind the other approach to increasing production is by increasing productivity in small areas. (AIM 2011)

In fact, according to the MCT minister, with the help of Chinese technology productivity is expected to expand from 1–1.5 tonnes per hectare to 9–10 hectare in some crops (AIM 2012).

CITTAU was officially handed over on 8 July 2011, witnessed by Mozambican President Armando Guebuza, the vice-minister and the Minister of Science and Technology for the Mozambican side and the Chinese ambassador in Mozambique (MCT 2011).

From the Chinese side, the government had to designate an enterprise or research institute to manage the centre in a sustainable way. In the case of Boane's centre, Hubei Lianfeng Agricultural Development Corporation was chosen. This enterprise was already present in Mozambique with a hybrid rice production project in the district of Xai-Xai, Gaza province (north of Maputo), before it was replaced by another Chinese company. There are also three Mozambican staff from the MCT indicated as working in the centre with the Chinese.

It was agreed that during the first three years the centre would be managed by the Chinese enterprise and would be supported by grants from Chinese government. MCT's engineer states:

> For the total construction of the project 40 million CNY (approximately US$6 million) were donated by the Chinese government. The Centre's functioning is assured for three years by the donation of 1 200 000 CNY (US$194 394) annually by the Chinese government. In every country the

Figure 7.1 Hu Jintao and Armando Emilio Guebuza at the unveiling ceremony of a Chinese agricultural demonstration centre in Maputo
Source: china.org.cn (2007)

demonstration centres work the same way: there is a Chinese enterprise designed by the Chinese government at the head of the project. The only exception is South Africa; they managed to negotiate with the Chinese so they could manage the centre by themselves. (Interview, Agricultural Engineer of IIAM, Maputo, 7 February 2012)

However, the Mozambican government was able to convince Beijing that due to its own lack of capacity, the Chinese government should continue to manage and finance the centre for an additional three years, even if the budget was to be reduced.

Institutional incoherence as CITTAU's bottleneck

Since the centre was handed over to Mozambique in 2011, the day-to-day management of CITTAU has been characterised by what might be called institutional incoherence. The concept of institutional incoherence is used here in the same way Booth (2010, 2012) uses it when he addresses the main bottleneck in provision of public good services in many African countries. For Booth (2010:8, 2012:36) institutional incoherence seen as 'persistently ill-defined mandates or overlapping jurisdictions among some or all of the organisations concerned; and perverse incentives confronting actors within particular organisations as a result of the incomplete implementation of a policy or the simultaneous pursuit of several policies that are, for practical purposes, in conflict'.

As previously stated, the agreement of CITTAU's implementation says that the Ministry of Agriculture, in particular IIAM, will be the main Chinese partner on the Mozambican side. But in reality neither IIAM nor other departments of the Ministry of Agriculture are involved in any aspect related to CITTAU's management; instead, they are reduced to mere 'spectators'. MCT, which was the subscriber of the agreement from the Mozambican side, is the only institution working alongside Hubei Lianfeng. As affirmed by one of the IIAM engineers, this institution was only involved in the discussions concerning the concession of the land to CITTAU. Apart from that, they are not even involved in the definition of the modalities of centre management (Ibid.).

The national head of agricultural services at MINAG asserted that he believed that behind this institutional uncertainty lay the search for political prominence and prestige of both ministers:

> I've heard something about this dispute between the two ministries. I find it difficult to believe, considering that we are talking about two institutions that make part of the Mozambican state. But what I think is the centre of commotion is the search of political influence and recognition by the two ministers through having in their power the coordination of a project with China. (Interview, MINAG national director of agricultural services, Maputo, 9 February 2012)

In spite of the dispute at the top level of the two ministries, it is clear among the ordinary IIAM and MCT technicians that CITTAU needs collaboration between the two institutions:

> The big question consists on what institution is going to coordinate the centre. Is it going to be the MINAG or the MCT? Both ministries want the centre. I think we can work together, because between technicians we understand each other. For me joint custody is possible. But political cooperation is different and doesn't work that way. (Interview, MCT engineer, Maputo, 8 February 2012)

This institutional ambiguity creates ignorance concerning the objectives and strategies of the centre among the technicians of both institutions. For example, one IIAM-Maputo technician said:

I think the biggest problem is the lack of clarity and transparency about this centre. There is a lack of clarity from the Mozambican ministries and from the Chinese authorities. Actually, we don't know who has to do what. I just know I have to go there, see what is going on to then write a report. (Interview, IIAM engineer, Boane, 17 February 2012)

Even if on some occasions it is said that in the future – after the Chinese leave – CITTAU will be managed by a joint team of the MCT and MINAG (MCT 2012), one can question how this will be possible since the latter has not actually been involved in the management of the centre.

Regarding this ambiguity the Chinese agricultural experts at CITTAU emphasised that this was one of the main obstacles for the normal work of the centre. Moreover, for the Chinese side, it is not comprehensible why the main partner of CITTAU is MCT instead of MINAG (interview, two Chinese agricultural experts, Boane, 18 October 2013). This creates problems since the main mission of MCT is not agriculture and, for most of the time, in order to solve the problems related to CITTAU, the MCT must first contact MINAG.

But the institutional ambiguities are not only between Mozambican institutions but also between the Chinese and Mozambicans. In April 2013, the Mozambican minister of MCT on a visit to CITTAU was quoted as saying that he was not happy with the centre's performance, because it was only testing Chinese seed varieties and not Mozambican, which was contrary to the instructions given by Mozambican authorities to the Chinese centre managers (Domingo 2013). Nonetheless, according to the Chinese managers, the main problem with Mozambican seed is its unavailability and high cost in the local market. In order to address this issue, the Chinese asked for help from MCT, who, to solve the problem, must ask for help from MINAG. Because of this complexity to date the problem has not been solved (Domingo 2013).

Another point, according to MCT technicians, is that the day-to-day CITTAU management and agricultural technology experiments are actually only done by the Chinese side with little participation of the local state officials. According to an MCT official, not one Mozambican state official is participating in land preparation, seed testing or in day-to-day centre management (interview, MCT State Official, Maputo, November 2013). However, the Chinese side blames the Mozambican side for their self-exclusion from the process. According to them, the MCT staff does not go to CITTAU even if they have offices there. According to our interviewee there are in theory six Mozambican technicians appointed to work at CITTAU but, actually, only three of them go there and they do so very rarely and under Chinese pressure (interview, two Chinese technicians from CITTAU, Boane, 18 October 2013).

Because of this, the Chinese consider the Mozambicans less committed to the centre, giving ridiculous excuses for not coming to work at CITTAU: 'The reasons given for the Mozambicans not coming to the centre are that the government [MCT] doesn't give them money to buy petrol'.

The fact of the matter is that the actual work done by Mozambican staff at CITTAU is not especially related to agricultural technology transfer but is more bureaucratic, like facilitating visas and work permits for the Chinese experts, facilitating Chinese imports of equipment and seeds, among other material used at CITTAU, and coordinating some events, like the opening and graduation ceremonies of the training courses (interview, MCT engineer, Maputo, November 2013).

Moreover, the problem exposes a difference in mentality between the Mozambican officials and their Chinese counterparts. It is difficult to ask a Mozambican agricultural expert to go to the farm to do 'dirty work' or a non-prestigious job; he is used to working in an office. In contrast the Chinese manager works on the farm every day.

We can also see this difference in mentality and commitment to agriculture between the two sides in the Chinese CITTAU head manager's words, talking about IIAM staff who work near the centre:

> [The Mozambican way of doing agriculture is] quite different from our Chinese way of doing agriculture, they [IIAM staff] devoted much less time and effort than us. For example, they start their work at 9:00 am and get off work at 3:00 pm. During the lunch time it's too hot in the field. And they rest over the weekends... but the crops don't have weekends. We have to keep a close eye on the crop growing whenever its necessary even over the weekends, but you can relax when things go well even on the week days. This is the nature of an agricultural job. (Interview, Chinese CITTAU manager, Boane, 18 October 2013)

The only Mozambicans who work closely and daily with the Chinese agricultural experts are the seasonal workers, who lack agricultural techno-scientific expertise. This also leads the Chinese agricultural experts to feel that the Mozambican officials are not recognising the importance of agriculture in the struggle against poverty and therefore attach less importance to this sector.

The language barrier is another issue that is hurting institutional relationships between the two sides. While this aspect is not specific to the Chinese because not all international cooperation or economic agents in Mozambique speak Portuguese, in the Chinese case it is worse because not one Mozambican working with them can speak Chinese and no Chinese can speak Portuguese or understandable English. The fact that not one of the ten Chinese working in the centre speaks Portuguese creates distance and misunderstandings between the Chinese and the Mozambicans. The young accountant is the 'official translator' and he only speaks very basic English, which is not enough to establish normal communication: 'I don't understand him at all. And he barely understands me. I don't want to say I speak perfect English or that he doesn't speak English at all. I am just saying communication is very difficult' (interview, IIAM technician, Boane, 18 February 2012).

The language barrier not only affects the institutional relationships but makes technical cooperation and exchange even more difficult. For example, the same interviewee stated:

> To communicate with the Chinese is very hard. So when we go there, we talk mostly with the Mozambicans that are working there. There are two of them who have been there for a long time and they are already used to understanding the Chinese. And when we want to explain something or give our technical advice we go to the fields and we show them.

Even though the scope for substantive cooperation between Chinese and Mozambican technicians seems negative at first glance, there are also some positive aspects, such as the recognition of the importance of Chinese agricultural technology and their productivity and efficiency:

> The agricultural techniques are really good. I am impressed with the irrigation systems they have installed. Most of the production is irrigated by gravity but they also have the drop to drop system, which allows a better control of water. I had already seen these types of irrigation systems but it is interesting to see how they implement them. (Interview, IIAM engineer, Maputo, 17 February 2012)

The Mozambican technicians also recognise the Chinese employees' high degree of diligence, in contrast with fellow Mozambicans, who are viewed as indolent:

> One of the advantages of Chinese in the field is efficiency. For example, for three workers, Mozambicans have three beds. But, Chinese, for three workers they only have two beds. So, there is always someone working. In agriculture, it is good to work this way. The Chinese boss is always on the field to make sure things are done. On the contrary, the

Mozambican boss would command from his home. (Interview, IIAM engineer, Maputo, 17 February 2012)

The Chinese are also seen as committed to African development, unlike Europeans or Americans:

> The Chinese have another point of view. They are interested in business and they are tougher. Why not? They are different to Europeans or Americans, who have been here for more than 30 years and Africa still doesn't develop. They [the Westerners] don't want Africa to develop. (Interview, IIAM engineer, Maputo, 17 February 2012)

Finally, there is the problem of CITTAU's sustainability which is not solved yet and perhaps this will be one of the biggest challenges of the CADC in Africa, since the majority of African states have limited material or financial capital to deal with this.

CITTAU managers envisage three options to guarantee the sustainability of the centre, some of which are already under implementation:

(i) to introduce paid training courses for the Mozambican farmers or for others who are interested. This system is already implemented in China where local farmers have to pay to get agricultural technological training. However, this option seems doomed to fail right from the start since many Mozambican farmers have limited resources;

(ii) to develop agro-industry which includes growing and processing crops like rice and maize, which are very popular on the local market due to the low price. Alternatively the centre could produce cotton seeds – one of the advantages of Hubei agriculture – which might be sold in the market; and/or

(iii) to develop a pig farm.

This last project is already under experimental implementation. At the time of our study there were about 600 pigs in the centre (interview, Chinese Manager, Boane, 18 October 2013). According to the Chinese managers, the idea of running CITTAU through a business model does not mean that this institution will become a pure commercial organisation, it will continue to maintain some degree of focus on social welfare issues.

It is not totally clear how all of these initiatives will fair when put into practice as they are still under research. What is certain is that the operating model of the CADC in African countries will be adjusted to the specificities of the host countries.

Conclusion

The way the agricultural demonstration centres were announced by Hu Jintao at FOCAC's summit shows the political and symbolic importance of them. These centres can be understood as political instruments to prove China's sincere commitment towards furthering Africa's agricultural development. But besides the political considerations, economic motivations are also central.

In this context, we wanted to illustrate through the example of the agricultural demonstration centre in Mozambique, the process of consolidation of this promised gift in order to have a more concrete and objective image of the implementation and operation of these centres. Despite the important political and economic motivations, the development of the centre has presented some obstacles, such as the dispute between MINAG and MCT over its control. This dispute underscores its political importance and significance within the Mozambican political context, where it is prestigious for a ministry to have a Chinese project in its profile.

But the lack of institutional coordination between both sides, particularly the Mozambican side, has consequences in the development of the project. The sustainability and the evolution of the centre do not rely only on Chinese capabilities but also depend on Mozambican competences to manage the project. If there is no institutional clarity on who should manage the centre and how, it will be difficult for the Mozambican side when the Chinese team leaves and the centre is handed over to the Mozambicans.

Institutional incoherence is not the only obstacle that CITTAU faces. There are also language and cultural barriers, which present even greater difficulties for the Mozambican and Chinese actors involved. Indeed, it is questionable how the very core task of this Chinese policy initiative – agricultural technology transfer – can be effective without written or oral communication.

It is still too early to make any definitive conclusions about the functioning of the centre. We will have to wait some years to see how it evolves and whether this model proves to be efficient and sustainable or not.

References

AIM. 2011. 'Centro de Investigação Agrária vai garantir auto-suficiência alimentar', 4 August. Available from: noticias.sapo.mz/aim/artigo/190104082011151138.html [Accessed on 7 November 2013].

AIM. 2012. 'China apoia transferência tecnológica', 1 April. Avalaible from: www.portaldogoverno.gov.mz/noticias/agricultura/abril-2012/china-apoia-transferencia-

tecnologica/ [Accessed on 11 December 2013].
Boletim do IIAM. 2009. *EAU. 100 Anos na Vanguarda da Pesquisa Agrária em Moçambique*. Maputo, MINAG.
Booth, D. 2010. 'Towards a Theory of Local Governance and Public Goods Provision in Sub-Saharan Africa'. *Working Paper* 13. ODI: London.
Booth, D. 2012. *Development as a Collective Action Problem: Addressing the real challenges of African governance*. London: ODI.
Bräutigam, Deborah. 2009. *The Dragon's Gift: The real story of China in Africa*. New York: Oxford University Press.
Bräutigam, D. & Xiaoyang, T. 2009. 'China's Engagement in Africa Agriculture: "Down to the countryside"'. *The China Quarterly*, 199:686–706.
China.org.cn. 2007. 'Hu Unveils Demonstration Center of Chinese Agricultural Technology in Mozambique'. Available from: www.china.org.cn/english/infernational/199602.htm [Accessed on 12 December 2013].
Domingo. 2013. 'Ministro insatisfeito com o desempenho do centro'. Available from: desafio.co.mz/index.php/economia/1036-ministro-insatisfeito-com-desempenho-do-centro-de-umbeluzi [Accessed on 5 December 2013].
FOCAC. 2006. Forum on China-Africa Cooperation Beijing action plan (2007-2009). Available from: www.focac.org/eng/ltda/dscbzjhy/DOC32009/t280369.htm [Accessed on 6 November 2013].
MAE. 2005. *Perfil do Distrito de Boane, Província de Maputo*. Maputo: Ministério de Administração Estatal.
MCT. 2007. *Memorandum de Entendimento sobre a Visita de uma Missão Chinesa para o Estudo de Viabilidade do Centro de Demonstraçoes de Tecnologias Agricolas Chinesas em Moçambique*. Maputo: Ministério de Ciência e Tecnologia.
MCT. 2011. *Comunicado de Imprensa. Assunto: Tem lugar a cerimónia de entrega do projecto de construção do Centro de Investigação e Transferência de Tecnologias agrárias Moçambique-China às autoridades moçambicanas*. Maputo: Ministério de Ciência e Tecnologia.
MCT. 2012. 'China vai reforçar cooperação no âmbito do CITTAU'. *MCT Notícias*, 26. Maputo, Ministério de Ciência e Tecnologia, 5 April.
MOFCOM. 2011. 'An Interpretation of New Measures on Economic and Trade Cooperation from 4th Ministerial Conference'. Available from: english.mofcom.gov.cn/article/policyrelease/Cocoon/201106/20110607621344.shtml [Accessed on 6 November 2013].

Chapter 8
Chinese Rice Farming in Xai-Xai: A Case of Mozambican Agency?

Sérgio Chichava

The Chinese commitment to support African countries in boosting agricultural development is one of the main promises made by the Asian giant to Africa. This commitment can be traced back to the first Forum on China-Africa Cooperation (FOCAC), held in Beijing in October 2000, and it was reiterated in the subsequent agreements (Addis Ababa in 2003, Beijing in 2006, Sharm El-Sheikh in 2009 and Beijing 2012)(FOCAC 2006a, 2006b; FOCAC 2009). Agricultural development is a primary concern for the majority of African states, particularly considering the food scarcity on the continent. It is estimated that in 2010 some 218 million people in Africa were struggling daily with hunger, a figure corresponding at the time to about 30% of the continent's total population (Garrity et al 2010:198).

Among the key measures taken by the Chinese government targeting the African agriculture sector is the construction of 30 agricultural demonstration centres in the same number of countries; the establishment of a special programme of food security in collaboration with the Food and Agriculture Organization (FAO) with a budget of US$30 million; the deployment of thousands of Chinese agricultural experts; and the training of African counterparts (FOCAC 2009). In addition, the China-Africa Development Fund (CAD Fund) has adopted the agricultural sector as a priority intervention area.[1]

Mozambique is one of the poorest African countries and its agricultural production is in crisis due to a variety of factors.[2] Prominent among these

---

1 This fund was established in March 2007 by the Chinese government through the China Development Bank (CDB) and is one of the eight promises made by the Chinese government at FOCAC 2006. The Fund will eventually reach US$5 billion support Chinese companies investing in Africa. In April 2012, CDB claimed that it had invested US$57 million in several agricultural projects in Africa, primarily cotton, leather processing, sisal, sugar, farm equipment assembly and sales (CDB 2012). Unfortunately, we did not find a non-Chinese source to support these figures.
2 According to the Mozambican Poverty Reduction Action Plan 2011–2014 (PARP 2011–2014), 54.7% Mozambicans are poor. Here poverty is seen as 'an inability by disability or lack of opportunity for individuals, families and communities to have access to minimum conditions, according to the inability, disability, or lack of opportunity for individuals, families and communities to have access to minimum conditions, according to basic rules of society, families and communities to have access to minimum conditions, according to the inability disability, or lack of opportunity for individuals, families and

is the devastation caused by the collapse of the economic system following Mozambique's independence in 1975. This was mostly due to the mass exodus of Portuguese settlers (who had comprised most of the qualified workforce), the devastating civil war that followed (1976–1992) and the poor policy-making during the 'Marxist-Leninist' period (1977–1990). Today, like many other countries, Mozambique is counting on external support for the recovery of its agriculture sector and to increase its production and productivity.

The purpose of this chapter is twofold: first, to map out and characterise the aid provided by the Chinese state, cooperation and investment in Mozambican agriculture since the early days of independence, and, second, to analyse the relations between Chinese investment and the local politics of accumulation by looking at the case of Hubei Lianfeng Mozambique Co Lda (HLMO Co Lda) in Gaza province,[3] a state-owned Chinese agricultural company which, between 2007 and 2012, was farming rice on the Ponela section of the Xai-Xai irrigation system. I argue that, like other foreign investment in Mozambique, Chinese investment is being primarily appropriated by local political elites for their own benefit. In fact, the arrival of the Chinese rice farm in Xai-Xai – the first and most significant Chinese investment into rice production in Mozambique after FOCAC 2000 – presented an opportunity to the local elites to direct it for their own benefit. This case illustrates the new China-Africa policy which, according Bräutigam (2010), emphasises 'mutually-beneficial agricultural cooperation', instead of being based on political or ideological motivations, which in the past have proven their unsustainability. In short, the Xai-Xai project seems to benefit the local elites more than the ordinary people.

From 'ideological aid to a 'mix of aid and business'

Frelimo, the former 'Marxist-Leninist' party that has governed Mozambique since its independence, has a long history of cooperation with China, which supported the liberation movement during the ten-year war against the Portuguese empire (see Taylor 2006; Henriksen 1978). In order to provide a comprehensive picture of the Chinese presence in Mozambican agriculture, it is necessary to distinguish between aid (bilateral or multilateral cooperation) and investment projects (by state-owned and private enterprises).

In terms of bilateral cooperation, Mozambique and China have engaged in agricultural cooperation since the early days of the country's independence in 1975. At that time, Mozambique, like other African socialist countries, benefitted

---

communities to have access to minimum conditions, according to basic rules of society' (GdM 2011a:5).
3 The Xai-Xai irrigation system covers an area estimated of 12 000 hectares. For its part, the area of Ponela block is estimated at 572 hadivided between the Chinese enterprise and ARPONE farmers. For a more in depth description of the Xai-Xai irrigation system see Ganho (2013).

from Chinese aid. According to Bräutigam (2010), in this period Chinese cooperation was motivated by notions of 'solidarity' as well as by 'ideology'. One of the most popular types of solidarity aid projects in the agriculture sector was the establishment of state farms by the Chinese government in Africa (Eadie & Grizzell 1979:224, Bräutigam & Ekman 2012). In Mozambique, the best-known example is the Moamba farm in the south, where vegetables (primarily potatoes) and maize were cultivated. Mozambican authorities considered this farm an important symbol of China's commitment to the country and it was one of the places visited in 1979 by the Chinese delegation headed by Li Sien-nien, then the vice prime minister (Voz da Revolução 1979). In addition to the Moamba state farm, the Chinese helped to develop the Matama state farm in Niassa (originally established by the Portuguese during colonial rule), northern Mozambique (Bräutigam & Ekman 2012).[4] In 1984, corn, beans, potatoes, wheat, sunflowers, garden vegetables, soybeans and bananas were the main products produced at the Matama state farm. At the time there were ten Chinese citizens working there as agronomist-engineers and mechanics (FBIS 1984).

Apparently the Matama state farm collapsed mainly due to the civil war, which forced Chinese agricultural engineers to flee in 1985, leaving behind agricultural equipment (*Mail & Guardian* 1997). The same is true of the Moamba state farm, which went into decline mostly due to the effects of the civil war. Nonetheless, given that the projects were ideologically driven, it is questionable whether the farms would have been able to succeed even in the absence of civil war (see Bräutigam 2010; Bräutigam & Xiaoyang 2009). Another argument in support of this point is related to the complete failure of Frelimo's agrarian policies which, during the Marxist-Leninist period, gave high priority to the state's large and heavily mechanised farms.

The present framework for bilateral cooperation in agriculture is based on a Memorandum of Understanding (MoU) signed between the two countries during the visit of the former prime minister of Mozambique, Pascoal Mocumbi, to China in 2002. According to its provisions, this MoU was valid for a period of five years (2002–2007) and was to be automatically renewed if there were no changes to report from either side. This MoU established cooperation in various areas, namely forestry, rice production, biotechnology, crops and livestock, processing, disease, pest control and research (Ministry of Agriculture (MINAG) 2002).

---

4 The Matama state farm is best known for having hosted the victims of '*Operação Produção*', launched in 1983 by the Mozambican authorities, with the aim of moving the urban unemployed people to the rural zones in order to work in the agriculture.

In order to solve the crisis in the agriculture sector, Mozambique borrowed from the China Exim Bank with the aim of rehabilitating and developing important agricultural infrastructure in regions considered critical to boosting the agriculture sector. These regions are Chokwe, in Gaza province (southern Mozambique); Zambezi valley, Zambézia province (central Mozambique); and Nguri and Chipembe, in Cabo Delgado province (northern Mozambique). A US$50 million concessional loan from China Exim Bank, targeting several agricultural projects, stands out among these loans. The first U$30 million, placed under the management of the *Gabinete do Plano de Desenvolvimento da Região do Zambeze* (GPZ),[5] was used to build three agro-processing factories (cotton, rice and maize) in the provinces of Manica, Zambézia and Tete, respectively (MINAG 2010). The remaining U$20 million was used to import agricultural equipment from China. The loan also aimed to help improve local farmers' production, with the intention of fuelling factories (MINAG 2010.). Yet, because of the inability of the Zambezi valley farmers to acquire the necessary equipment, officials decided to place available funds at the disposal of all Mozambican farmers with the capacity to buy the requisite materials. As a senior MINAG official explains:

> [As you know] it is a concessional credit, so the GPZ couldn't give it for free to the farmers. According to the parameters defined by GPZ, many of our brothers from Zambezi valley were not eligible. It was necessary to pay 40% as the first tranche. First, the opportunity was given to the Zambezi valley farmers, but the equipment was not sold so it was exposed to the rain and sun. This coincided with the process of restructuring the GPZ and it was decided that the equipment could not be left abandoned, so it was decided to sell it to the farmers of other regions: Moamba, Nampula and Chokwe – all over the country. (Interview, MINAG, 3 August 2012)

It should also be mentioned that the three agro-processing factories were built by China Engineering Co Ltd (CAMCE). The cotton-processing factory in Guro district (Manica province) and the maize agro-processing factory in Ulongué (Tete province) were completed in 2012 and are presently managed by Instituto de Algodão de Moçambique (IAM) and Instituto de Cereais of Moçambique (ICM), both public institutions. It is important to stress that this concessional fund was channelled to Mozambique through Moza Banco, a bank

---

5 As GPZ (Office of the Zambezi Development Plan) was unable to reach their goals, the Mozambican authorities closed it in 2010 and replaced it with the *Agência de Desenvolvimento do Zambeze* (AGZ).

created in 2008 by the Macanese businessman Stanley Ho through the holding group Geocapital and the Portuguese politician António d'Almeida Santos in association with a small number of Mozambican political figures close to Frelimo, such as Prakash Ratilal (see Alves 2012).[6] Although the circumstances surrounding the choice of Moza Banco to implement this loan remain obscure, the GPZ reported that it had signed an agreement with Geocapital in 2005 in order to develop several socio-economic projects in the Zambezi valley (GPZ 2005).

In 2012 Mozambique signed another long-term credit line from China Exim Bank of US$60 million to develop an agricultural project in Chokwe, one of the most important agriculture regions in the country. Named Chokwe Agro-Processing Complex, the project aims to develop several projects, primarily a processing, packaging and conservation unit; a cattle breeding and processing farm; rice-processing factories (costing US$16.6 million); rehabilitation of the irrigation system; and establishing an irrigation maintenance unit (US$41.7 million) and agricultural service centres (US$1.7 million) (MINAG 2012).

In addition, it is important to note that in 2011 Mozambican authorities were negotiating two loans of US$25 million and US$12 million, with China Exim Bank in order to rehabilitate the Chipembe and Nguri dams in Cabo Delgado province to boost its agriculture sector (GdM 2011b).[7] According to a key informant at MINAG, at the time this chapter was written the Mozambican government was still in negotiation with the Chinese and prospects seemed promising (interview, MINAG, Maputo, August 2012).[8]

The current dynamics of Chinese-Mozambican cooperation should be considered with reference to FOCAC measures. Mozambique was granted one of the 30 Agricultural Technology Demonstration Centres established in Africa in the framework of FOCAC, with the main objective of transferring Chinese technology to boost the agriculture and livestock sectors. Mozambique was the

---

6 Ratilal was a former central governor of the Bank of Mozambique and vice minister of Commerce. The alliance with foreign capital has been one of the ways used by the new Mozambican bourgeoisie to do business in Mozambique. The alliance between Chinese entrepreneurs and the Mozambican political elite is not a secret. The best known and most controversial is the alliance in the timber sector. However, there are strong indications of linkages in other sectors, especially mineral resources. Due to its importance, this issue merits a thorough study that is not the subject of this chapter.

7 These two dams were considered, after independence, to be the future of the Cabo Delgado province. The former president of Mozambique, Samora Machel, wanted to build a city in Chipembe thanks to the insights created by this dam (FBIS 1983). The Chibempe dam (or irrigation system of Chipembe) was constructed in the 1970s with the support of North Korea.

8 It was also made clear that the Chipembe dam (paralysed during the civil war) will be rehabilitated by the Brazilians through the Câmara de Comércio e Indústria Brasil-Moçambique (CCIBM), which will work with EMBRAPA to develop agricultural activities (JM Online 2012). Moreover, *Notícias* (2012), affirmed that the Chinese have already agreed to finance these two irrigation systems. This information was unconfirmed by our source, who is the same source quoted by this newspaper.

first country to receive this type of Chinese aid in Africa.

The cost of the Agricultural Technology Demonstration Centre of Umbeluzi (CITTAU) (located in Boane, southern Mozambique) was estimated at CNY40 million (approximately US$6 million) (Durán & Chichava 2012). Construction started in 2008 with technical assistance from the government of Hubei province. CITTAU is managed by HLMO Co Lda, the same company that was managed the Ponela rice farm in the Xai-Xai irrigation scheme.[9] CITTAU was officially inaugurated in July 2011 by the Mozambican president, and it launched its first training course in Chinese agrarian technologies in July 2012. According to the Ministério da Ciência e Tecnologia (Ministry of Science and Technology) 30 local farmers attended the course (MCT 2012). One of the main objectives of CITTAU is to take advantage of Chinese technology to increase Mozambican rice production from estimates of two to three tonnes per hectare a year to nine to ten (Durán & Chichava 2012). In addition to rice varieties, some others varieties of cotton and maize are also being tested (Durán & Chichava 2012). As is evident from these examples, China-Mozambique interactions in this area surpass bilateral agreements, loans or grants and, as a result, various institutions have become involved.

Patterns and trends of Chinese investment in the Mozambican agricultural sector

In order to provide a comprehensive view of Chinese investments in the agricultural sector, this section presents a synthesis of all Chinese investments approved by Centro de Promoção de Investimentos (CPI), the public agency responsible for promoting private investment in Mozambique. The data used for this purpose includes projects approved between 2000 and 2012. However, not all private investments are channelled through CPI, only those seeking fiscal incentives. It is also not possible to confirm through the CPI data whether a project actually got off the ground. Despite these shortcomings, the CPI database is the only reliable database which can be used to examine patterns and trends in private investment in Mozambique.

---

9 It is important to note that thanks to the establishment of CITTAU, Chinese firms – mainly from Hubei – have received some privilege to invest in Mozambican agriculture. In fact, Lianhe Africa Agriculture Development Co. Limitada, with the headquarters at CITTAU is planning to invest large sums in Mozambican agriculture (Boletim da República 2012a).

It is also important to underline that companies from Hubei province are investing in other sectors besides agriculture. Between 2011 and 2012, according to research in Boletim da República (an official bulletin), we found some companies from Hubei: Aqua-Alliance Co Limitada (Boletim da República 2010b); Joyo Industrial e Comércio (Boletim da República 2011a); Tiamo Indústria e Comércio-Sociedade Unipessoal Limitada (Boletim da República 2011b; Gomesol Limitada (Boletim da República 2011c), dedicated to the import and export of several products.

Table 8.1 Chinese investment in Mozambique's agriculture sector (2000–2010)

Investor	Objective	Year	Province	Intended Jobs Created	IDE (US$)	Total (US$)
Exploração, Transformação e Comércio de Madeira	Wood exploration and commerce	2001	Cabo Delgado	1 803	400 000	63 699 600
União dos Trabalhadores de África (UTA)	Wood exploration and commerce	2003	Cabo Delgado	150	1 000 000	1 000 000
China Grains & Oils Group Corporation Africa (CGOG Africa) (a)	Planting, distribution, processing and trade in agricultural products; forest cutting, distribution, processing; relevant trade; tourism and transport	2005	Sofala	150	5 500 000	6 000 000
Biworld International Limited	Purchase and sale of timber, sale of various kinds of industrial machinery and agricultural, import and export	2006	Tete	215	200 000	2 000 000
Xin Jian Companhia	*	2006	Zambézia	200	195 000	200 000
Hubei Lianfeng Mozambique	Import and marketing of industrial machinery and equipment, agricultural fertilisers and other agricultural chemicals; Development of agricultural activities, namely the production of all sorts of grains, legumes and vegetables, farming of small animals, among others	2007	Gaza	6	1 200 000	1 200 000
Weng Chen Liao	*	2009	Sofala	60	60 000	60 000
Sunway International Mozambique Lda	Production and industrial processing of peanuts and sesame	2010	Nampula	50	500 000	500 000

Source: CPI (2010)
* *Unknown*

What is perhaps most interesting about this data is the fact that the majority of Chinese companies have invested in timber, not in food crops. It is also important to note that the Wen Cheng Liao Company and China Grains & Oils Group Corporation Africa (CGOG Africa) – a subsidiary of China Grains and Oils Group Corporation (CGOG), a state-owned enterprise – projects failed due to reasons that are unclear (CPI 2009). In 2009, the Mozambican government suspended the approval of all large land concessions in order to carry out an inventory, leading to the Wen Cheng Liao Company not being able to carry through their investments (Centro de Promoção de Investimentos 2009).

CGOG Africa was planning a joint venture with a Mozambican enterprise, Aruangua Agro-Industrial Limitada. This enterprise is owned by a local businessman with close ties to the Frelimo party, and the project was planned to be one of the largest Chinese investments in agriculture in the country. The project, however, never materialised for reasons that remain undisclosed. CGOG Africa was among a list of 11 investment projects listed as on hold in 2008. Among several explanations advanced for the failure of this project, potential accounts include the withdrawal of investors, lack of clarity on sectoral regulations, lack of financial liquidity and investors' financial dependence (CPI 2009) on access to credit. In 2008, CGOG Africa surrendered its stake in the joint venture to China Begbu Lisheng Chemical Technology Development Co Ltd (Boletim da República 2008).

According to CPI data, between 2000 and 2010, agriculture, agro-industry and construction were the sectors that received the least investment, accounting for only 4%; the majority of Chinese investment targeted the manufacturing sector (77%), followed by aquaculture and fisheries (12%) (see Chapter 2). Investment in aquaculture and fisheries is important to note particularly because it constitutes one of the sectors prioritised by the Mozambican government in its fight against food insecurity (GdM 2011a).

The pattern evident here is not dissimilar from other non-Chinese foreign direct investment (FDI) in the agriculture sector. Indeed, between 2000 and 2010, although agriculture and natural resources were the sectors that attracted the most investment, the largest part of the FDI in agriculture was concentrated in forestry (67%) and biofuel production (18%) (Mandlate & Castel-Branco 2012).

Nonetheless, recent developments point to dramatic changes in patterns and trends in Chinese investment in agriculture in Mozambique, with an increasing number of companies looking to invest in this sector. According to some sources, the CPI approved two big new investments in 2012. The first project, Agrícola CCM, features an investment of $50 million in agriculture and livestock in Barué, Manica province (Zambezi valley) (email, personal communication, 17 July 2012). Barué is considered by GPZ as the location with the most potential in the Zambezi valley to develop livestock. The Agrícola CCM is an enterprise created by Construções CCM Limitada, a joint venture between Nanjing Construction Group and John Kachamilla, a former minister of the Ministry of Mineral Resources (Boletim da República 2012a; 2012b).

The second project is headed by China Wanbao Oil & Grain Co Ltd, which took over the Hubei Lianfeng rice concession in the Ponela block in Xai-Xai. In addition to China Wanbao Oil & Grain Co Ltd, the Lianhe Africa Agriculture Development Co Ltd (another company based in Hubei) is also planning to invest in food production (Durán & Chichava 2012).

Mozambique is one of the main destinations of Chinese investment in cotton in Africa in addition to rice. In fact, China-Africa Cotton Moçambique Ltd (CACM) plans to invest US$20 million in cotton growing and cotton processing in the provinces of Manica, Sofala and Inhambane. CACM is the result of an association between Chipata Cotton Company Moçambique and China-Africa Cotton Development Ltd. This company also purchased the Companhia Nacional de Algodão (CNA), a former French cotton production company.[10] In 2011, CACM inaugurated its cotton-processing factory in Beira, the capital of Sofala province. China-Africa Cotton Development Ltd is also operating in other African countries, namely Zambia, Malawi, Zimbabwe and Tanzania (CACDL 2010).

The next section will analyse the China Wanbao Oil & Grain Co Ltd. This choice is justified by the fact that this is the biggest Chinese investment in Mozambican agriculture and is currently at an advanced stage of implementation.

From Hubei Lianfeng Company to Wanbao Grain and Oil Investment Limited: delivering on FOCAC promises?

The initial contacts between Chinese and Mozambican representatives from the respective provincial governments of Hubei and Gaza started in 2005. An initial agreement was signed in 2007, shortly thereafter replaced by a new one in 2008, valid for a period of five years (DPAG 2008). As a result of this bilateral agreement, a rice production project was established in the Ponela block in the Xai-Xai irrigation system by Moçambique Lianfeng Desenvolvimento de Agricultura Co Limitada (also referred to as Hubei Lianfeng Mozambique Co Lda, HLMO Co Lda). Lianfeng Overseas Agricultural Development Co Ltd, a

---

10 More information about CACM is available on its website: mozambique.ca-cotton.com/Indexe.asp?id=10.

state-owned enterprise, is the parent company of this enterprise.[11] According to CPI data, the project was costed at US$1.2 million and is currently being carried out in an area of only 300 hectares. It was expected, however, that this area would increase to 10 000 hectares. Under the Gaza and Hubei governments' agreement, there was also a proposal to develop horticultural production in Moamba, in Maputo province (DPAG 2008).

During the period 2008–2009, a group of Chinese scientists from the Chinese Academy of Agricultural Sciences (CAAS) visited Xai-Xai to perform some yield tests, with the support of the Bill & Melinda Gates Foundation (BMGF) under its 'Green Super Rice Project' (Bräutigam & Ekman 2012:7, CAAS 2009). Thirty varieties of Chinese hybrid rice and one Mozambican variety, called 'Limpopo rice', were tested with success. The yields of the Chinese rice varied between 7.64 and 10.26 tonnes per hectare while the average of the Mozambican rice variety was 7.61 tonnes per hectare (CAAS 2009:5). Besides Mozambique and other Asian countries, CAAS is also developing similar research projects in two other African countries (Nigeria and Uganda) and a number of Asian states, with the continued support of BMGF. In Nigeria the rice tested poorly because of 'the poor water management and land preparation', and in Uganda the tests were not implemented due to unknown reasons. In Africa, only tests in Mozambique had favourable results (CAAS 2009). Under the Hubei and Gaza province agreements it was established that the HLMO Co Lda was obliged to help local communities by transferring technology to boost their productivity and by employing local people.

The analysis will now shift to the process of technology transfer, which has caused a certain amount of disillusionment with Chinese agricultural interventions within the local farmer communities. The main local community that benefits from Chinese agricultural technology transfer is a group of local farmers organised in an association named Associação dos Agricultores e Regantes do Bloco de Ponela para o Desenvolvimento agro-pecuário e Mecanização agrícola de Xai-Xai (Ponela Block Association of Farmers and Irrigators for Agri-Livestock Development and Mechanization in Xai-Xai, ARPONE), which includes 46 farmers selected from a group of approximately 150 candidates.[12] The non-selected candidates have to wait as suppliants. According to our sources linked to ARPONE, the initial selection process was fair and was publicised in the press. ARPONE farmers were attributed

---

11 Apart from agriculture, Hubei Lianfeng Company, in partnership with Hubei State Zhouji Farm, is also investing in the construction sector through a society called Lianfeng Building Materials, Limitada (Boletim da República 2010).
12 Interview, the head of ARPONE Association, Xai-Xai, May 2012.

an area of 285.5 hectares at Ponela block.[13] Nonetheless, farmers must pay for access to the Chinese technical assistance and many ARPONE members were not able to do so. There are several other features of this interaction that are worth noting, especially concerning the modalities and the meaning of Chinese technology transfer. In addition, the agreement is silent about the rights and obligations of Mozambican farmers.

In order to indicate the nature of the relationship between ARPONE farmers and HLMO Co Lda, we can look at an agreement signed in 2011 between both sides. The objective was to cooperate and help Mozambican farmers with the preparation of an area of 100 hectares.

In addition, in the framework agreement, ARPONE farmers were obliged to sell their production for 10 mts/kg (≈US$0.34/kg) to HLMO Co Lda.

Nevertheless, it must be underlined that the payment for Chinese technical assistance is in the framework of a new Chinese policy which emphasises the sustainability of developmental projects not only based on 'ideological' or diplomatic issues after years of their failure in Africa. As stated by Bräutigam & Xiaoyang (2011:692), 'while diplomacy remains a major purpose of aid, significant reforms in the 1990s and 2000s positioned China's official engagement in Africa to bolster China's long-standing policy that aid should generate "mutual benefit".' Nonetheless, the financial weakness of the major members of ARPONE, as will be addressed below in more detail, will deprive them of receiving technical assistance from the Chinese.

The HLMO Co Lda failure at Ponela block

The problem was not only ARPONE's inability to pay for Chinese technical assistance, but also the inability of HLMO Co Lda to manage or even to develop its own project at Ponela, mainly due to financial and material difficulties. Table 8.3 shows the evolution of the production of HLMO Co Lda during the first three years (2007–2010), according to the agricultural authorities of Gaza.

As can be seen, until 2010 HLMO Co Lda achieved more or less the production objective of ten tonnes per hectare. Nevertheless, they never reached the full use of the 300 hectare plot, which was one of the conditions recommended by the MoU in order to have the concessional area extended. DPA reports indicated that, even though the global production results could

---

13 Normally, the area attributed to each farmer is five hectares. Nonetheless, there are seven farmers with ten hectares and one with 20 hectares. It should be noted that the Ponela irrigation system is managed by a public enterprise called Regadio do Baixo Limpopo (RBL) created in 2010, which, among other things, has the duty to assist the local farmers and other users of the irrigation system. RBL was created some years after the arrival of the Chinese and the establishment of ARPONE and it is therefore still too early to draw any conclusions on its role.

Table 8.2 Cost of Chinese technical assistance

Activity	Cost (mt/$)
Assistance with trenching services	5 000 mts p/m (≈$180 p/m)
Land levelling	3 000 mts/m (≈$100)
Supplying seeds	24 mts/kg (≈$0.86/kg)
Assistance in sewing process	Not mentioned
Supply and herbicide assistance	3 000 mts/m (≈$100)
Mechanised cutting followed by machine threshing	3 000 mts/ha (≈$100)
Rice transportation from the farmers to the factory for processing	1 000 mts/ha (≈$30)

Source: Associação dos Agricultores e Regantes do Bloco de Ponela parao Desenvolvimento agro-pecuário e Mecanização agrícola de Xai-Xai 2011

be considered positive, HLMO Co Lda failed to respect one of the agreement clauses related to technology transfer, namely the testing of seeds and the introduction of new methods of irrigation (DPAG 2010).

To reinforce this argument, we can look to the 2011 agreement between ARPONE farmers and HLMO Co Lda. As was previously stated, in 2011 HLMO Co Lda committed to help ARPONE farmers to prepare an area of 100 hectares, but this failed to materialise because of the lack of equipment to assist all the farmers simultaneously, so they only worked with two farmers.[14] As we can see in the following statement, HLMO Co Lda was not able to assist the local farmers or to fully exploit its own concession:

> The Chinese enterprise that is there [at Ponela block], is obliged to transfer technology according to the agreement, but it wasn't even capable of exploiting the entirety of its 300 ha concession. They used to exploit 40 ha, 60 ha, 80 ha. Only last year they did a little bit more... Also because when they arrived here their team was very small and they were not well-equipped. So they could hardly help all local farmers... they tried to do their best, but it was difficult; the areas are too big... Besides, technology transfer is not free; it has costs. (Interview, HC, Xai-Xai, May 2012)

This is one of the main reasons why in 2012 a Chinese private enterprise, Wanbao Grain & Oil Investment Limited, undertook the Hubei Lianfeng project in Xai-Xai, with an investment of US$95 million that created a new

---

14 Interview with HC, Xai-Xai, May 2012.

Table 8.3 HLMO Co Lda: Evolution of the rice production

Campaign year	Area (Hectares)	Productivity (Tonnes/Hectare)	Production (Tonnes)
2007/2008	20	9	180
2008/2009	30	9	270
2009/2010	40	9.5	380

Source: DPAG (2010)

company called Wanbao Africa Agriculture Development Limited (WAADL). Nonetheless, in terms of the direction of management, the structure remains more or less the same, with Haoping Luo – the former head of HLMO Co Lda – still as the head of WAADL.[15]

The transfer was made under an agreement with the Bureau of Reclamation of Hubei. It is considered to be the 'first and the largest overseas agricultural investment from Xiangyang city' in Hubei province and to represent a 'major success' as well as a 'microcosm of successful "going out" of Hubei agriculture' in the implementation of Chinese government policy (*Hubei Daily* 2012; Danqing & Yongsheng 2012). The achievement of Wanbao Grain & Oil Investment Limited also permitted the entry of another giant Chinese enterprise, Liugong, specialising in the manufacture of construction equipment. Liugong signed an agreement with Wanbao to supply equipment for this project, estimated at CNY27.582 million (China Lifting Network 2012). It is worth noting that this is part of Hubei province's strategy to invest in other African countries such as Sierra Leone and the Democratic Republic of Congo (DRC).

Equally, in Mozambique, Wanbao's is seen as an opportunity to overcome the country's rice deficit:

> Against all [bad] things that are said or are propagated, this is a strong investment which will catapult rice production in Mozambique… in 5 000 ha, according to my calculations as an agronomist, if they produce seven or eight tonnes per acre minimum twice a year… they can produce 70 or 80 thousand tonnes of rice. This alone will reduce the Mozambican rice deficit by a fifth… This is strategic thinking. In the MoU, they are obliged to help our farmers to boost their productivity. They are doing this without any problem… (Interview, MINAG, Maputo, 1 August 2012)

---

15 Our source from CPI said that the Wanbao Grain & Oil Investment Limited is estimated in US$200 million.

In contrast to the official view, the ARPONE farmers, whose experiences with HLMO Co Lda were not entirely positive, remain sceptical and are anxious to see what will happen (interviews, Xai-Xai May 2012).

In spite of this, one cannot blame only the Chinese for the poor performance of ARPONE's farmers; a better understanding of the ARPONE association and the profile of its members is also needed to understand the situation.

In fact, it can be said that ARPONE farmers are not yet equipped to develop agriculture projects of this kind: they do not have the required agriculture equipment, they do not have easy access to credit and they lack the necessary training or experience in the field. Even if they reach the production stage with their limited means, they must face the lack of agricultural market chains as they do not have access to harvest equipment or processing factories.[16] According to ARPONE farmers, the 2010–2011 rice campaign was one of the most successful, but because of the lack of harvest equipment, production deteriorated.[17] For example, among the 46 ARPONE members only one in five owns a tractor.[18]

The lack of access to credit was cited as one of the main problems by almost all the farmers. According to them, during the last five years access to credit has been very restricted, not available to all, and typically disbursed outside the recommended rice-planting timeframe. As a result, rice planted in the wrong season was plagued by birds and rats, leaving Mozambican farmers with significant losses. This makes them less eligible for new credit and creates a vicious cycle. The problems faced by the ARPONE farmers are not an exception in the Mozambican agriculture sector; they are the main obstacles to the development of the sector, as illuminated by this statement:

> The *Associação dos Agricultores e Regantes de Ponela* [Ponela Association of Farmers and Irrigators, ARPONE] has neither stores nor even hoes, not to mention a tractor. But it is an association that nevertheless wants to produce in 361acres, now we are only using 275 acres. (Interview, Xai-Xai May 2012)

To complete the picture, the main people who created the ARPONE association are Frelimo's locally important members, such as the current vice minister of Territorial Administration and the former provincial secretary-general of the party in Gaza, as well as various provincial directors like those of Agriculture

---

16 Interviews, the RBL employers and ARPONE farmers, Xai-Xai, May 2012.
17 Interviews, ARPONE farmers, Xai-Xai, May 2012.
18 Ibid.

and Social Services who are also farming in Ponela. We can also add to this list the provincial governor's wife, who is considered one of the most successful farmers in Ponela block. Most of these people do not have any agricultural experience, and they are using their positions, either in the party or in the state, to acquire land or to use state means to cultivate their farms or to gain Chinese favours. This suggestion is illustrated in the statements below:

> ... I am very critical of the government's land concessions. It is not right to see our leaders allocating land to themselves because they have an obligation to ensure people's livelihoods. For example, the [provincial] governor is obliged to resolve our problems, the administrator [of the district] also should resolve our problems, the primeiro-secretário [head of the party] idem, the secretária-permanente [third provincial government figure] idem. We can only go to the government when we have complaints about our financial partners. It's up to them to resolve this. How can they monitor themselves if they have no impartiality? (Interview, an ARPONE farmer, Maputo, 3 August 2012)

Those senior figures of the party or the state are the only ones who are able to easily obtain bank credit or pay to obtain Chinese technical assistance, which, as has been stated, is not bilateral technology transfer but paid consultancy services. My interlocutor insisted on this point, giving the case of the provincial director of agriculture:

> For example, the provincial director of agriculture is the person to whom we have to address our problems of seeds. But he has a parcel [at Ponela block] and he has the possibility to use the state equipment and means, so he is not concerned with our problems. He has the power to decide where and how to allocate the DPA equipment. He can use the seeds and the tractors of the DPA for his parcel; he is not like us, and he doesn't have the same problems... he has never had the same problems we do. In the first [agricultural] campaign he was the first to harvest the rice and in this campaign also, because he has the conditions to do this... he doesn't fight to improve our conditions... He is the person who has the obligation to deal with the banks, with MIA [Moçfer, one of the enterprises helping the ARPONE farmers with seed supply], in order to help us, but he is only concerned with his own business. (Interview, ARPONE farmer, Maputo, 3 August 2012)

What is more, the number of Frelimo political figures and state officials (usually

Frelimo party members) farming in Ponela block is growing because they are replacing the ordinary members of ARPONE, who are not able to do agriculture because they lack money and equipment. Additionally, the 'new arrivals' do not follow the waiting list and are often able to jump the queue. As stated previously, the initial list of local candidates for parcels at Ponela block was composed of 150 people. Those not selected in the initial phase joined a waiting list for suppliants. This 'new group' includes the current *secretário provincial* (head of the Frelimo party at provincial level); the *secretária-permanente da Direcção Provincial da Agricultura*, DPA (third in the DPA hierarchy); the administrator of Xai-Xai district; the director of agrarian services; and some RBL engineers (a public company charged to manage the Xai-Xai irrigation system), who at the time of this study were undertaking their first agricultural campaign:

> The process of land allocation to our leaders did not follow scrupulously and strictly what was on the list… do you think that the Secretária Permanente provincial [premier secretary of the province], second in the hierarchy after the governor [of the province], the Administrador, supreme chief of the territory, followed the criteria [of the list]?… The people [the alternate candidates] are very angry with the process, I know that they are very angry, but what can they do? (Interview, ARPONE farmer, Maputo, 3 August 2012)

However, according to Mozambican bureaucrats from RBL and Direcção Provincial da Agricultura de Gaza (Provincial Department of Gaza Agriculture, DPAG) and to some politicians, the main problem was not HLMO Co Lda, which was transferring technologies to the Mozambican farmers and was encouraging them to boost their productivity. The main problem was that this group of Mozambican farmers was not committed to agricultural tasks and they showed limited interest in learning with the Chinese (Ibid). Evidently, this kind of statement does not please ARPONE farmers, as shown by this statement:

> At this moment the only ones producing are the Chinese and some people supported by them. But the authorities say in the media that we are all producing, that everything is going well. I read in the newspaper that the administrator [of Xai-Xai, who owns a parcel at Ponela] said that we are producing. He is exaggerating. If he says this, the government will not help us in Gaza [because they take his word]. He shouldn't say that everything is okay, because it isn't. But he says that because of

his [personal] interests. (Interview, ARPONE farmer, Maputo 3 August 2012)

The elite using state resources for their own benefit is not specific to this case. It must to be understood in the general framework of the logic and process of bourgeoisie formation in Mozambique, or within the context of Frelimo's objective to co-opt opposition political members, independent and critical civil society or to develop the Frelimo party in the Renamo stronghold (see Forquilha 2009, 2010; Cahen 2011; Castel-Branco 2010).

For instance, the Fundo de Investimento de Iniciativa Local (OIL) was established in 2006 with a budget of '7 million meticais' (≈US$230 000) and officially with the aim of promoting development at the district level by supporting local individual initiatives. Forquilha (2009, 2010) shows that most of this fund is not distributed according to the merits of the projects but according to political influence. The general members or sympathisers of the Frelimo party are favoured, unlike the opposition sympathisers or members. Clearly, being a member or sympathiser of the party, or a senior state official, is the best way to take advantage of opportunities at all levels, control access to natural resources, to influence decisions, organisations and institutions or to anticipate or to 'facilitate' access to natural resources for foreign investors (Ibid.; Cahen 2011:4; Castel-Branco 2010:58).

It is easy to understand in the context where the state is seen by local elites as the only way to realise success, wealth and political power and where Frelimo has been in power since independence and is today without any real challenger from civil society or other political parties.

Is the arrival of WAADL a new hope?

As said above, WAADL started its activities in 2011, after replacing HLMO Co Lda. Even though its activities are still at an early stage, some concerns are already being voiced by local civil society organisations and press. The first negative reports about the WAADL project appeared at the end of 2012 when the Fórum das Organizações Não-Governamentais Nacionais de Gaza (FONGA), an NGO platform based in Xai-Xai, was quoted by the independent daily *Canal de Moçambique,* claiming that the company was displacing more than 80 000 small farmers to put their project in place (an improbably large figure that they later reduced to a still unsubstantiated 38 000) (Nhacuahe 2012; FONGA 2013a). Besides allegations of forced resettlement of the local population, another concern was related to water management in Limpopo River. According to FONGA, the project's high-level requirements for water usage are likely to contribute to drought in Baixo Limpopo (Ibid.).

While only a matter of discussion in 2013, things took a serious turn the following year. On 16 August 2013, a group of around 400 local farmers armed with blunt weapons took to the streets to protest against the Chinese project, which brought WAADL activities to a halt (FONGA 2013b). Intervention by the police was required to break up the demonstrations. Protesters accused the provincial governor and other local political leaders, in cahoots with the Chinese company, of contributing to the deprivation of the local populace. In an echo of old prejudices, the Chinese were even accused of stealing dogs by the locals (Ibid.). This action was followed by an open letter to President Armando Guebuza, who was visiting the region, written in October 2013 by FONGA on behalf of the local farmers. According to FONGA, the local populace was angry because they weren't consulted about the project and found themselves to be summarily deprived of their land. FONGA divided the affected people into two groups: one was composed of cattle herders and another of farmers. The first group, who lost grazing land, were not asking for the suspension of the project but for fair compensation; the second was asking for the project to be terminated and for their land to be returned. According to FONGA, this divergence of opinion was also creating conflicts between the two groups (Ibid.).

Moreover, WAADL was also accused of multiple violations. For example, the Chinese company was accused of not transferring agricultural technology to the local farmers, but of only selling services at unaffordable prices; of not respecting local labour law; of paying salaries below the local minimum wage; of terminating contracts unilaterally without any reason and of obliging workers to work extra hours without being paid (Ibid.).

Interestingly, there are different accounts of the number of farmers that were displaced. Even FONGA provides contradictory figures in different reports. For example, during the demonstrations of 16 August 2013, FONGA stated that the dislocation affected almost one thousand families whereas in its open letter to the Mozambican president the same organisation mentioned 38 000. It is difficult to know the reasons behind these different accounts, but it is possible that FONGA is exaggerating the numbers in order to focus public attention on this issue.

Furthermore, the recent surge of significant investment into the Mozambican agricultural sector, particularly from China and Brazil, is giving prominence to some civil society organisations, which have claimed that those investments will not help the people but local elites and big capital. The *União Nacional dos Camponeses* (UNAC), one of the most active NGOs against Prosavana,[19] is also

---

19 Trilateral agricultural programme between Brazil, Japan and Mozambique which aims to transform the Nacala Corridor in the North into one of the most productive region in the world.

starting to criticise the Xai-Xai project.

However, the reality is more nuanced. Those affected by the project consist of a heterogeneous group. To fully understand this, it would be necessary to study the history of the Xai-Xai irrigation scheme since its construction in the colonial period until the arrival of the Chinese project, something that is outside the scope of this chapter. Here, it is important to remember that those affected by the project could themselves be further divided into two groups: the first is composed of people who were allowed to work in the irrigation scheme during the colonial period, and who continued to use the land after the independence even with the establishment of state farms; the second group who arrived after the collapse of state farms in 1980s and has since then used the land on the irrigation scheme.

The RBL Company dismisses FONGA's claims suggesting that they are not only unfounded but they reflect a 'hidden agenda' (interview, RBL manager, Xai-Xai 2014). For the Chinese company, the dissatisfaction of the locals was a result of lack of transparency and nepotism of the local government which failed to inform the local community about the project and, when asked to select some people to work alongside the Chinese, selected only their friends and family:

> The problem is the [Mozambican] government. We've asked them to select some people to work with us. In the first stage we asked for 25 persons. But only two people came from Chimbonhanine [one of the areas affected by the project]. The other 23 are from the city; this is the problem of the government. (Interview, RBL manager, August 2013)

It is interesting to note that the request of WAADL to select local farmers to work alongside them in the project is part of the company's business strategy. In fact, as distinguished from HLMO Co Lda, the Chinese company that preceded it, WAADL is an agro-processing company and does not intend to produce rice alone. WAADL selects local farmers to work on its land and guarantees that they will buy the production; there is no salary paid. Apart from the Mozambican farmers, WAADL has also selected some Chinese companies (three at the time of this study) to produce rice. Regarding the Mozambican farmers, the Chinese company is providing them with training in Chinese techniques of rice production. This first group comprising 25 persons began training in 2012, while the second group, comprising 70 persons, started their training in 2013. As noted earlier, the selection of local farmers is done by the Mozambican government. The farmers are trained to farm an area of 2 hectares and it is expected that, after having acquired the required skills in rice production, they will be moved to areas of 5 hectares, where they will become 'commercial' farmers, selling their production to the Chinese company.

WAADL is also concerned with communication with these local farmers as it has been a source of many conflicts. To minimise this problem, WAADL recruited three Mozambican agricultural experts to work with the selected local farmers. Equally, in order to build its image, WAADL has embarked on corporate social responsibility activities such as constructing schools for the community.

It is too early to say whether this will help to change the perceptions of the local population towards the Chinese, or if it will appease their concerns. In any case, there are deeper problems that might hamper the success of this initiative. For example, regarding the local farmers selected to be trained by the Chinese and later sell their production to the company, it will be hard for them to be successful since their activities ultimately depend on accessing bank credit. To facilitate the process, RBL requested *Fundo de Desenvolvimento Agrário* (FDA), a state agency responsible for agricultural credit, to help the farmers. However, at the time of this fieldwork, the first group, which had already terminated their training course, was awaiting credit from FDA. According to them, the period of rice plantation was almost over. As we've seen in the case of ARPONE farmers, poor access to bank credit is one of the key bottlenecks in this whole process.

Chinese land grabbing in Mozambique?

As is the case in other African countries, rumours concerning the hoarding of land by Chinese investors in Mozambique are widespread. The most spectacular episodes occurred in 2007 and 2008, when researcher Loro Horta published news indicating that the governments of Mozambique and China had signed an agreement to transform the Zambezi valley into the first Chinese agriculture 'colony' in Africa (Horta 2007, 2008). According to Horta, the Chinese were interested in producing rice, and they had plans to send, initially, 3 000 farmers (the number would rise later to 10 000) to the provinces of Zambézia and Tete. The apparent aim was to produce rice to export to China.

Horta argues further that this was part of a Chinese plan to modernise the Mozambican agricultural sector. This project was estimated at US$800 million and it aimed to boost Mozambique's rice production over five years, from the current 100 000 tonnes of rice to 500 000 tonnes. Apparently the concession of funds by the Chinese, for major projects like the construction of the Catembe Bridge and the Mphanda Nkuwa Dam, depended on the granting of land to the Chinese.

However, the Mozambican government immediately denied this, claiming that 'in Mozambique, the land is not being sold or leased' (Rádio e Televisão Portuguesa 2008), which does not fully correspond with the truth. Indeed, Horta was harshly criticised by some researchers, especially in light of the fact that there was no evidence of any Chinese plan either to modernise Mozambican agriculture or to invest in the Zambezi valley (Bräutigam & Xiayang 2009:697–698; Bräutigam 2012; Bräutigam & Ekman 2012; Ekman 2010, 2012).

In fact, while the evidence from Zambezi valley does not confirm Loro Horta's assertions, the former representative of GPZ, Sérgio Vieira, was nevertheless very enthusiastic about bringing Chinese investment to the Zambezi valley and he worked hard for it. The most important achievement of Vieira was the aforementioned concession of US$50 million from China Exim Bank, to be used in the development of agricultural projects in the Zambezi valley.

Also, if Horta was wrong about the Chinese plans to invest heavily in the Zambezi valley agriculture, the truth is that the GPZ and Chinese companies signed different agreements in order to develop the valley. In 2006, the media quoted Sérgio Vieira as saying that GPZ signed agreements in 2006 with three Chinese companies, namely China Minmetals, Zhen Hua Harbour Construction and Construction and Agriculture Machinery Import and Export in order to develop several activities in the port, mining and agricultural equipment sectors in Zambezi valley (Macauhub 2006; Agência LUSA 2006).

During Hu Jintao's visit, the official Bulletin of GPZ, *O Vale Online*, reported that GPZ signed a MoU in 2007 with the Chinese enterprise, Zhen Hua, to develop different projects in the Zambezi valley and because of the high potential of this region they hoped to see large-scale Chinese investment in this area (*O Vale Online* 2007). According to Macauhub (2011), Sérgio Vieira was also quoted in a 2011 interview by the Mozambican weekly *Magazine Independente*, saying that, thanks to the support of China Exim Bank's loan of US$50 million, the Zambezi valley was experiencing improvements never seen before. However, despite the desire and the efforts of the GPZ to attract Chinese investment to the Zambezi valley, these were nothing more than mere intentions (interview, MINAG, Maputo, 1 August 2012). The former provincial director of agriculture in Zambezi explains what happened with the negotiations between the Chinese and GPZ. He also explains why the Chinese preferred to invest in Xai-Xai instead of Zambézia:

> The Chinese have shown some interest in investing in rice production in the region of Zambézia. The Chinese government has shown a keen interest in the region, but things did not work and nothing has

happened yet. Why? The main reasons are the following, and I can say this because I have participated in the negotiation process with the Chinese. In the first phase, the Chinese wanted 50 000 hectares (this was the first condition). So we went to visit the land and we identified some possible sites for the investment. The Chinese therefore sent a team to study the soil, the infrastructure requirements, etc. After this study, they imposed new requirements. For example, they analysed the closer river to the investment zone and they found that this river is a seasonal river. This means that there are seasons where there is water and some seasons where the river is dry. This was a problem for the Chinese. They also noticed that the necessary infrastructure was not in place... They required minimal infrastructure, otherwise the investment would be too expensive. There is a need for irrigation, communication, roads, ports, etc. So after this experience they said that they preferred to invest in Nampula where the port is more important. What we have in Xai-Xai is different. It is different to rehabilitate an existing infrastructure than to start from zero [in the Zambézia case]. In Xai-Xai the irrigation system exists since colonial times and the Chinese had only to rehabilitate it, repair the channels... so if at Xai-Xai rice production per hectare could cost between US$2 000 and US$3 000 (considering the investments made to improve roads, canals, etc.), in Zambézia the cost per hectare could be between US$7 000 and US$10 000. So the Chinese withdrew... But the [Chinese] interest in investing in Zambézia agriculture, especially for the rice production, has not disappeared, because the region presents very good conditions for this crop. (Interview, MINAG, Maputo, February 2012)

To further substantiate the idea of Chinese interest in Zambezi valley, the former director of Zambézia DPA said:

In Zambézia there is large-scale Chinese private investment, especially in the forestry sector. These are private investments but fall within the scope of cooperation. The cooperation agreement or the MoU between China and Mozambique establishes that Chinese investors can exploit Mozambican forest resources in exchange for Chinese know-how. I don't know the names of these companies, but most of them are from Guangzhou, near Hong Kong.

In the end, even though we cannot confirm the existence of Chinese land grabbing, or talk about a 'Chinese agricultural colony', in Loro Horta's words, the WAADL investment in Xai-Xai will have profound economic and socio-cultural impacts on the region.

Conclusion

This chapter leads to three conclusions: first, the Mozambican case shows that Chinese engagement in agriculture either through investment or bilateral or multilateral cooperation is becoming increasingly important, even though it is too early to estimate its political, economic or social impact. The pattern of this interest is quite varied, including food crops, especially rice, cash crops like cotton and silk, and others. It must be stressed again that this is one of the main Chinese promises to Africa. Second, Mozambican farmers' difficulties in accessing agriculture credit is one of the main obstacles to development in the sector. Third, like other modes of FDI or international aid, Chinese aid and investment in the agriculture sector is mostly used by local Frelimo and state elites to improve their own lives or to strengthen the party in the opposition stronghold through buying the conscience of either its members or sympathisers to improve those of the ordinary people. Here, the major beneficiaries of these Chinese rice investments are the local political state elites, their families and friends. It was not a major surprise that when Xai-Xai farmers protested violently in August 2013 against the project, the Gaza provincial governor was named as one of the land usurpers along with the Chinese. If this logic continues to persist or if the political or state elites continues to use their position to accumulate wealth, the widely anticipated development of agriculture in Mozambique, or an emergence of an important and strong group of Mozambican farmers in the Xai-Xai irrigation scheme, will remain a mirage.

References

Agência LUSA. 2006. 'Empresas chinesas anunciam investimentos no Vale do Zambezi', 3 July.
Alves, A. 2012, 'Os interesses bancários chineses em Moçambique: o caso da Geocapital'. In: S Chichava & C Alden, eds. *A Mamba e o Dragão: Relações Moçambique-China em perspectiva*, IESE/SAIIA, Maputo, 49–60.
ARPONE. 2011. *Contrato de Assistência Técnica e compra e venda*, Associação dos Agricultores e Regantes do Bloco de Ponela para o Desenvovimento Agro-Pecuário e Mecanização Agrícola de Xai-Xai, Xai-Xai, 6 December.
Bambo, V. 2012. 'GAZA: Forte presença de chineses no regadio do Baixo Limpopo', *Notícias*, Maputo, 3 June.
Boletim da República. 2008. *China Grains & Oil Group Corporation*, 49, III Série Maputo, 4 December.
Boletim da República. 2010a. *Lianfeng Building Materials Limitada*, 9, III Série, Maputo, 20 May.
Boletim da República. 2010b. *Aqua-Alliance Co Limitada*, 49, III Série, Maputo, 14 December.
Boletim da República. 2011a. *Joyo Industrial e Comércio*, 6, III Série, 3º Suplemento, Maputo, 14 February.

Boletim da República. 2011b. *Gomesol, LDA*, 46, III Série, 4° Suplemento, Maputo, 22 November.
Boletim da República. 2011c. *Tiamo Industria e comércio*, 43, III Série, Suplemento, Maputo, 27 October.
Boletim da República. 2012a. *Lianhe Africa Agriculture Development Co Limitada*, 24, III Série, Maputo, 16 May.
Boletim da República. 2012b. *Agrícola CCM Limitada*, 23, III Série, Maputo, 13 June.
Boletim da República. 2012c. *Construçõs CCM Limitada*, 40, III Série, Maputo, 3 October.
Bräutigam, D. 2010. *The Dragon's Gift: The real history of China in Africa*. New York: Oxford University Press.
Bräutigam, D. 2012. 'The Zambezi Valley: China's first agricultural colony? Fiction or fact?' Available from: www.chinaafricarealstory.com/2012/01/zambezi-valley-chinas-first.html [Accessed on 21 June 2012].
Bräutigam, D & Xiaoyang, T. 2009. 'China's Engagement in African Agriculture: "Down to the Countryside". *The China Quarterly*. Cambridge: Cambridge University Press, 686–706.
Bräutigam, D & Ekman, S. 2012. 'Briefing Rumors and Realities of Chinese Agriculture Engagement in Mozambique'. *African Affairs, 111(444)*, Oxford, Oxford University Press, 483–492.
CAAS. 2009. 'Green Super Rice for the Resource Poor in Africa and Asia (BMGF grant ID#: 51587)'. *Semi Annual Report Submitted to the Bill & Melinda Gates Foundation* (BMGF). Beijing, Chinese Academy of Agricultural Sciences, July.
CACDL. 2010. 'China-Africa Cotton Development Limited. The best Chinese agriculture enterprise in Africa'. China-Africa Cotton Development Limited. Available from: www.ca-cotton.com/Indexe.asp?id=10 [Accessed on 18 June 2013].
Cahen, M. 2011.'The Enemy as a model. Patronage as a crisis factor in constructing opposition in Mozambique'. *Oxpo Working Papers* n°10. Oxford.
Castel-Branco, C. 2010.'Economia extractiva e desafios de industrialização em Moçambique'. In: L. de Brito et al. (eds.). *Economia Extractiva e Desafios de Industrialização em Moçambique*. Maputo, IESE, 19–109.
CDB. 2012. '$57 Million Invested in Agriculture by China-Africa Development Fund'. China Development Bank. Available from: www.cdb.com.cn/english/NewsInfo.asp?NewsId=4159 [Accessed on 2 July 2012].
China Lifting Network. 2012.'Liugong successful agricultural projects in Mozambique 71 sets of equipment orders', 6 April. Available from: www.qzj123.com/news/201206/04/52768.html [Accessed on 8 July 2012].
CPI. 2009. *Relatório anual de Actividades 2008*, Maputo, Centro de Promoção de Investimentos.
CPI. 2011. *Investimento Chinês 1990–2010*, Maputo, Centro de Promoção de Investimentos.
Danqing, X & Yongsheng, C. 2012. 'Xiangyang's First Overseas Investment of $95 Million in Agricultural Project in Mozambique'. *Xiangyang Daily*. Available from: en.xiangyang.gov.cn/publish/cbnews/201205/04/cb416_1.shtml [Accessed on 21 July 2012].
DPAG. 2008. *Acordo de Gemelagem específica para a área da agricultura entre a Direcção provincial de Gaza e a Direcção provincial de administração das farmas estatais de Hubei (Hubei Lianfeng Mozambique Co Lda), para execução do projecto de produção agrícola alimentar no regadio de Xai-Xai*. Direcção Provincial de Agricultura de Gaza, Xai-Xai, 20 October.
DPAG. 2010. *Informe do estágio de cooperação entre Moçambique e República Popular da China em Gaza*. Direcção Provincial de Agricultura de Gaza, Xai-Xai, 10 May.
Durán, J & Chichava, S. 2012. 'Centro de Investigação e Transferência de Tecnologias Agrárias de Umbeluzi. A história de um 'presente' chinês a Moçambique'. In: S Chichava & C Alden, eds. *A Mamba e o Dragão: Relações Moçambique-China em perspectiva*. IESE/SAIIA, Maputo, 125–148.

Eadie, G & Grizzell, D. 1979. 'China's Foreign Aid, 1975–78'. *The China Quarterly*, 77. Cambridge: Cambridge University Press, 217–234.
Ekman, S. 2010.'Who is Loro Horta?' *Shanghaisigrid*, 4 May. Available from: http://shanghaisigrid.typepad.com/blog/2010/03/who-is-loro-horta.html [Accessed on 21 July 2012].
Ekman, S. 2012. 'Searching for Loro Horta', 23 April. Available from: starvingcritic.wordpress.com/2012/04/23/searching-for-loro-horta/ [Accessed on 21 July 2012].
FONGA. 2013a. *Mais de 400 camponeses erguem enxadas e catanas para impedirem usurpação das suas terras pelos chineses.* Xai-Xai, Fórum das Organizações Não-Governamentais Nacionais de Gaza, 17 August.
FONGA. 2013b. *Senhor Presidente da República. Petição 1*, Xai-Xai, Fórum de Organizações Nacionais de Gaza, 30 August.
FBIS. 1983. *Work on Chipembe Dam continues.* Rosslyn, Foreign Broadcast Information Services, 10 October.
FBIS. 1984. *Profile of Niassa Province.* Rosslyn, Foreign Broadcast Information Services, 13 January.
FOCAC. 2006a. 'Forum on China-Africa Cooperation-Addis Ababa Action Plan (2004–2006)'. Forum on China-Africa Cooperation, 20 September. Available from: english.focacsummit.org/2006-09/20/content_630.htm [Accessed on 17 August 2010].
FOCAC. 2006b. 'Forum on China-Africa Cooperation Beijing Action Plan (2007–2009)'. Forum on China-Africa Cooperation, 16 November. Available from: www.fmprc.gov.cn/zflt/eng/zyzl/hywj/t280369.htm [Accessed on 19 July 2010].
FOCAC. 2009. Forum on China-Africa Cooperation Sharm El Sheikh Action Plan (2010–2012), Forum on China-Africa Cooperation, 12 November. Available from: www.focac.org/eng/dsjbzjhy/hywj/t626387.htm [Accessed on 19 July 2010].
Forquilha, S. 2009. 'Reformas de Descentralização e Redução de Pobreza num Contexto de Estado Neo-patrimonial. Um Olhar a partir dos Conselhos Locais e OIIL em Moçambique'. In: L Brito et al, eds. *Pobreza, Desigualdade e Vulnerabilidade em Moçambique*, Maputo, IESE, 19–48; Forquilha, S. 2010. 'Governação distrital no contexto das reformas de descentralização administrativa em Moçambique. Lógicas, dinâmicas e desafios'. In: L de Brito et al, eds. *Desafios para Moçambique 2010*, Maputo, IESE, 31–50.
Forquilha, S. 2010. 'Governação distrital no contexto das reformas de descentralização administrativa em Moçambique. Lógicas, dinâmicas e desafios'. In: L de Brito et al, eds. *Desafios para Moçambique 2010*, Maputo, IESE, 31–50.
Forquilha, S. 2010. 'Reformas de Descentralização e Redução de Pobreza num Contexto de Estado Neo-patrimonial. Um Olhar a partir dos Conselhos Locais e OIIL em Moçambique'. In: L de Brito et al, eds. *Pobreza, Desigualdade e Vulnerabilidade em Moçambique,* Maputo, IESE, 19–48.
Ganho, A. 2013. '"Friendship" rice, business, or "land-grabbing": The Hubei-Gaza rice project in Xai-Xai'. *Working paper 32.* LDPI.
Garrity et al. 2010. 'Evergreen Agriculture: A robust approach to sustainable food security in Africa'. *Food Security*, 2:197–214.
GdM. 2011a. *Plano de Acção para a Redução da Pobreza, 2011–2014 (PARP)*. Maputo, Governo de Moçambique.
GdM. 2011b. *Matriz dos projectos com a República Popular da China.* Maputo, Governo de Moçambique.
GPZ. 2005. *Acordo para o Vale do Zambeze aproxima Macau de Moçambique. Geocapital selou parceria com empresas moçambicanas.* Gabinete do Plano de Desenvolvimento da Região do Zambeze. Available from: www.gpz.gov.mz/noticias2.htm [Accessed on 23 January 2013].
Henriksen, T. 1978. 'Marxism and Mozambique'. *African Affairs*, 77(309). Oxford, Oxford University Press, 41–462.
Horta, L. 2007. 'China, Mozambique: Old friends, new business', 13 August. Available from:

www.isn.ethz.ch/isn/Security-Watch/Articles/Detail//?id=53470&lng=en [Accessed on 26 June 2012].

Horta, L. 2008. 'The Zambezi Valley: China's first agricultural colony?' Available from: csis.org/blog/zambezi-valley-china%E2%80%99s-first-agricultural-colony [Accessed on 31 August 2010].

Hubei Daily. 2012. 'Hubei Achieves Progress in Overseas Agricultural Development', 1 July. Available from: english.rikes.gov.cn/4/288/291/4085.html [Accessed on 21 July 2012].

JM Online. 2012. 'Seminário realizado em Uberaba tem resultados práticos em Moçambique', 13 July. Available from: www.jmonline.com.br/novo/?noticias,2,CIDADE,63554 [Accessed on 21 July 2012].

Lin, X. 2010. 'China, Africa cooperate on agriculture, forum shows', 12 August. Available from: www.china.org.cn/world/2010-08/12/content_20694264.htm [Accessed on 12 December 2010].

Macauhub. 2006. 'Chinese Companies Announce Investments in Mozambique's Zambezi Valley', 5 June. Available from: www.macauhub.com.mo/en/2006/06/05/1121/ [Accessed on 8 July 2012].

Macauhub. 2011.'Empréstimo do Banco da China a Moçambique permitiu desenvolver diversos projectos na Zambézia e em Tete', 13 July. Available from: www.macauhub.com.mo/pt/2011/10/13/emprestimo-do-banco-da-china-a-mocambique-permitiu-desenvolver-diversos-projectos-na-zambézia-e-em-tete/ [Accessed on 16 July 2012].

Mail & Guardian. 1997. 'South Africans "Weirdest" Settlers In'. Available from:mg.co.za/print/1997-08-15-south-africans-weirdest-settlers-in [Accessed on 19 July 2012].

Mandlate, O & Castel-Branco, C. 2012.'Da economia extractiva à diversificação da base produtiva: O que pode o PARP utilizar da análise do modo de acumulação em Moçambique?' *Desafios para Moçambique 2012*, Maputo, IESE, 117–144.

MCT. 2012. *Comunicado de Imprensa. Assunto: Ministro da Ciência e Tecnologia lança oficialmente no Centro de Investigação e Transferência de TecnologiasAgrárias do Umbelúzi (CITTAU) Ciclo de Capacitações aos Produtores Agrários moçambicanos*, Ministério de Ciência e Tecnologia Maputo 5 June.

MINAG. 2010. *Projecto âncora de implantação das fábricas de processamento e do estabelecimento das cinturas de produtores* Maputo: Ministério da Agricultura, 7 July.

MINAG. 2002. *Memorando de entendimento sobre a cooperação no domínio da agricultura entre o Ministério da Agricultura e Desenvolvimento Rural da República de Moçambique e o Ministério da Agricultura da República Popular da China*, Ministério da Agricultura: Maputo.

Nhacuahe A. 2012. 'No Vale do Limpopo: Chineses desalojam 80 mil pessoas para projecto Wambao Agriculture'. *Canal de Moçambique*. Available from: www.canalmoz.co.mz/hoje/23854-chineses-desalojam-80-mil-pessoas-para-projecto-wambao-agriculture.html [Accessed on 11 February 2013].

O Vale Online. 2007. *GPZ assina memorando com chineses*, 27 February. Ano 2, Maputo. [Accessed on 16 July 2012].

RTP 2008. 'Governo nega intenção de vender terras à China', Rádio Televisão Portuguesa, 13 de Mai, http://macua.blogs.com/moambique_para_todos/macau/page/2/ [Accessed on 15 August 2010].

Taylor, I. 2006. *China and Africa: Engagement and Compromise*. London: Routledge.

Voz da Revolução. 1979. *Vice-primeiro ministro da RPC em Moçambique. Estreitar laços de cooperação*, 64. Maputo: Frelimo.

Chapter 9
Mozambican Perspectives on the Chinese Presence: A Comparative Analysis of Discourses by Government, Labour and Blogs

João Feijó[1]

The Chinese presence in Mozambique is not a recent phenomenon. Just as in several other parts of Africa, in South Africa (Park 2008:9–31), Mauritius, Madagascar or Reunion, as from the late 19th century, Chinese immigrants have set themselves up in the city of Lourenço Marques, today's Maputo (Medeiros 2007). The construction of public buildings and private homes, of the port, the railway, and other colonial undertakings required minimally skilled and low cost labour. This was the context in which Chinese 'coolies'[2] formed a much cheaper alternative to expensive European labour. In these and in other tasks, the Chinese distinguished themselves for their knowledge, skills and work quality, and competed strongly with European workers. The Chinese community was concentrated in the cities of Beira and Lourenço Marques and, like the communities of Indian and Pakistani descent, the Chinese were marginalised by the white population of Lourenco Marques.[3]

It was said that the Chinese were servile and unhygienic, and, in the early 20th century, the press depicted them as 'filthy farmers who put public health at permanent risk' (Zamparoni 2000:200). As from the 1930s, Chinese traders became established in the cement city of the settlers. Later, in the 1950s and '60s, they set up small clothing stores. On leaving Portuguese schools, the younger Chinese came to work in public and private institutions (Medeiros 2007). Following Mozambican independence in 1975, many of these Mozambicans of Chinese descent emigrated to Portugal, Brazil or

---

[1] The research is included in the project 'Business configurations in African and in China: A study of four countries', financed by the FCT (PTDC/AFR/72258/2006).

[2] 'Coolies' was the name given by the British in the second half of the 19th century and first decade of the 20th century to Indian and Chinese contract labourers in their possessions in the Indian Ocean and South-East Asia.

[3] The Asians were clearly segregated. Although the Indians had a major presence in trade, and the Chinese in construction, both communities were excluded from the trade associations, such as the Chamber of Commerce, and the Commercial Association of Shopkeepers, as well as from other class, civil, charitable, recreational and political associations of Lourenço Marques (Zamparoni 2000:210).

South Africa.⁴

The contact between the Mozambique Liberation Front (Frelimo) and the People's Republic of China date to the first half of the 1960s. China made efforts to influence the ideological thinking of Frelimo with the aim of extending its prestige and influence, which became more evident after the death of Eduardo Mondlane. The provision of support in the form of military training for Frelimo guerrillas was effective (Taylor 2006; Henriksen 1978; Jackson 1995). After Mozambican independence, the two countries formalised diplomatic ties. Although the Soviet Union demonstrated a more decisive role in relations with Mozambique,⁵ China maintained relations of cooperation, in terms of financial support, the provision of technical staff, and even of food aid (Taylor 2006:94). A new generation of Chinese citizens entered the country, in various projects concerned with health, agricultural mechanisation, the textile and footwear industry or wind energy (Liu 2009:226).

Economic relations with Mozambique received a new push at the turn of the new millennium. Following the adoption of the 'Going Out Strategy',⁶ Mozambique received the largest wave ever of Chinese migration and investment. According to data made available by the Investment Promotion Centre (CPI), US$1.3 million of direct Chinese investment entered Mozambique in 2003, US$5.5 million in 2005 and US$61 million in 2007, when China was the 6th largest foreign investor. Although quantifying the Chinese population resident in Mozambique is a problematic task, the total number of immigrants was around 10 000 in 2009,⁷ which would be about 0.05% of the total

---

4 In the late 1960s, an elite of Chinese origin with economic and cultural capital benefitted from a certain prestige in colonial society, so that the collapse of the colonial society and economy precipitated several diasporas (Medeiros 2007:180). In interviews held with Mozambicans of Chinese origin in 2010, in Maputo, it was found that the Marxist-Leninist model of development imposed shortly after independence was one of the main reasons for emigration. According to the interviewees, many families had memories (lived or told) of the Maoist experience, frequently associated with precarious living conditions.

5 Mozambique opened a second embassy in Moscow (Taylor 2006:110), visits of high-ranking government representatives of the two countries were stepped up and various agreements were signed, not only with the USSR, but with other Warsaw Pact countries. Ian Taylor (1996:99–105) argues that the Chinese support for the National Front for the Liberation of Angola (FNLA), the Chinese invasion of northern Vietnam in 1979, as well as the Mozambican refusal to condemn the Soviet invasion of Afghanistan, had a negative impact on Sino-Mozambican diplomatic relations. China was insisting on non-alignment with regard to the two superpowers (the United States and the Soviet Union), which were competing for influence in southern Africa, and China also favoured the adaptation of Marxist theories to local reality.

6 The strategy promoted by the government of the People's Republic of China to encourage Chinese companies to invest abroad.

7 It is not easy to obtain this information, not only because there are no systematised data in the Mozambican immigration services, but also because of the reluctance of the Chinese consular services to supply this information. The number given is an estimate provided both by a diplomat in the Chinese embassy in South Africa and by the chairperson of a Maputo-based association of Chinese

population of Mozambique. Throughout Africa, China has been strengthening a range of diplomatic relations, this time for motives that are much more economic than political.

Following this investment and migration, academic articles and the mass media have reported the rise of anti-China or anti-Chinese feelings in several African countries.[8] The rebel forces in Ethiopia, Sudan and the Democratic Republic of Congo (DRC) have expressed these attitudes, based on the links between China and the regimes the rebels oppose (Sautman & Park 2009:258). A feeling of antagonism towards Chinese immigrants in Africa was also expressed by market traders in Mali, Senegal, Cameroon, Ghana, Togo, Uganda (Sautman & Park 2009:258), Namibia (Dobler 2008:244) and the DRC (Vircoulon 2009:313). In most cases, these reactions result from competition for access to resources of power, and the targets are foreigners (investors and workers) in general, and not the Chinese community in particular. Hence these attitudes should be understood, not so much as ethnic (particularly anti-China) reactions, but as nationalist responses, within a discourse of defending majority but unfavoured groups. Sautman and Park (2009:258) stress that both the mass media and researchers are insisting on an anti-China sentiment, based on what they report in southern Africa, particularly in Zambia and Lesotho, but also in Zimbabwe, South Africa and Namibia. However, a range of enthusiastic attitudes towards China and the Chinese can also be identified, concerning, for example, their economic contributions and their capacity for work.[9] For Sautman and Park (2009:258), the anti-China and anti-Chinese attitudes that have been expressed are not something entirely spontaneous, but form part of party political struggles and the manipulation of public opinion against the ruling parties. These are movements, sometimes of a populist inclination,[10]

---

from Fujian. The latter estimates that there were about 5 000 Chinese in Maputo and a similar number scattered across the other provinces.

8 In Zambia, after the publication of the 2006 election results, the Patriotic Front party attacked several Chinese businesses (Sautman & Park 2009:276). Lesotho also has a history of periodic eruptions of anti-Chinese violence and, in 2008, Chinese were the target of xenophobic attacks in South Africa. Meanwhile, the Portuguese paper *Público* of 17 November 2009 mentioned that a number of Chinese companies and workers had been assaulted in Luanda, where at least four Chinese citizens were killed last year. Sautman and Park (2009:259) mention that violence against Chinese citizens has also occurred in Pacific states, such as the Solomon Islands (in 2005), Tonga (in 2006) and Papua New Guinea (in 2007 and 2009), where the *Chinatowns* and most of the shops managed by Chinese were burnt. A feeling of apprehension about Chinese immigration is even felt on other continents, such as Europe and in the United States.

9 Sautman and Hairong (2009) show that in a questionnaire addressed to university students in ten African states (including Zambia and South Africa), most of those surveyed had a positive attitude both to China and to the Chinese.

10 The most prominent anti-China and anti-Chinese mobilisation began in Zambia, in mid-2006. As Sautman and Park (2009:275–281) show, the anti-China campaign unleashed by Michael Sata, leader of the Patriotic Front party, was part of a political struggle, which sometimes took on a particularly

which compare the Chinese presence in Africa to neo-colonialism, holding it responsible for the exploitation and degradation of local economies.

Despite the multiplicity of research on China in Africa, there is still a deficit of information on relations between China and Mozambique. The published work deals mainly with the diplomatic relations between China and Mozambique (Taylor 2006), with Chinese investment in the country (Liu 2009) or in agriculture in particular (Chichava 2011), with development opportunities (Chichava 2010) and the impact of the Forum on China-Africa Cooperation (FOCAC) (Hon et al 2009). There are some reports, written by non-governmental organisations (NGOs), about the environmental impact of the economic activities of Chinese companies, namely the studies by Lemos and Ribeiro (2007) and by Mackenzie (2006). Although these matters are reported in the Mozambican media, the social representations and labour relations in Chinese companies in Mozambique are still shrouded in mystery. The rumours that circulate among people in various strata of Mozambican society – such as the claim that most of the Chinese workers in Africa are prison labour – illustrate the distance between the cultures and the consequent lack of knowledge of each other. In this scenario, this chapter intends to contribute with an analysis of the different Mozambican perspectives on the Chinese presence in Mozambique. This analysis intends to distinguish between the social representations of three social groups that issue opinions: first, Mozambican staff in ministries; second, actors in the mass media; and finally, the Mozambicans working in companies with Chinese capital.

Methodology

This chapter results from two items of research and a consultancy undertaken between 2008 and 2010 in Maputo city. In the first place, it was part of doctoral research into intercultural relationships in an organisational context. During this research, eight companies with Chinese capital were analysed, in construction (three), restaurants (one), industry (one), printing (one), telecommunications and personal care (one). Among other stakeholders, 13 Chinese in leadership positions, 21 Mozambican workers, two trade union delegates,[11] two labour inspectors, and the executive director of the Industrial Association of Mozambique (AIMO) were interviewed. Apart from the interviews, countless observations were made during the 12 months of work in the field.[12]

---

populist shape.
11 In this area, four trade union delegates were interviewed, representing the National Union of Building, Timber and Mine Workers of Mozambique (SINTICIM) and the Union of Hotel, Tourism, Restaurant and Allied Workers (SINTIHOTS).
12 The first conclusions of this research are summarised in Feijó (2010).

At the same time, and in order to gather information about the discourses in the Mozambican mass media about the Chinese presence in Africa in general, and in Mozambique in particular, a content analysis was undertaken of the discourses published in the Mozambican blog *Diário de um Sociólogo*. Started by Carlos Serra (a sociologist and professor at the Eduardo Mondlane University) in April 2006, *Diário de um Sociólogo* rapidly became one of the most widely read of the Mozambican blogs. It became popular among the internet users of Maputo, although it is mostly accessed from abroad.[13] Following a 'sociology of rapid intervention', the discourses in this virtual space made an important contribution to an increase in social participation, even though several comments are made anonymously or with the use of pseudonyms. The editor is interested in matters concerned with social exclusion, with Mozambican politics and with Mozambique in general. The blog is constantly updated with short posts covering the news, reproducing various social facts taken from the mass media or from personal observation, normally with brief comments, but sometimes with longer reflections. There are two reasons for the choice of this blog as an object for analysis: first, it has paid a lot of attention to Chinese investment and the Chinese presence in Mozambique and is thus a space with a great deal of information for analysis; and second, most of the posts spark off many comments from the readers, making the blog a privileged space for debate on Sino-Mozambican relations. The research consisted of a content analysis of the posts, links and comments[14] published in the *Diário de um Sociólogo* blog from November 2006 to January 2009, in which China or the Chinese presence in Africa is mentioned. The sample contains 67 posts and 359 comments (with an average of 5.4 comments per post). The 67 posts under analysis contain links to 78 Internet pages (mostly online newspapers or documents for reading, news agencies, portals of non-governmental organisations or research centres, reports on the Internet or other blogs) which were also taken into consideration in the analysis.

Finally, a work of consultative support for the Centre for Chinese Studies of Stellenbosch University was undertaken, concerned with assessment of the undertakings made by FOCAC in Mozambique and the dissemination of the results[15] (Hon et al 2009). During this exercise, several meetings were held

---

13 According to the sitemeter, in the second half of 2008 there were, on average, between 19 000 and 26 000 visitors a month. In July 2009, most of the visitors were from Brazil, 24% were from Mozambique and 11% from Portugal. This information is available from: www.sitemeter. com/?a=stats&s=s25oficina&r=36 (accessed on 1 July 2009).

14 As from the first half of 2009, Carlos Serra began to moderate comments on the blog, which had not happened in earlier years.

15 This occurred in December 2009 and its purpose was not only to collect data on the ground, but also to disseminate the conclusions of the preliminary report.

with a range of senior staff from four ministries in Mozambique, namely the Ministry of Foreign Affairs and Cooperation (MINEC), the Ministry of Public Works and Housing (MOPH), the Ministry of Agriculture (MINAG) and the Ministry of Industry and Trade (MIC). As part of the doctoral research, other Mozambican staff were also interviewed, from the ministries of Youth and Sport (MJ) (sent to accompany the construction of the Zimpeto national stadium) and of Labour (labour inspectors). The analysis also took into consideration various statements by members of the Mozambican government, published in the media.

The semi-official discourse – representations of government representatives
The main finding during the interviews with representatives of the Mozambican government was that their discourse was particularly formal, cautious and defensive. Aware of the sensitive character of the matter, and of the media interest, several of the staff were reluctant to have the meetings taped. The answers were given in a neutral tone and with an unofficial nature.[16]

The interviewees took an attitude of valuing the diplomatic relations between the Chinese and Mozambican governments. José Morais, a former Mozambican ambassador to China (cf. Hon et al 2009:69), stressed the historical friendship between the two countries. He believed that this facilitated an atmosphere of mutual trust. According to several interviewees, the two countries have strengthened their bilateral relations, shown by the visits of high-ranking Chinese government representatives to Mozambique,[17] and of important Mozambican leaders to China.[18] According to the deputy foreign minister, these high-level meetings have created good channels of communication, facilitating dialogue, negotiation and bilateral cooperation.

---

16 During the research, attempts were made to interview various Chinese diplomats, but the reaction was still more laconic. The reactions of Chinese embassy staff in Maputo or staff of the Centre to Promote Investment, Development and Trade with China (CPIDCC) were always evasive or negative, despite our insistence.
17 According to Hon et al (2009:70), several senior Chinese officials have visited Mozambique since the Beijing summit of 2006, notably Chinese President Hu Jintao in 2007, Foreign Minister Li Zhaoxing in 2007; Deputy Trade Minister Fu Ziying in 2007; Deputy Health Minister Chen Xiaohong in 2007; Minister of Science and Technology Wang Gang in 2008; Director of the Foreign Aid Department Wang Shichun in 2008; the Deputy Governor of Jiangxi province, Xiong Shengwen in 2008; and Deputy Trade Minister Jiang Zengwei in 2009.
18 Hon et al (2009:71) mention the visits of Armando Guebuza, president of the Republic of Mozambique in 2006 and 2008; Alcinda Abreu, Minister of Foreign Affairs and Cooperation in 2006; Aiuba Cuereneia, Minister of Planning and Development in 2007; Fernando Sumbana, Minister of Tourism in 2007; Felício Zacarias, Minister of Public Works and Housing in 2007; David Simango, Minister of Youth and Sport in 2007 and 2008; António Fernando, Minister of Industry and Trade in 2008; Eduardo Joaquim Mulémbwè, chairperson of the Assembly of the Republic in 2008; Esperança Machavele, Minister of Justice in 2008; Eduardo Koloma, Deputy Minister of Foreign Affairs and Cooperation in 2008; and Filipe Nyussi, Minister of Defence in 2009.

Likewise, in February 2007, after receiving a group of Chinese business people who were accompanying the visit of Hu Jintao, Prime Minister Luísa Diogo praised the 'unconditional and unreserved support' provided by China to the African continent. According to Diogo, China is 'the only international partner who never displayed any reservations about the priorities indicated by Mozambique'. By way of example, Diogo pointed out that 'when we say that the [construction of a new building to house] the Attorney-General's Office is a priority in Mozambique they agree with us, unlike other partners who, despite recognising the importance of the Attorney-General's Office, when there is no money for it, they simply do not disburse the sums necessary' (Portal of the Government of Mozambique 2007).

The information published in the press at that time, which declared that the China Exim Bank would finance a major hydro-electric project on the Zambezi river (the Mphanda Nkuwa dam), helped strengthen the position that the Chinese government is an important alternative for obtaining loans. The former Minister of Public Works and Housing, Felício Zacarias (Mangwiro 2007), argued that the project would allow better management of the water resources in that part of the country, avoiding floods and periods of drought.

The development opportunities that China offers Mozambique were mentioned several times, namely the level of technical and financial support in the building of infrastructures. The interviewees from the MOPH, MJD (Ministry of Youth and Sports) and MINEC stressed the role of Chinese companies in building a range of public buildings, including the Ministry of Foreign Affairs, the Joaquim Chissano Conference Centre, the Attorney-General's Office, the new national stadium and Maputo International Airport, among others. Chinese companies have also taken part in renewing the Maputo water supply system, in repairing part of National Highway No 1, and in expanding the coverage of the state telecommunications company, TDM.[19]

At the Investment Promotion Centre, the role of China was stressed in investment in Mozambique. In 2008, China became the second-largest foreign investor in the country, with 15 investment projects presented, assessed at US$76 million. Similarly, trade between the two countries has, over the last ten years, recorded sharp growth, making China the third most important trading partner of Mozambique, after South Africa and Portugal.[20] Despite various rumours about large investments of Chinese capital in agriculture in the

---

19 The company Telecomunicações de Moçambique announced in August 2008 that it was negotiating funding of US$25 million from China. Through this agreement, it was intended to expand, by 2010, TDM's coverage from 82 to 128 of the country's districts (Hon et al 2009:82).

20 According to the African Forum and Network on Debt and Development (2007), the sum increased from US$13 million in 1998, to US$422 million ten years later.

Table 9.1 Representations of China in the blog Diário de um Sociólogo

	No	%
Illegalities and lack of respect for human rights	102	34.1%
Exploitation of raw materials in Africa	92	30.8%
Development opportunities	44	14.7%
Conflictual relations with Mozambican workers	31	10.4%
Chinese strategies in Africa	13	4.3%
Dependence on and bad use of Chinese investment	11	3.7%
Chinese cultural influence	6	2.0%
Total	299	100.0%

provinces of central Mozambique, Rafik Vala, the Zambézia Provincial Director of Agriculture, categorically denied any such interest on the part of Chinese investors. He mentioned instead the request for agricultural land by investors from several countries of South-East Asia.[21] Nonetheless, the construction of an agricultural research centre in Boane, about 20 kilometres from Maputo, with Chinese capital and know-how, was stressed (see Chapter 6).[22]

A series of labour disputes in Chinese companies caused clear embarrassment among the representatives of the MJD sent to accompany the work on the Zimpeto national stadium. Put in a delicate situation – between the protests of the workers, sometimes echoed in the media, and in a very sensationalist way[23] (Macuácua 2009:16–17) and good government relations – these Mozambican officials never openly criticised the Chinese employer. They say that the Chinese officials work for results established in advance, which they try to attain at any cost. For the interviewees, the knowledge and capacity for work of the Chinese people meet Mozambican needs, and may be an advantage in comparison with other foreign companies. They opted for praising the professionalism of the Chinese workers who, they say, should be a source of learning for local staff:

> The Chinese have a different rhythm of work. It is the desirable rhythm of work for an undertaking of this scale, and indeed for any kind of construction. Look, the Chinese contractor, when building a hotel, or

---

[21] As Chichava (2011:392) notes, although Brazil, India and China have all defined agriculture as a priority in their cooperation with Africa, the investments of these countries in Mozambique have mostly focused on other areas, such as the extractive industry and construction.

[22] The project was budgeted at US$55 million (Xinhua, 2007), and ten Chinese technicians supervised construction of the demonstration centre. The project leader worked in Nigeria, in the International Institute for Tropical Agriculture (IITA), as a specialist in cooperation projects under the Food and Agriculture Organisation (FAO) – (Hon et al 2009:72).

[23] In the report in question the journalist mentioned a work accident in which a worker fell from a height of 35 metres. But there was no point that high anywhere on the building site.

housing, can build two or three floors in a week. But if we take the same building and give it to a Portuguese, it can take two, three, four weeks to do two or three floors. (Interview, technical director of the national stadium building job, Ministry of Youth and Sport)

Similarly, another high-ranking MJD official stressed the difference between Mozambicans and Chinese in this regard:

Why? Because the Mozambican works from 7:30 to 12:00 and from 14:00 to 17:00. Whether the job's done or not, at 17:00 he's off... but what do I present at the end of the day? That doesn't count. Now for the Chinese it's not like that. (Interview, deputy director of the national stadium building job, Ministry of Youth and Sport)

The high levels of physical and verbal violence were explained by the existence of different work cultures:

In my understanding [violence] results from the difference in cultures, the culture of work. For us in Mozambique, absenteeism, arriving late, that is, whether we do things or don't do them... is normal. For the Chinese, the culture of punctuality, the culture of working for results is completely different from our Mozambican behaviour. (Interview, deputy director of the national stadium building job, Ministry of Youth and Sport)

Most of the Chinese companies in Maputo (Feijó 2010:276) operate with a number of foreign employees that is clearly higher than the established quota.[24] In many companies, particularly in the building industry, the number of Chinese workers is close to 40% of the total staff (Feijó 2010:276). According to the MJD interviewees, non-compliance with the employment quotas on the work building the national stadium was justified on the grounds that Mozambique lacks the skilled labour needed for jobs with high technical demands and tight deadlines. This opinion was supported by the fact that these are projects of public interest, approved by the Mozambican government.[25] In any case, the

---

24 Article 31, paragraph 5, of the Labour Law stipulates a maximum limit for the hiring of foreign workers – namely 5% of the total workforce in large companies, 8% in medium companies and 10% in small companies.

25 Article 31, paragraph 6, of the Labour Law states that in this type of project, where the hiring of more foreign workers than the percentage stipulated in the law is envisaged, authorisation to work is not required, and it is enough to inform the ministry that supervises the labour area within 15 days of the worker entering the country.

existence of this type of inter-government agreement[26] cannot but place state officials in a delicate situation.[27]

The discourses of the *Diário de um Sociólogo* blog

In a second level of analysis, it was intended to analyse the perspectives about the Chinese presence in Mozambique in one of the main Mozambican blogs. This is a second field of analysis which reflects the representations of two specific sectors of Mozambican civil society,[28] namely what Boaventura de Sousa Santos (2003) calls *secondary civil society* and *extraterritorial civil society*. *Secondary civil society* consists of the leading political class which, through associations, seeks to pursue the same interests that are pursued publicly through the state.[29] *Extraterritorial civil society* consists of foreign non-governmental organisations and their staff, both Mozambican and expatriate. These two sectors of civil society comprise a series of well-informed actors, aware of their rights and duties of citizenship, and who are more active politically.[30] These are two

---

26 A request was made of the Ministry of Youth and Sport to consult the Memorandum of Understanding between the Mozambican and Chinese governments on the construction of the Zimpeto national stadium. Despite insistence, the replies were always vague, laconic and useless.

27 At a conference entitled 'Rethinking Development', jointly organised by the NGO, the Friedrich Ebert Stiftung, and by the Frelimo Party, in September 2010, after presenting a study precisely on the representations of the mass media and of the Mozambican workers about Chinese investment in Mozambique, the participants provided me with three clearly defensive comments. A first comment noted the existence of an anti-Chinese movement, explained by 'prejudice' and 'Western fear' of Chinese competition. A second comment relativised the poor labour relations in the Chinese companies, arguing that this was normal in companies that have recently installed themselves in Mozambique, just as happened with Italian and Portuguese building companies in the 1990s. The third comment stressed the professionalism, pace and capacity for work of the Chinese workers, and the consequent advantages for Mozambique.

28 By civil society is understood the non-governmental organisations and institutions, normally noted for opposition to the structures supported by the force of the state. It is an expression used to designate a range of organisations connected with development or philanthropy, community groups and associations, women's or environmental organisations, religious organisations, professional associations, trade unions, social movements, trade associations or media independent of the state.

29 Biza (2008:58) and Francisco et al (2008:26) argue that any form of organisation – be it political, economic, trade union, religious, cultural, sporting or of any other kind – tends to be understood as a site for necessary penetration by the party. As Groelsema et al (2009:30) show, the mass organisations such as the trade unions and the business associations (normally the solid base of opposition forces) in Mozambique are among those most aligned with the ruling party. In this context, a climate of fear of the authorities develops, strengthening a political culture of subjection, expressed in paternalist and clientelist shapes (Chabal & Daloz 1999:31–44).

30 Gabriel Almond and Sidney Verba (1963) defined three types of culture regarding political participation, which they called *parochial, subjection* and *participatory*. The *parochial* culture unfolds in structures of traditional power, politically decentralised and marked by poor visibility of the state in the daily lives of the population. Individuals are not involved in political and administrative procedures. The culture of *subjection* develops in the context of an authoritarian and highly centralised political structure. The subjects are aware of the normative structure imposed by the state, but are not involved in decision taking and have no expectation of participation. On the contrary, in the culture of subjection, individuals adopt passive and obedient attitudes towards the law. *Participatory* culture

sectors that are distanced from what Boaventura de Sousa Santos (2003) calls *non-civil society*, namely local communities organised along lines very different from those of modern civil society.[31]

From the analysis of 67 posts, 359 comments and 78 links to other pages, 299 references to China in Africa were found, as described in Table 9.1. When China or the Chinese were motive for debate, the matter was normally dealt with negatively, stressing the illegalities and lack of respect for human rights (34.1%) or the exploitation of raw materials in Africa (30.8%), as well as the conflictual relations with Mozambican workers (10.4%). The most optimistic perspectives concerned the development opportunities (14.7%) offered by China to people on the African continent.

Exploitation of raw materials in Mozambique
China and the Chinese were often the subject of debate in the *Diário de um Sociólogo* blog in terms of the search for raw materials in Africa. In fact, a substantial number of entries in the blog concerned the theme of the exploitation of Mozambican natural resources by foreign economic interests. These references dealt with the unsustainable exploitation of forestry resources in central and northern Mozambique, the exploitation of land by Chinese farmers, and hunting and trafficking in wildlife (such as the trade in elephant ivory and shark fins). Forestry exploitation was a subject repeatedly mentioned in the mass media in a clearly alarmist fashion. Expressions such as 'looting of timber' and 'Chinese takeaway' became common, particularly after publication of the polemical report by the American Catherine Mackenzie (2006). As Carlos Serra (2007b) wrote 'whether we like it or not, the looting exists, whatever the origin of the looters. And this looting has been reported more by journalists than by the environmentalists, whose origin, as is known, is very recent'. This was the context in which two open letters were published: the first, by Carlos Serra himself, was addressed to the president of the Republic

---

(characteristic of the two sectors under analysis) is proper to democratic systems, where individuals are more active and participate. Citizens recognise their rights of citizenship and the duty of the state to submit to the general will. The authors stress that reality is not watertight and that individuals act according to traits of these three political cultures.
31 Indeed, several reports assessing democracy and civil society in Mozambique (Francisco et al 2008; Groelsema et al 2009) note a series of social factors that limit the development of civil society, at least in the way it is understood in Western contexts. Negrão (2003:15) shows that in countless African contexts, participation in associations and decision-making procedures is limited by questions of kinship, gender or age, so that associations tend to be organised vertically (Chabal & Daloz 1999:17–30), according to patriarchal logic. The presence of the appointed traditional authorities – whose power has been used by the central government to dominate rural majorities (Lourenço 2007:64–74), and even some urban strata – limits the formation of a broader public voice, generating forms of 'decentralised despotism' (Mamdani 1996:25).

of Mozambique, and requested the appointment of a commission of inquiry to analyse the phenomenon, and the second, by journalist Marcelo Mosse, was addressed to the President of China. In the same year, two songs were recorded (one of which had a video clip) in Mozambique which dealt directly with the destruction of Mozambican forests (one was by the musician Azagaia[32] and the second was by a group of Mozambican singers[33]). Through the mass media, various sectors of Mozambican civil society (journalists, teachers, musicians, environmentalists) expressed their concern, not only with the sustainable exploitation of the forests, but also with the development of the forestry industry. Various commenters on Carlos Serra's blog warned that containers carrying unprocessed wood were being exported illegally to China, while on the other hand Chinese furniture was being imported, in clear breach of the law and damaging Mozambican industry.

Based on research undertaken by the Timorese Loro Horta, the project that became known as 'Chinese granary' in the Zambezi valley was a subject that generated intense debate. According to Horta, the growth of the Chinese middle classes and the consequent increase in the demand for foodstuffs (including rice) has been accompanied by a decline in arable land in China. Hence the search for land to exploit on other continents has become a reality. From this perspective, the Chinese interest in financing the construction of the Mphanda Nkuwa dam would fit into that goal, envisaging the development of large areas of agricultural production and the migration of hundreds of Chinese workers and families. This news was widely commented on, and a concern was expressed that Zambézia would be transformed into a 'Chinese province' or a 'dumping ground for Chinese who are surplus to requirements in their own country'. Several commenters on the blog compared this project to the system of crown estates and companies of the colonial epoch,[34] forecasting that the

---

32 The song was entitled 'Letter to Father Christmas', and Azagaia sang 'and we received the polemical eastern visit / The President of China Hu Jintao / and obviously we signed several pragmatic agreements / A dam on the Zambezi, and the construction of the new stadium / And China is generous... / it only wants wood in return / And it cuts down our forests, with our cheap labour / and is not boycotted as in Zambia / Let the people just speak while our business goes on'.
33 With lyrics by Mia Couto, in 'Let Mozambique stand up' they sang 'There goes the board of a coffin / The deceased is the forest of a nation / All the wealth for export / Nothing remains for us, no, no / Nothing remains for us, no, no / It's way past time, put your hand on your head / And now see how the land weeps / The chainsaw saws and saws / It steals the green, in another war'. It is sung by the Mozambicans Gorwane, Xtaca Zero, Gprofam and Pipaz Forjaz and the video is available at www.youtube.com/watch?v=4vJpyox9guA, (accessed on 9 August 2009).
34 The estates were a feudal system through which, in the 17th century, territories in the Zambezi valley were rented by the Portuguese crown to Portuguese settlers, many of them of Indian origin. In the 19th century, in order to ensure the occupation of its overseas territories (in a context of imperialist competition for mastery of the African continent), Portugal granted huge territories to crown companies, such as the Mozambique Company and the Niassa Company. These were trading

people living in the valley will become cheap labour and will be banned from practicing agriculture for their own sustenance.

This perception of a Chinese economic threat was also the result of a fear of globalisation on the part of the fragile Mozambican industrial fabric. According to the faxed newssheet *Pátria* (2007), several Mozambican businessmen in construction fear Chinese competition, which is seen as a threat to the weak national business class.

Ethics and human rights – considerations on 'the pragmatic Chinese style'
As Table 9.1 shows, the Chinese government and Chinese economic actors were associated above all with a lack of ethics or with disrespect for democracy or human rights. These representations derived from a series of news items concerning the exploitation and illegal export of Mozambican products, or environmental problems, or the poor quality of Chinese foodstuffs.

In the *Diário de um Sociólogo* blog many illegalities committed by Chinese companies in the timber sector were reported. Based on letters from readers, the daily press, news agencies or official reports, the Chinese presence in the timber sector was, on most occasions, associated with violations of the law, notably illegal logging and the export of unprocessed wood. Taking on a sensationalist character, the matter was stressed in several headlines of the daily paper *Notícias* (cf. Carlos Serra 2007b).

The association of Chinese citizens with illegality in the timber sector began in 2007, when Serra (2007e) published a letter from a worker in Cabo Delgado, Heike E Meuser, addressed to the provincial governor, with a photograph of a Chinese worker beside a truck laden with logs. Chinese companies were associated with logging valuable or protected tree species (jambirre, umbila or *mondzo*) and with the illegal export of hundreds of containers full of unprocessed wood, allegedly using forged documents (news item in *Wamphula Fax*, reproduced by the *Imensis* portal 2007, cf. Serra 2007c) and with the connivance of the local authorities (Alan Ogle & Isilda Nhantumbo,[35] cf. Serra 2007d). The situation in northern Mozambique even involved scenes of violence (Heike Meuser, cf. Serra 2007e) or death threats (Serra 2007f).

Also in the environmental area, the Chinese were associated with the illegal export of ivory – notably in the *New York Times* (2008, cf. Serra 17.07.2008a) – or fishing for protected species and exporting them to Asian markets, in the

---

companies which were granted political power and the monopoly on the economic exploitation of territories in the provinces of Sofala, Manica and Niassa.

35 The report, in English, and dated October 2006, is entitled 'Improving the Competitiveness of the Timber and Wood Sector in Mozambique' and was written for the Confederation of Economic Associations of Mozambique (CTA).

daily paper *Notícias* (2007c, cf. Serra 2007g).

A further polemical question arose from the news that the China Exim Bank would finance the construction of a dam on the Zambezi river. In an interview in *Notícias* (2007a, cf. Serra 2007p), Daniel Ribeiro (a specialist in water matters for the NGO Environmental Justice) claimed that construction of the dam would have negative implications for the Zambezi delta, as well as on protected areas. Ribeiro argued that Chinese banks should only finance projects that met international environmental standards.

The suspicion that Chinese milk products were contaminated with melamine – including the British Cadbury brand of chocolates (JMS 2008, cf. Serra 2008b) – did not pass unnoticed in Carlos Serra's blog (2008c). According to the *BBC News* (2008, cf. Serra 2008c), 22 Chinese companies exported milk to two African countries: Burundi and Gabon. This situation generated great concern in the blog's comment boxes. One of the comments drew the attention of the Mozambican authorities to Chinese products:

> The entry of China into liberalised international trade has allowed the marketing of many products of poor or doubtful quality. When we are talking about foodstuffs, public health could be at stake, Consumers would be thankful if the administration takes measures! (Paula Araújo, cf. Serra 2008c)

Another comment stressed the fact that products (in this case contaminated milk) rejected by China were exported to Mozambique:

> Dr Serra, one thing concerns me. It is known that many Chinese containers enter Mozambique illegally in order to take back wood from the north. Don't these same containers (entering illegally) bring into Mozambique banned products, rejected by the Chinese market? (Kimmanel, cf. Serra 2008c)

Yet another comment claimed that China was the country that produced the most counterfeit goods in the world, putting people's lives at risk:

> If I'm not mistaken, China is the country that most falsifies products, even food. I am afraid of consuming anything that is Chinese. (Nelson, cf. Serra 2008c)

Chinese products were often associated with low cost, but also with poor quality. *Pátria* (2007) wrote that most of the Chinese buildings in Mozambique have not stood the test of time, and, in less than five years, have begun to show small cracks. The commenter 'Chapa 100' (cf. Serra 2007i) stated:

> The Chinese are building infrastructure but nobody goes to the public to talk about their maintenance. Are we going to ask for aid from the Chinese to maintain the infrastructures? Should this partnership not be concerned about the transfer of knowledge?... with these cyclical floods and droughts, will these infrastructures respond to this future dynamic of natural disasters?

A further question that caused protest in the mass media concerned the sale of weapons made in China to African countries. Indeed, the attempt to unload a ship with containers of weapons from China destined for Zimbabwe was an episode that seriously damaged China's image in Mozambique. After the Zimbabwean elections, and following the repressive policies against the Movement for Democratic Change (MDC), in April 2008, *Mediafax* (cf. Serra 2008d) reported the attempt to unload a container with 77 tonnes of military material in a Mozambican port and later in Durban, South Africa. In Mozambique, the government diplomatically refused to allow unloading using 'technical arguments' (Serra 2008d) and in Durban, the South African authorities banned the unloading, backing the position of the dockers and the local trade unions. The *Mediafax* editorial (cf. Serra 2008d) was particularly critical not only of China but also of the Southern African Development Community (SADC) and of the regime of Robert Mugabe.

Serra (2008e) commented on the pragmatic relations which the Chinese rulers establish with their African counterparts, with clear sarcasm:

> As for our Chinese and Russian brothers, it is already known how to proceed, since they do not use that sermonising music about human rights and give us the money we want, it's just a matter of letting them use your gold, your platinum, your timber and charging them the patriotic rent.

In the words of Carlos Serra, Chinese diplomacy adapts with clear skill to the rentier character[36] of the Mozambican economy.

---

36 Beblawi (1987:51–52) defines a rentier economy based on four fundamental aspects, including the predominance of rents in the overall economy, the predominance of the external character of the rents, the small number of figures involved in productive activities, as well as the centralisation of wealth creation in a small fraction of society. In a rentier economy, the state, in its dual administrative and business function, is the element that receives the external rents (Abdel-Fadil 1987:86). In this system,

Conflictual relations with Mozambican workers

A further question reported in the news concerned the conflictual labour relations between Chinese employers and Mozambican workers. Complaints occurred mainly in the timber and construction sectors. Labour problems were reported in building work on the Foreign Ministry, the Joaquim Chissano Conference Centre and the Zimpeto national stadium. The reasons for the protests concerned low wages, long working hours, lack of individual protective equipment (helmets, boots or gloves), work accidents, insults and physical violence against Mozambican workers:

> Some workers who spoke to *Magazine* [local weekly], on condition of anonymity, said that, during the period in question, they were subjected to ill-treatment by the employer, violations that include excessive hours of work, and refusal to grant compassionate leave, among others. (*Magazine* 2007:10, cf. Serra 2007j)

> There have been reports of gunshots on building sites for various reasons... sometimes I wonder: is it the language that creates an abysmal gap between the parties involved? Or is it differences in the pace of work and the level of demands that we are not used to, and this irritates the Chinese? Or are the shots which we are used to seeing in kung fu movies really normal situations in the life of the Chinese? (Wetela, cf. Serra 2006)

In the journalistic pieces and in the comments boxes it was thought that the Chinese behave in a racist way. One anonymous commenter (cf. Serra 2006) said: 'Unlike other races, they are extremely racist. Anyone who has gone into a Chinese shop can witness this'. The description of how Mozambicans are treated by Chinese employers today contains a reminder of how they were treated in the past by the former colonisers. As Henning Mankell stated in an interview with *Le Nouvel Observateur* (cf. Serra 2008c), 'China is full of poor people and exports them to Africa. Here, the Chinese behave like real colonisers, like the Portuguese. It's a terrible form of colonisation. The Africans are maltreated by them'.

In the building industry and in the timber sector, complaints were sometimes presented to the local authorities. However, the workers have also complained of the inefficiency of the Mozambican inspectors and that the

---

access to benefits does not result from the remuneration of factors of production (capital and labour), voluntarily employed in a logic of maximising productivity.

law is not being applied. *Notícias* (2007b, cf. Serra 2007l) reported that the government does not have the resources to respond adequately to the situation: 'with a total of 50 forest wardens who face various difficulties in terms of work equipment, such as patrol vehicles…'. The lack of inspectors on the ground was noted in the report of Alan Ogle and Isilda Nhantumbo (cf. Serra 2007d). The government reactions were regarded as sporadic, and in most cases just promises to investigate. On the other hand, it was reported that the Chinese businesses are protected by powerful Mozambican political and economic interests, which makes it difficult to enforce the law on the ground:

> Workers from many companies and concessions say they are victims of ill-treatment and when they try to protest, they are thrown out of their jobs. To avoid becoming unemployed, the workers say they can do nothing and don't know who they can turn to, because whenever they try to do something to defend themselves, it's the bosses who win the cases in court, all because they can pay, and thus the institutions of justice just put a full stop to the cases… The workers denounced that in many cases the bosses shout at them. A worker told me that he had heard an employer say 'Go and complain wherever you like, because some of our partners are veterans and here in your poor country you are afraid of them'. (Aunício da Silva 2008, cf. Serra 2008f)

Development opportunities
Although the Chinese presence has been heavily criticised, there were also several comments in favour of the Chinese presence and investment in Mozambique. Several commenters denied that the forest is being destroyed, and stressed the granting of Chinese loans, the building of infrastructures and of an agricultural training centre.

Despite all the protests, some opinion pieces denied the environmental consequences of forestry activities. In an article published in the daily paper *O País* (cf. Serra 2007m), Lázaro Mabunda said that the Mozambican authorities have shown that logging is well below the officially fixed limit, so that the future of generations yet to come is guaranteed. Mozambique is thus serving merely as 'an echo chamber for us to make a noise about what does not exist'. For Gabriel Muthisse, rather than Chinese forestry companies, it is the peasants who are mostly responsible for deforestation. According to several commenters on *Diário de um Sociólogo*, these criticisms resulted from a general campaign against China, particularly in the forestry sector, manipulated by an 'outside hand'. For these voices, behind the published reports a European concern about Chinese competition in Africa is hidden, as well as the fear of losing political and economic influence on the continent. Taking into account the European colonial experience, the current Western interest is a false attitude. For Muthisse, the supposed campaign is promoted by Western countries who are taking advantage of these political episodes and alleged environmental problems, supposedly with xenophobic attitudes:

> Just look at the great mobilisation started around the visit of the President of China to Africa. This visit is being preceded by real campaigns of xenophobia against China. Specific aspects of China/Africa cooperation are raised, with the purpose of presenting this Asian giant as the enemy of Africans... Appeals to moralism, to some xenophobia, or even to noble causes (such as the environment) will be waved to attract our attention. (Gabriel Muthisse, cf. Serra 2007n)

An opinion article published by Adelino Buque (2007) in *Notícias*, (cf. Serra 2007b) on the 'supposed friends of the forests'[37] was particularly illustrative. Buque thought that Serra's open letter 'is no more than a false text smelling of xenophobia' and asked the Mozambican president to remain calm and continue 'with his busy agenda of the fight against poverty'. Using official data on the forests, Buque wrote that everything was being done to disturb the local authorities during the visit of a Chinese delegation to Mozambique. For him, 'an anti-Chinese movement has used people with credibility in analysing social questions, people from the academic sector and also from cooperation institutions'. Buque recalled that, when he was a child, there was talk of 'the danger of the Chinese because they ate human beings, preferably children, and people were educated by the colonial system to look at the Chinese with distrust'. From Buque's perspective, there is clear evidence of an international anti-Chinese campaign. Several commenters have questioned the agenda of the funding agencies allegedly behind the academic reports published in Africa.

Furthermore, the granting of loans by the China Exim Bank was also regarded as an important aspect for the development of Mozambique. On 18 May 2007, when Serra mentioned a news item published in the *Imensis* portal, entitled 'Environmentalists Contest the Impact of the Mphanda Nkuwa Dam', some commenters stressed the importance of the Chinese loan. Several commenters argued that, for a weak economy such as Mozambique, the China Exim Bank loan represents a great development opportunity:

---

37 The friends of the forests was a civil society movement, consisting of several Mozambican non-governmental organisations – the Centre for Public Integrity (CIP), Centro Terra Viva (CTV), Cruzeiro do Sul, FONZA, Environmental Justice (JA), Livaningo, ORAM and Pro-Ambiente. Its objective was to promote defence of the Mozambican forests, by raising the awareness of civil society.

There are people going without sleep in the four corners of this world to persuade at least one financial institution to release money for that dam. The Exim Bank almost did not release the amount because Mozambique has no guarantees for such a large amount of funding. Were it not for efforts at the table and under the table it would never have been successful... I was never a great fan of Chinese resources, and I have said this openly, but now I am obliged to accept that this time Mozambique needs that money... the World Bank refused to finance the project. (cf. Serra, 2007p)

For Muthisse (cf. Serra 2007b), the Chinese support in granting loans makes many Western countries less fundamentalist in laying down conditions concerned with good governance, human rights or the defence of the environment. China is a new alternative for access to credit and developing African countries now have a new negotiating partner, which is an important advantage.

The *Diário de um Sociólogo* blog mentioned the design and implementation of several large infrastructures by various Chinese companies. The construction of a residential area for Mozambican parliamentary deputies was announced by the president of China and *Pátria* (2007, cf. Serra 2007o) referred to the construction of several public buildings, such as the Joaquim Chissano Conference Centre and the Foreign Ministry.

According to statements by Horta (2008) to *Macauhub*, China is investing in improving African agricultural production, with rice as the main priority. According to Horta, in 2008 the Chinese government promised to invest US$800 million to the modernisation of Mozambican agriculture, with the main purpose of increasing rice production from 100 000 to 500 000 tonnes a year by 2013. Loro Horta believed that the foreign exchange resulting from the export of rice would allow Mozambique to acquire goods produced in China, as well as other raw materials on the world market.

Although the investment in agriculture has been analysed with concern (by environmentalists, journalists and university lecturers), some comments stressed the advantages of these projects, particularly the rational use of land, the increase in agricultural production and of exports, job creation, and the generation of tax revenue:

Without doubt it's a worrying story, containing between the lines the claims about a 'Chinese province', and a dumping ground for Chinese who are surplus to requirements in their own country, but on the other hand it's better to see the Zambezi valley productive and producing food, rather than unproductive or turned into a vast jatropha plantation, as our Italian, Spanish, Portuguese and similar friends would like. (Anonymous in Serra 2008g)

As for me, I have no problems in using our fertile land rationally, because only thus will we be able to develop, jobs will be created, agriculture will be mechanised, and our economy will be strengthened, by increasing exports. (Reflectindo, cf. Serra 2008g)

Obviously I'm not saying it's a market of astronomical size, but as production increases, so the market will grow, thanks to the increase in income of more people who would pay taxes, spend, save and invest, thus making the market grow. (Chagas in Serra 2008g)

As Muthisse noted (cf. Serra 2007i), the Chinese are also investing in sectors where Western investors have not paid much attention – such as the long deactivated copper mines of Zambia – to the benefit of African populations. As Obed Khan commented (cf. Serra 2008g), across the world there is an increase in demand for agricultural products, and a need for new areas of production. Mozambique has thus become a strategic region, and should take advantage of the Chinese interests. For Bhalane (cf. Serra, 2008g), the question is also uncontroversial. He argues that Mozambique has an enormous territory, with low population density, and so land is not a national problem.

An anonymous commenter (cf. Serra 2007i) said that Mozambique should learn from growing economies, such as those of China, India or Brazil, who have managed to reduce poverty levels. He argues against ridiculing 'everything that comes from China, as I see happening, even with the use of demagogy'. However, as was mentioned in the *Notícias* supplement, *Economia e Negócios* (cf. Serra 2007p) Chinese expansion in Africa can only be a development opportunity, if the Chinese are careful and do not repeat the past mistakes of the Western countries. As Muthisse mentions (cf. Serra 2007i), Africans will be able to benefit from Chinese investment if they stop lamenting and learn to negotiate.

Perspectives of Mozambican workers on labour relations
Analysis of the interviews held with 21 Mozambican workers and two trade union delegates showed the existence of a series of representations related to the low economic rewards, with low expectations of participation, promotion or even of learning, with defective health and safety conditions, with despotic

management, with the high capacity for work of the Chinese workers, and with the various illegalities committed by the employers.

Low economic rewards

In the manufacturing industry, construction and restaurants, the wages of most Mozambican workers were precarious. Normally the minimum wage is the reference point for most of the staff. Even in a printing company, which demands higher levels of skill, the most highly paid worker interviewed did not earn more than 2 500 meticais a month. In the cases analysed, even working on Saturdays (working a total of 48 hours a week, in the case of the plastics industry) or working overtime (as in the case of construction) the monthly wage did not go higher than 2 300 or 2 500 meticais respectively. However, because they often suffer deductions for arriving late, many workers receive even less than the national minimum wage. By way of example, in a large building company, ten meticais were discounted from a worker's wage for every minute that he was late. As one Mozambican worker mentioned, bearing in mind that the daily wage was 65 meticais, 'if you arrive at 7:05 it's not worth going in'.

In five of the eight companies analysed, performance prizes were instituted. However, from observing the wage charts or from conversations with the Chinese employers, it was noted that the Mozambican workers who achieve the objectives stipulated are a small minority.[38] According to the workers, the award of the prize is not usually accompanied by any explanation, which raises many criticisms of the system.

Even with overtime, the wages paid in the large Chinese building companies were about half the sums paid in other companies of the same size.[39] Taking as a reference point the monthly cost of a basic basket of goods and services (budgetted at the time at 5 229 meticais by the trade union federation, the Organisation of Mozambican Workers, OTM) the dissatisfaction of the workers is understandable. Daily survival is only possible by cutting essential expenses on food, health and transport and through involvement in a series of parallel activities. Many workers interviewed arrive at work on an empty stomach (or having just drunk tea) and after travelling for about 60 minutes, often on foot.

Similarly precarious is the granting of social benefits[40] to the workers. No

---

38 By way of example, if they are never absent from work, in a building company in the private sector, the workers win an annual prize of 1 000 meticais. However, when asked about the number of workers who reach the objective, the employer's reply was: 'No. Very few. Maybe one per cent'.
39 According to the trade union delegates, when wages, incentives and benefits are added together, many workers manage to obtain monthly remuneration of more than 5 000 meticais in companies such as CETA or Teixeira Duarte.
40 Compensation granted to the workers (sometimes in money and sometimes in kind), normally (but

worker benefitted from a transport or food allowance.[41] In one of the large construction companies, each worker was offered a simple bread roll during the lunch break, and at the end of the day a second piece of bread for anyone doing overtime. With the exception of one building company – which, at the end of the year, offered a basket of foodstuffs to its workers – in the small and medium companies analysed, only a kettle was available. The workers drank water with sugar (which is rarely offered), sometimes accompanied by bread if the worker brings it from home. This situation caused particular discontent in one of the restaurants analysed, where most of the employees have no right to meals.[42] Some staff ate leftovers abandoned by the customers, but were obliged to do so with great discretion:

> We can work with them from 9h to 22h, without them giving us any food. They don't give us anything to eat. They don't agree to give us anything. The Chinese can see you eating, take your food and throw it away. So that you don't eat. Yes! Yes! This all happens... Not even the food of the clients. If you're seen eating it, you're fired, accusing of stealing it. (Mozambican kitchen assistant)

For many workers, the absence of this type of benefit causes more indignation than the low wages. In a clear expectation of paternalist management,[43] the

---

not necessarily) to deal with expenses related to their professional activity. These benefits may include meal allowances, meals and foodstuffs, transport (individual or collective) petrol, company car, among many others.

41 The Labour Law does not oblige the employer to provide transport or meal allowances to his workers, and this question depends on a collective labour agreement. In any case, negotiation is extremely difficult in all the companies analysed, which are not every open to workers' participation, particularly when it comes to workers' demands.

42 In the establishment analysed, only two Mozambican workers receive a meal, because they work the full day, from morning to night. The company employs 17 workers. The Chinese employer justified this measure by the potentially treacherous behaviour of his staff. He claimed that many Mozambicans consume food and drink of dubious quality in the informal bars. He argued that, if the Mozambican worker contracts food poisoning in one of these establishments, he might blame the meal offered by the restaurant, and denounce the situation to the labour inspectorate or demand compensation from the employer.

43 Émile-Michel Hernandez (2000:99–100) defines paternalist management as a practice that consists of making available to workers a range of social benefits (concerning, for example, food, housing, health or even training) in exchange for reduced wage levels, thus perpetuating the worker's dependence on the company. According to the author, the African economic context provides fruitful terrain for maintaining the paternalist system. On the one hand, it is a model which is adaptable with greater ease to social contexts of a collective nature, characterised by the greater importance of the family and the group. On the other hand, in a system marked by the weakness or absence of the welfare state, workers' expectations for protection develop around the company, expecting it to fill the gaps in a socially precarious context. Maricourt (1996) classifies this model of reciprocity, observable in developing counties (African or Asian), as *'père protecteur'*. In this model, the system tends to be accepted by the majority of the subordinates, who not only perceive the existence of mutual benefits,

Mozambican workers regard these practices as inhuman and offensive. As a printing industry technician put it:

> Yeh, they take care of him as a son. Not exactly as a son, but with respect. The way they treat him is with respect. Our Chinese, they don't respect you. Sometimes they have no consideration. Sometimes they have no heart. Since I had spoken that day, I am there because I have nowhere else to go. If a better place should appear, we'll go there.

One positive aspect on which the interviewees were unanimous concerned punctuality in paying wages. As one building worker said, 'in Mozambican companies, you reach the end of the month and there's no money, but here you reach the 30th and you've already been paid. You don't need to say anything'.

According to the Mozambican workers, the rewards for national workers contrast with those for their foreign counterparts. The Mozambicans stress that, apart from the wages, the Chinese benefit from accommodation, water and electricity, daily meals, biscuits, cigarettes, fruit or free medical treatment. Freed from these obligatory expenses, the Chinese have greater room for savings and accumulation:

> They don't spend! They don't spend anything! They have cigarettes from the company, food from the company. Those guys don't buy anything. These cigarettes come from the company. The food comes from the company. The fruit, bananas and oranges, come from the company. Omo [washing powder], water, everything. (Mozambican building worker)

The idea that the Chinese are economically privileged or that 'they like living here because they live well' is strengthened by observing some consumer goods.[44] In this area the fact that most of the Chinese workers own their own portable computers, on which they watch films or communicate over the internet, stands out. However, the ascetic behaviour of the workers and their motivation to transfer money to China prevents them from displaying outward signs of wealth, such as buying a car. As one Mozambican engineer said:

---

but contribute to a climate of greater consensus and social stability. The effectiveness of this model thus lies in the stability of the chain of relations and in the creation of clientilist networks.

44 This is a representation that should be understood based on the way in which foreigners in general are represented in Mozambique. The association of the populations of European origin with wealth and prosperity has been found in several studies (Serra 2000:23; Ribeiro 1999:121–122; Feijó 2011:167–176).

It's difficult to have this here. They can't go outside (the building site). Those who do leave all have to enter the bus, or minibus, to go to the beach and then come back here. The director, yes, he shows that he has... he rides in luxury cars, he rides in a Mercedes. He's the director of the job. They leave, they have various jobs here, but he's the leader of the building jobs. He has to show that he has something.

Lack of expectations of participation and promotion
In the companies analysed, particularly in construction, restaurants and industry, there are very few expectations of mobility and promotion. The existing perception is that Mozambican staff are condemned to undertake tasks that are directed by the expatriates who do not trust anybody except themselves to do any complicated tasks. During a focus group meeting, the question even provoked irony from the participants:

'Inside there!?' – Mozambican waiter
'No! (laughter)' – Mozambican kitchen assistant
'Not at all!' – Mozambican waiter
'It seems they don't even know what this is!' – Mozambican kitchen assistant

Likewise, there were very few expectations of participating in decision taking. In fact, various problems were identified in vertical communication (between Chinese chiefs and Mozambican workers), which have an impact at the horizontal level (between the Mozambicans themselves). Most times, these problems were explained by linguistic differences, and by the fact that few Chinese speak European or African languages. Apart from the language question, it is thought that the Chinese are not predisposed to communicate with the Mozambicans, devaluing the entire communication procedure, both verbal and non-verbal (smiles, nodding one's head depending on the discourse, eye-to-eye contact, etc.):

He never pays attention... He doesn't look at you... practically he doesn't listen to you. He doesn't want to know. If you need something and speak, he walks away. He's not paying attention. He pays no attention to any of the Mozambicans. (Mozambican kitchen assistant)

A SINTICIM delegate said:

And more! What also makes the situation worse is communication!

> Communication is a serious blockage. The great majority of the Chinese there don't speak English, much less Portuguese. They speak Chinese. Mozambicans are very distanced from them. Because the link between the Chinese worker and the Mozambican worker here is a serious problem. Sometimes a Chinese says… for example… '*saiu, saiu, saiu, casa, casa, casa*' [left, left, left, house, house, house]. Why? You don't understand. The Chinese doesn't know. He can only say '*saiu, saiu, saiu, saiu, casa, casa, amanhã não anda cá*' [left, left, left, left, house, house, tomorrow not coming here]. But why? Isn't that it? Did he tell you to do this? If that's not it, how am I going to make him understand?

Furthermore the supposed distrustful and insecure character of the Chinese makes communication with the Mozambicans difficult. In the opinion of one waiter, when any attempt is made to draw closer 'they think it has to do with some mischief, someone is looking for something that they're talking about'. In a company in the telecommunications sector, opportunities for participation were much greater because the working language is English, because highly skilled labour is involved, and because of the director's participatory style of leadership. The managing director makes a point of holding weekly meetings with the workers, of keeping his office door constantly open, and of organising a dinner with the workers every four months.

Perception of the learning possibilities
Although several Mozambicans recognise the merit of Chinese colleagues in training local staff, the dominant representation was exactly the opposite. Apart from the language barrier, the lack of patience of the expatriate staff in training local workers was stressed.

> They don't teach. They only argue. 'Take here, take here'. He teaches you to stay watching everything, to deliver, to carry wood. And delivering wood, is that good? (Mozambican building worker).

> The employer's son is very intelligent, but he has no patience to teach. He has no patience to teach… When we ask the employer's son, he gives us the explanation, but he has no patience. He has no patience. (Mozambican printing technician)

According to the Labour Law, one of the objectives of hiring foreign workers is precisely the training of Mozambican workers. But for the Mozambican staff interviewed, this objective is not being achieved, particularly in the large public works. A human resource official in the company that built the national stadium said:

> The Chinese do everything on their own, the Chinese engineers plan everything. The Mozambicans only follow orders. That way, there's no learning. I think that, if tomorrow the Minister says 'I want to build a stadium like this in Beira', nobody would know how to do it.

Poor work health and safety conditions
In terms of health and safety, working conditions in the Chinese companies are precarious. According to a Maputo city labour inspector, this is one of the greatest problems detected on the building sites of Chinese companies, particularly when compared with the other large companies in the sector. By way of example, at the national stadium building site, in April 2009, safety helmets were the only individual protection equipment used by most of the workers. The workers had footwear that was inappropriate for the type of work they were doing, mostly shoes, sandals and flip-flops. Workers who were handling iron bars 30 millimetres in diameter were given painting gloves, without the resistance needed for this kind of work. Problems of the lack of individual protective equipment were also experienced in other sectors, notably in the plastics industry. In countless situations there were work accidents that resulted in amputations, as well as skin lesions from handling toxic products, where the packaging only contained information in Mandarin. These situations caused strong discontent among the workers, particularly because of the employer's slowness in providing assistance for the victims.[45] In the restaurant sector there were also complaints about the lack of hygiene. One waiter said that in the restaurant 'there were drains and the Mozambicans… without protective material did that work of cleaning [the drains], at the same time as we were making the food'. In all the companies analysed, various stories were told about the lack of hygiene of the Chinese workers. Handling food after urinating (without washing their hands), coughing and spitting alongside colleagues at lunch (a common practice, even in the offices) or chain smoking are practices that scandalise many Mozambicans. In a clear continuity with the representations of the coolies in the early 20th century, the image of the Chinese is that of an 'uncivilised' citizen. Not only in Mozambique, but in other countries of the region,[46] the idea predominates that in China there is no

---

45 At about 10:00 on a Sunday, while he was working in a ditch on the national stadium site, a block fell onto a worker breaking his legs. Despite the complaints, the worker was left without assistance until about 17:00, when he was taken to Maputo Central Hospital.
46 Likewise, Sautman and Park (2009) identified a whole range of health and safety problems reported in

culture of hygiene and safety, so that the Chinese place values such as profits and productivity ahead of the protection and safety of the workers.

Representations of the Chinese leadership style

In most of the organisations analysed, particularly in construction, the manufacturing industry or restaurants, the labour relations are very hierarchical. According to the interviewees, the Chinese chiefs tend to exercise their authority in a despotic, intransigent and even violent manner. Often this attitude was justified by the existence of a military discipline inside Chinese organisations. This idea was frequently repeated by senior officials of the MJD or of the Mozambican police stationed at the national stadium building site in Zimpeto,[47] as well as by several Mozambican restaurant workers. Resorting to the memory of the period of the one-party state in Mozambique, this military discipline is not really anything new for the older Mozambican staff:

> They always have a form of respect… they are soldiers, a type of soldiers. It's the bearing of military command. This is plain to see, we live it. The chief has spoken, amen. What if the chief wants a cup of coffee… Two situations can happen. Either the servant sees the chief sitting there and runs over to him with a tray carrying everything, because the chief asked him, or then he gives a shout [in a voice of military command] *'txé txé!!!'* That military manner. *'Txá txá!!!!* Give me that!!!!'" (Deputy director of the national stadium building job, MJD)

> I believe that they have their own internal regulations. They have rules, severe rules among themselves. They feel the boss here doesn't want something. They speak in Chinese then… there is a regime here… a law… internal regulations. (Mozambican waiter)

According to the MJD official, the immigration of people from a single party regime, which adopts a 'policy of iron, a governance of iron' generates a series of conflicts and contradictions in a more democratic country. He added that this phenomenon tends to cause rumours about the characteristics of the labour relations and about the freedom of Chinese workers. Thus 'we later end up falling into those speculations, and I don't know if they're true or not,

---

Chinese companies in Namibia (in the construction sector), in Zambia (in mining), and in Lesotho. The matter has raised a great deal of polemic in the mass media.

47 The testimony of the Mozambican police present at the national stadium was collected before 1 May 2009. After that date, following the disturbances in which two Mozambican workers were shot, the attitude of the security forces became much more laconic and unavailable.

that these individuals are prisoners, and they've come here as a form of I don't know what and I don't know how many'.

This idea that the Chinese building workers are prisoners, serving their sentence in Mozambique, is widely spread not only among the population of Maputo,[48] but in many other African cities. The same rumour was observed in Zambia (Sautman & Park 2009:277), Namibia (Dobler 2008:243), Angola (Liu 2009:219) and Equatorial Guinea (Esteban 2009:683), among other African countries. This representation is encouraged not only by the low level of interaction between the Chinese expatriates and the local workers, but also by the language barrier to communication. This representation can be explained by a series of four factors: in the first place, by the historical memory of forced labour (known commonly as 'chibalo'); a second factor is to do with the fact that many Africans are not familiar with people of non-African origin doing manual work (driving machines on building sites, carrying buckets, etc.) and sleeping in dormitories, as many Chinese workers do; third, because of the strict working conditions to which the Chinese workers are subject, and the extreme labour discipline which is largely unknown in Mozambique; and finally, this stereotype is encouraged by the lack of interaction between the Chinese expatriates and the local workers, resulting not only from language barriers, but also from the mistrustful character of the Chinese, particularly when spoken to by non-Asian counterparts.

Just as in other companies of European or South African capital (Feijó 2009), relations of power and authority in the Chinese companies seem strongly racialised. During the discussion groups and through observation of the labour dynamics it could be seen that, in any company, any and every worker of Chinese descent holds indisputable authority in the eyes of his Mozambican counterparts. As one Mozambican waiter said, 'we regard all of them as our bosses'.

For most of the workers interviewed, motivation is not based on reward, but above all, on coercion. It is said that the Chinese are intolerant towards any kind of failing committed by their local colleagues, an attitude that becomes worse in situations of protest or labour demands. According to the workers interviewed, in these situations the Chinese become nervous and irritated, which tends to be expressed in the summary dismissal of or physical and verbal aggression towards Mozambican staff. This phenomenon generates an environment of fear and silence among the local workers:

---

[48] This rumour was reproduced, sometimes with great conviction and certainty by some of the ministry staff, business people, journalists, taxi drivers and even researchers and university lecturers.

> You've got a big mouth, you talk a lot, you can't come to work. You can't complain. You keep quiet. You can't complain... He can send you away. Anyway he likes. He hits you, beats you. (Mozambican building worker)

> Ah no, the chief doesn't shout, he just passes and looks. But to us, if we're just standing there, he screams, 'Aiinaaaa!' as if we were dogs! (Mozambican building worker)

Setting up a trade union committee in a Chinese company is very difficult. On the one hand, the provincial officials responsible for setting up trade union bodies face enormous passive resistance whenever they initiate contacts with a company. Delegates from both SINTICIM and SINTIHOTS said that the Chinese employer was most unwilling to receive them. There were also language incompatibilities when faced with inconvenient matters.[49] Furthermore, workers in the companies who spontaneously organised a group to press demands were either sacked, or their contracts were not renewed. As a worker at the gate of the future national stadium said, 'there is no union here. Here when a union representative was elected, the Chinese threw him out'. In May 2009, following the second strike at the national stadium building site,[50] the MT (Ministry of Labour) charged SINTICIM with sending a representative to the site, in order to mediate in labour disputes. According to the trade union representative, relations remained tense four months after the strike. The labour relations were described as follows:

> Beatings, malicious conduct. They mistreat the union. They mistreat the union. How often do they say 'Machava no good'. They are violent people. They hit. They tell us, you have to hit a bit, hit more. And they say no, we are educating. You are not in line, you don't understand this or that. Just like that... shouting at the workers. It shouldn't be like that! There are some complaints, but it is not as open as before. Now they complain in the shadows.

Feeling unprotected and without the support of the government or the unions, the workers interviewed adopted strategies of obedience and apparent passivity:

---

49 The interviewees shared several episodes concerning the presentation of phony apologies by the Chinese employers, normally entrusting Mozambican workers with this task. In other situations, the Chinese workers feigned total lack of knowledge of the Portuguese language, allegedly in order to discourage the formation of a trade union committee. These episodes were confirmed by various Mozambican workers.

50 In South Africa, in Zambia (in the mines) and in Namibia (in construction) labour stoppages in Chinese companies have also been recorded (Sautman & Park 2009:262).

We have to accept everything. That's our role. Even complaining. Where can we complain? The police don't come in. When they come in, they ask for money. They just come to the door to take money. (Interview, building worker)

However, the apparent resignation of the Mozambican workers does not mean there are not various strategies of passive resistance to their employers. Obedience is a way of winning the trust of the chiefs in order to allow relaxation of vigilance and, consequently, autonomy of the workers. But the resistance strategies diagnosed rested above all on theft, sabotage, irony and peaceful expressions of protest.[51] However much the Chinese leadership style may be considered despotic and overbearing, the fact is that it does not invalidate the existence of reciprocal actions in the form of spontaneous resistance strategies, which is revealing of the complexity of these relations of superiority and subordination. One notes, however, that thefts and the use of nicknames do not only take the Chinese community as the target, but often affect other Mozambican work colleagues.

There were cases where labour relations were much less distant, shown at the level of formality of relations or of the display of power. Despite the brusque and rigid attitude, relations between Mozambicans and Chinese can take on an informal nature. During her pregnancy, a Mozambican printing technician was invited by the manager's wife for lunch at her house. After the birth, she held the baby tenderly when the mother brought the child to the workplace. In the construction industry, it is possible to witness lively discussion between Chinese and Mozambican workers who, despite the difficulties in communication can be seen laughing together.[52] Furthermore, it is said that the Chinese do not have habits of ostentation but, on the contrary, take an ascetic and simple attitude.[53] As one industrial worker remarked, the Chinese rarely

---

51 On the strategies of resistance and adaptation used by Mozambican workers in Maputo, see João Feijó (under preparation) "They Pretend to Pay Us, We Pretend to Work – resistance and adaptation of Mozambican workers in Maputo" *in Estudos Moçambicanos*. Maputo: Eduardo Mondlane University.

52 However, these situations can cause conflict for various reasons. On the one hand, Chinese playfulness is often rough (slaps on the head, squeezing the neck with a hand, kicking, spitting out a cigarette on top of clothing, etc.). And on the other hand, often the conversations involve complying with orders given by the Chinese colleagues (go and buy something nearby, etc.), which often ends in accusations of swindling and theft. For this reason the SINTICIM union delegate at the national stadium building site seriously advised the Mozambican workers not to become involved in this type of interaction.

53 This situation was noted by several of those interviewed by Sautman and Park (2009), in several African countries, notably in Zambia and Namibia. By way of example, the Zambian historian Webby Kalikiti (cf. Sautman & Park 2009:276) said that in Zambia, the Chinese prefer to drive their own cars, instead of hiring Zambians of African descent, as do their European, Indian or Lebanese counterparts. According to the historian, for Zambians it is inconceivable that an expatriate should undertake manual work, yet on a building site a Chinese engineer can be seen driving a drag-shovel. Kalikiti

buy new clothes but continue using the clothes they bought many years ago.

Although the Mozambican workers recognised undeniable authority in the Chinese employers, the failure to display wealth deprives them of social status, at least when compared with employers of European descent.[54] As one Mozambican interviewee said 'the Chinese is not a traditional boss in Africa. The European, the American, the Westerner is a traditional boss. The Chinese is not. So there is this initial difficulty in looking at the Chinese as a boss'.[55] In this perspective, the word 'boss' carries two meanings: on the one hand, it expresses a relationship of authority and domination of an employer over a subordinate. On the other hand, the concept carries a more symbolic meaning, which reveals ostentation and social status. Just as, or even more important than 'being a boss' is precisely 'looking like a boss', and this recognition comes from the public demonstration (before family, neighbours, friends) of outward signs of wealth, both in property (top of the range mobile phone, four-wheel drive vehicle, hi-fi apparatus) and in relations with subordinates (giving loud orders in public) and even in terms of possessing cultural capital (group celebration of a university graduation).

Representations of work capacity

In the images constructed about the Chinese workers in Mozambique, one clearly structuring element concerns their extraordinary capacity for work, organisation and undertaking complex engineering tasks:

> They sit at the computer, they discuss, four of them come there... They discuss... They go to the job... but go and see the perfection with which they work. I take my hat off to them. He's come to work! He's not someone who's come to chatter. None of that! He's come to work! (Mozambican human resources technician)

---

said that, in the same situation, a Japanese engineer would sit and watch the Zambians working. Other interviewees noted that the Chinese arrived in Namibia with a much more humble attitude than people of European descent. For a local trader (cf. Sautman & Park 2009: 265), "*Chinese were much better than the Germans or the Boers. He said that the Chinese lived, worked and walked amongst them (as equals and in the townships), as opposed to the whites who only lived in town in their big, fancy houses. He stated that the Chinese did not look down on them; they took local taxis*".

54 Unlike the Chinese, the population of European descent are known for living in the richest parts of the city (Polana and Sommerschield), for driving good cars, for valuing fashion and image, and for going to the beaches at Ponta do Ouro, Bilene or Tofo.

55 According to a Mozambican citizen of Chinese origin, the Chinese immigrants in Mozambique are treated with less respect than their European counterparts, particularly by agents of authority or by customs staff at Mavalane airport. According to this interviewee, these officials would not dare to address or search Europeans in the rude way they treat Asians, particularly those of a more humble origin.

Extreme dedication to the task at hand is stressed by the hours spent on it after the end of the working day (including during the night), on Sundays[56] and on public holidays. Particularly during their first months in Mozambique, the Chinese workers tend to dedicate all their time to the company. Long weekly workloads, sometimes in excess of 80 hours, have been frequently witnessed, in sectors such as construction, restaurants and the manufacturing industry. This is a life dedicated exclusively to work, where no time is left over for leisure, or even for recovery from an accident:

> Not at all. If he leaves [the building site] it's to go there on foot and come back. He's not going far. (Mozambican building worker)

> [Even seriously injured] he went to work, [laughter] he went, he went! [Laughter] It's funny, it's something I admire about the Chinese, they don't know what illness is, they don't respect it... Yes, because the next day he ought to be at home resting a bit. Resting. But no! [laughter] He was there. (Mozambican waiter)

The qualifications of the Chinese were, however, represented with some reservations by some local workers, particularly in the restaurants and in construction.[57] The fact that these are workers with rural characteristics,[58] without much education, not very literate, not very fluent in Mandarin and not very familiar with writing[59] – all this did not go unnoticed by some Mozambicans, particularly the better educated. Likewise, several building workers relativised the efforts of the Chinese worker. They claimed that their Chinese colleagues only guide and direct, while the Mozambicans do the heaviest work.[60]

---

56 Work on Sundays is most frequent in the manufacturing industry and in construction, where, according to reports by the Mozambicans, the Chinese only have one or two days off a month. In restaurants, work at the weekends is inherent. In the services sector, a standard working day tends to be followed, and weekends and public holidays are respected, at least in Maputo city.

57 As a prominent businessman in Zambia said (cf. Sautman & Park 2009:272) most of the Chinese immigrants come from a working class or peasant social stratum.

58 The rural characteristics of many Chinese workers, particularly in construction and even in the printing industry, are reflected in their calloused hands, in their faces (marked by the sun and by climatic conditions), and in their way of eating, looking and walking.

59 A Mozambican waiter said, 'This manager, he's writing the menu, and he's copying what's on the computer. He was writing things that the others, who are also Chinese, couldn't read. Then he had to go to the kitchen to find out what he had to write. He wrote badly. They don't understand anything that he wrote. So he didn't learn how to write at school… But on those contracts, it says they've got degrees. They're lies they invented in order to be in charge. I had a look at this. It's also obvious from the behaviour of the other Chinese'.

60 According to a Mozambican building worker, 'on the days when we went on strike we saw the way

While the Mozambican chiefs found the performance of the Chinese workers a motive for admiration, for the Mozambican workers it was normally a reason for dissatisfaction. In fact, it is thought that the Chinese bring to Mozambique their culture and professional demands, imposing on the local population intensive work rhythms out of line with the remuneration paid. The way a Mozambican is represented in the eyes of the Chinese is as a simple machine for working, completely dehumanised. The Chinese are represented as people obsessed with results and who devalue the emotional relationship between the workers and their working environment.

The high attention paid to work and to production is incompatible with valuing traditional questions, such as 'respect for illness', for the family or for the dead. In these situations, the management restricts itself to strict compliance with the labour legislation. Since most of the Chinese are unable to read Portuguese, the justification of an absence, even with an official declaration, can become a problematic task.[61] The officials protest that the Chinese workers in Mozambique are away from their wives and so have no family duties. As a Mozambican waiter said:

> They are looking at each other as a family. But they are not at home. We are. We have our relatives here. And nobody plans death, it happens… they don't understand, somebody falls ill, he's ill, but they discount his wages for the days he doesn't come, although they know he's not well. You feel unwell there, they look at you, and they don't say go home… I have colleagues who have children, they have families, the child falls ill, they take him to the hospital, he goes to explain… what do they answer? 'I don't want to know about the hospital'… But they have no feelings… none at all!

The Chinese orientation towards tasks and production contrasts with the

---

they work. For example, the iron bars they oblige us to carry. It takes two of us to carry one of those iron bars. But when they carry them, it takes four of them. The bars are 12 metres or 15 metres long. Where it takes two of us to carry the bar, it takes four of them'.

61 Obtaining a declaration justifying an absence is also no easy task. One waiter said, 'the other day I had a death in the family and I had to go to Chokwe. But there it's difficult to get a document, proof… of the death. It's not like here in Maputo. I arrived here and I explained to him but he didn't want to know. They discount from your wages. But they know these things! Because one of them has businesses in Nampula. When they need to deal with documents, they have to come here to Maputo. All the documents they need, they ask for here, and later send up there.' Furthermore, many workers resort to traditional medicine, where it is not the practice to request a justificatory declaration. According to the national survey on causes of mortality, held by the National Statistics Institute (Mazive 2009:41), the traditional healer was the second most used source of health care by patients who died of HIV/AIDS (33% in urban areas and 44.2% in rural areas).

importance granted in Mozambique to the domain of the spiritual. Pressed by their employers to work on Sundays, some Mozambicans try to explain their religious commitments, invariably without success. According to a building worker, 'when I tell them I want to go to church, they ask: you're going to church? Do you think you'll get money there? You could come and work here to increase your take-home pay.'

Representations of the legality of Chinese conduct

Finally, another representation frequently made by local workers concerned non-compliance with Mozambican law. Most of the Chinese companies analysed operate with a number of foreign workers clearly above the stipulated quota.[62] As mentioned previously, in many companies, particularly in construction,[63] the proportion of Chinese workers is close to 40% of the total permanent workforce. In large public works, the hiring of Chinese workers takes place under the diplomatic agreements between the governments of the two countries and with government funding. Without these advantages, the small and medium companies in the private sector face greater difficulties, including legalisation of their expatriate workers. As mentioned previously, in these cases, many Chinese operate without work contracts, normally with tourist visas, or temporary residence permits.[64] The increase in foreign investment in Mozambique, accompanied by a quota system which limits the hiring of expatriates, generated dissatisfaction in a series of parallel services, on the part of the Mozambican middlemen. As in other African countries,[65] the system functions as a network through the work of a group of intermediaries who have good contacts in the immigration and frontier services and in other ministries, who charge various amounts for the provision of assorted services, such as the renewal of visas, the legalisation of foreign citizens with expired visas, or even obtaining Identification

---

62 See note 24.
63 Given the characteristics of the construction industry, the number of workers on a building site may oscillate greatly, depending on the job that is being undertaken. Most contracts are thus signed for a specific time, with the purpose of finalising part of the job (iron folding, pouring cement, building scaffolding, etc.), and may possibly be renewed. On 7 November 2009, about 500 Mozambican and 300 Chinese were working on the national stadium building site.
64 By way of example, in one of the companies analysed, there were 34 Mozambicans and seven Chinese (which is more than 20% of the workforce). Of the seven foreigners, only two had a work contract. A further two operated with a temporary residence permit, and the others were on tourist visas. Some of the Chinese workers had expired visas.
65 In Namibia, in a context of public opposition and consequent increased rigour by the Interior Ministry in the granting of work permits for Chinese traders, more creative ways of obtaining work visas have been developed. According to Gregor Dobler (2008:248), many arriving traders do not come alone, but as part of organised schemes, in which established traders act as immigration brokers and agents for work permits.

and Residence Documents for Foreigners (DIRE).[66]

The hiring of workers was done in a very disorganised and flexible manner. Many of the workers did not sign contracts and said they had no proof of paying social security contributions, including in some public works. The failure to comply with labour norms was very frequent. According to one labour inspector, these situations were encouraged by the fact that the Labour code is not available in Mandarin. As a lawyer for the Human Rights League said, even if the Chinese have access to this information in their own language, they continue to make 'a Chinese interpretation of Mozambican law'. This situation was confirmed on the ground by a representative of SINTICIM, stationed at the new national stadium building site. According to him, the Chinese have created a series of artifices to facilitate the sacking of Mozambican workers (without paying any compensation), or to apply deductions from their wages. According to the union delegate, physical assault against Mozambican workers has also been handled very lightly by government officials.

In a small private sector company, the behaviour of the Chinese was considered very sinister, leading to countless suspicions of illegal activity:

> Then they meet there and gamble. Outside this place, sometimes some mulattoes appear, they go in the back, we don't know what's there, they go into a warehouse where no Mozambican has ever entered. There are private warehouses there. We don't know what's inside them. Suddenly they can go in with any bag... (Mozambican waiter)

> In fact, he can't be seen... Mmmm, one of them I have seen, he had make-up, and used a beret, that normally hides the face, and he can't be recognised. I don't know if he's afraid of being recognised. I don't know. He goes in with a very large rucksack. He goes in, and when the boss arrives, he has to go up there with a set of scales... They are very strange kids who have come in with those rucksacks. Very strange. (Mozambican waiter)

The mistrustful character of the Chinese, keeping themselves to themselves, strengthens the suspicions of the Mozambicans about the legality of their

---

66 This is a lucrative business for the middlemen and the state officials. Regularising a foreigner with an expired tourist visa (which involves a fine of 1 000 meticais for each day the foreigner overstays) normally costs more than 3 000 meticais. These sums were always paid in advance, and often the service promised was not completed, leaving the foreigners hostage to the fixers, who either demanded more money, or simply returned the documents without regularisation. Several of the Chinese interviewed were distraught at this situation.

activities. According to one local waiter, 'they are very closed! This shows that there is always something that is not right. I think the Chinese is the only race that is distrustful in any country... they are distrustful... expect everything of the Chinese.'

Chinese employers and workers were frequently associated with corrupting labour inspectors or Mozambican police officers. The Chinese even recognised this corrupt behaviour in talking to the Mozambican workers. According to one waiter, 'they dare to say that they are not afraid of the police because Mozambicans like money'. The version of the employers, however, rather paints a picture of the Chinese as victims, stressing the vulnerability of the Chinese population to the greed of local corrupt and opportunist police.[67] Indeed, most of the Chinese interviewed presented themselves as the main target of the agents of Mozambican law enforcement.[68] In any case, Chinese management strategies tend to bypass Mozambican law, attempting to capitalise on their economic power to bribe government officials. Several Mozambicans in influential positions, taking advantage of the power resulting from their functions, also seek to draw benefits from this situation.

Conclusion

From the comparative analysis of the various representations, it may be noted that the discourses expressed by senior government staff tend to stress the good diplomatic relations between the two countries, as well as the characteristics of Chinese cooperation. According to Mozambican diplomats, because it does not impose conditions on investment in Africa, the Chinese government encourages a 'win-win' relationship. These actors also stress the importance of Chinese investment and knowledge for the economic development of Mozambique.

The apparently good relations that can be noted at the top contrast with the tense character of relations at the grass roots, and this is particularly sensitive in labour relations. At this level, the low wages, the difficulties in participation (made worse by the language difference), the enormous work pressures, and

---

[67] Note that opportunism was not attributed solely to the Mozambican police, but also to other Mozambican citizens. One story told by a Chinese worker concerned a policeman who asked to see his passport on the public highway. Since he was not carrying the document with him, the foreign worker decided to bribe the policeman. However, other Mozambicans were watching and began to argue loudly with the policeman, so that he ended up having to divide the money with these members of the public.

[68] A Chinese technician in the plastics industry said, 'the policemen especially like to stop the Chinese. It is easy for them to ask money for Chinese... Policemen ask for money like beggars and the police ask for money without reason... They use to ask normally for 200 or 500 meticais. They say 50 is little. Increase it.'

the commandeering, despotic and sometimes violent behaviour of the Chinese workers lead to dissatisfaction, which has been expressed with strikes or passive resistance. In order to better understand the conflictual character of labour relations in the Chinese companies, it is important to mention two aspects: first, most of the companies analysed are in the construction, restaurant or manufacturing industry sectors, which are marked by demanding work conditions, the dominance of an unskilled workforce, and the payment of low wages (Lopes 2006). On a building site, or on an assembly line, channels of communication tend to be vertical and possibilities for participation are infrequent. To understand the labour relations in these sectors, it is important to bear in mind the relations in other areas, characterised by the presence of a more skilled workforce. In the telecommunications company analysed, the fact that several workers were more skilled and were minimally fluent in English, that regular work meetings were held, and that above average wages were paid, all contributed to the existence of a much more satisfactory work environment, when compared with the other sectors. Second, while Chinese investment and employers have been severely criticised by Mozambican workers (with echoes in the mass media), the fact is that these criticisms have also been made of other investors, and not only of foreign capital (above all Portuguese[69] and South African), but also Mozambican. In this context, the voices of protest do not necessarily have an anti-Chinese character, but are a reaction to the strong asymmetries in the distribution of resources of power, or to what is called the dehumanisation of labour relations, with the connivance of state agents (allegedly policemen and labour inspectors). Thus criticism of Chinese investment often expresses a critical attitude towards the Mozambican government or to local political figures, usually belonging to the ruling party.[70]

The series of rumours about Chinese activity in Mozambique (concerning investment in agriculture, the contractual ties of the Chinese workers, or the illegalities committed) illustrate the enormous distance between the Chinese population and Mozambican civil society. In comparison with various Western countries,[71] the Chinese embassy in Maputo has not shown the same dynamism

---

69 Criticisms of the investment and the labour relations in companies of Portuguese capital were particularly prominent in the media in the late 1990s and the start of the new millennium (Feijó 2011).

70 According to Chichava (2010:343), in addition to involving Chinese business people, the exploitation of timber also involves Mozambican businesses, a far from negligible proportion of whom are linked to the ruling party, but some are also linked to the opposition. In fact, Afonso Dhlakama, leader of the main opposition party, is mentioned as a shareholder in Socadiv Holding Lda, a company that specialises in exploiting timber.

71 By way of example, the Brazilian Studies Centre, the Camões Institute, the Franco-Mozambican Centre, ICMA or the Spanish Embassy sponsor and promote a range of projects and cultural events that bring together specific sectors of Mozambican society.

in opening channels of communication, and so does not contribute to reducing preconceptions and stereotypes. Intercultural communication is made more difficult by the language differences.

For their part, the unofficial and laconic character of the Mozambican government's reactions bear a sociological meaning that is interesting to analyse. In fact, several non-governmental organisations have expressed their concern about a series of environmental practices financed by funds from countries that contribute directly to the Mozambican state budget. Exposed to a noisy sector of civil society, which, albeit in a limited way, is expressing fears about the lack of transparency of Chinese investment in Africa, members of the Mozambican government face a particularly delicate situation. On the one hand, they express disquiet and discomfort when confronted with questions concerning governance or public accountability. But on the other hand, silence expresses a desire not to compromise economic relations with large capital (not only Chinese, but also Western capital).

References

Abdel-Fadil, M. 1987.'The Macro-Behaviour of Oil-Rentier States in the Arab Region'. In: H Beblawi & G Luciani, eds. *The Rentier State*.Vol. II. London: Croom Helm, 83–107.

AFRODAD. 2007. *Chinese Development Assistance in Mozambique*. Fact Sheet Available from: www.afrodad.org/downloads/publications/Mozambique%20Factsheet.pdf [Accessed on 22 May 2011].

Almond, G & Verba, S. 1963. *The Civic Culture*. New Jersey: Princeton University Press.

BBC News. 2008.'Chinese to tighten dairy testing', 17 July. Available from: news.bbc.co.uk/2/hi/asia-pacific/7621651.stm [Accessed on 1 May 2009].

Beblawi, H. 1987.'The Rentier State in the Arab World'. In: H Beblawi & G Luciani, eds. *The Rentier State*,Vol. II, London: Croom Helm, 49–62.

Biza, A. 2008. 'Associações de jovens, Estado e política em Moçambique – da herança a novos desafios (1975–2004)'. *Cidadania e Governação em Moçambique*, Maputo: IESE, pp. 49–70.

Buque, A. 2007. 'Compulsando sobre exploração de madeira'. *Notícias*, 14 February. Available from: www.jornalnoticias.co.mz/pls/notimz2/getxml/pt/contentx/26825 [Accessed on 8 May 2011].

Chabal, P & Daloz, J-P. 1999. *Africa Works: Disorder as political instrument*. Oxford, James Currey.

Chichava, S. 2010.'Moçambique na rota da China – uma oportunidade para o desenvolvimento?' In: L de Brito, CN Castel-Branco, S Chichava & A Francisco, org. *Desafios para Moçambique 2010*. Maputo: IESE, 337–351.

Chichava, S. 2011. 'As economias emergentes no sector agrícola moçambicano – leituras, implicações e desafios'. In: L de Brito, CN Castel-Branco, S Chichava & A Francisco, org. *Desafios para Moçambique 2011*, Maputo: IESE, 371–400.

Dobler, G. 2008. 'Solidarity, Xenophobia and Regulation of Chinese Businesses in Namibia'. In: C Alden, D Large & R Oliviera. eds. *China Returns to Africa: A rising power and a continent embrace*. London: Hurst Publishers, 237–255.

Esteban, M. 2009. 'The Chinese Amigo: Implications for the development of Equatorial Guinea'. *The China Quarterly*, 199:667–685.

Feijó, J. 2011. *Do passado colonial à independência – discursos do semanário* Savana *nas celebrações das datas históricas de Moçambique (1998–2003)*. Maputo: Alcance Editores.

Feijó, J. 2011. 'Eles fingem que nos pagam, nós fingimos que trabalhamos – resistência e adaptação de trabalhadores moçambicanos em Maputo'. *Estudos Moçambicanos*, 22:122–138.

Feijó, J. 2010. 'Relações sino-moçambicanas em contexto organizacional – um estudo de empresas em Maputo'. In: C Serra, ed. *A Construção Social do Outro – perspectivas cruzadas sobre estrangeiro e moçambicanos*. Maputo: African Studies Centre of the Eduardo Mondlane University, 245–316.

Feijó, J. 2011. 'Biscates, Manobras e Boladas – estratégias de compensação salarial de trabalhadores moçambicanos em Maputo'. In: C Maneschy, Ana Gomes & Ida Gonçalves, eds. *Nos Dois Lados do Atlântico – trabalhadores, organizações e sociabilidades*. Belém: Editora Paka Tatu, 95–112.

Francisco, A, Mucavele, A, Monjane, P & Seuna, S. 2008. Índice da sociedade civil em Moçambique 2007 – avaliação, desafios, oportunidades e acção. Maputo: Community Development Foundation.

Groelsema, R, Turner, M & Shenga, C. 2009. *Avaliação da Democracia e Governação em Moçambique – Relatório Preliminar*. Maputo: USAID.

Henriksen, T. 1978. 'Marxism and Mozambique'. *African Affairs*, 309:441–462.

Henriksen, T. 1983. *Revolution and Counter-revolution: Mozambique's war of independence 1964–1974*. Connecticut: Greenwood.

Hernandez, E. 2000. 'Afrique: L'actualité du modèle paternaliste'. *Revue française de gestion*, 128: 98-106.

Hon, T, Jansson, J, Shelton, G, Haifang, L, Burke, C & Kiala, Carine. 2009. *Evaluating China's FOCAC Commitments to Africa and Mapping the Way Ahead*. Stellenbosch, Centre for Chinese Studies of Stellenbosch University.

Horta, L. 2008. 'China e Moçambique apostam no Vale do Zambeze para fazer "celeiro" chinês'. diz investigador, *Macauhub*, 21 July. Available from: www.macauhub.com.mo/pt/news.php?ID=5748 [Accessed on 17 May 2011].

Imensis. 2007. 'Exportação ilegal de madeira envolva filho de ministro', 9 November. Available from: www.imensis.co.mz/news/anmviewer.asp?a=10806&z=15 [Accessed on 1 May 2009].

Jackson, S. 1995. 'China's Third World Foreign Policy: The case of Angola and Mozambique, 1961–93'. *The China Quarterly*, 142:388–422.

JMS. 2008. 'Autoridades de Hong Kong confirmam presença de melamina em chocolates Cadbury', *RTP*, 5 October. Available from: ww1.rtp.pt/noticias/?article=149886&visual=3 &layout=10 [Accessed on 17 May 2011].

Lemos, A & Ribeiro, D. 2007. 'Taking Ownership or Just Changing Owners?' In: M Firozi & M Stephen, eds. *African Perspectives on China in Africa*. Cape Town: Fahamu – Networks for Social Justice, 63–70.

Liu, H. 2009. 'Stepping into Africa: More internationalized or not – Chinese Companies in Angola, Mozambique and Uganda'. *Chinese in Africa / Africans in China – Conference Papers*. Centre for Sociological Research, University of Johannesburg, 217–242.

Lopes, M. 2006. *Os empresários da Construção Civil e as Relações de Trabalho*. Maputo: Imprensa Universitária.

Lourenço, V. 2007. 'Do conceito de *campo político* em África: contornos teóricos e exercícios empíricos'. *Cadernos de Estudos Africanos*, 13/14:49–80.

Mackenzie, C. 2006. 'Forest Governance in Zambézia, Mozambique: Chinese Takeaway! Final Report for Fongza'. Available from: www.illegal-logging.info/uploads/Mozambique_China.pdf [Accessed on 17 May 2011].

Macuácua, S. 2009. 'Na construção do Estádio Nacional – Moçambicanos escravizados e discriminados'. *Público*, 16 March.

Mamdani, M. 1996. *Citizen and Subject: Contemporary Africa and the legacy of late colonialism*.

Oxford: James Currey.
Mangwiro, C. 2007. 'Mozambique, China in talks on hydro-power Project', 20 March. Available from: planetark.org/dailynewsstory.cfm/newsid/40957/story.htm [Accessed on 8 May 2011].
Maricourt, R. 1996. 'Paternalisme au Japon et en Occident'. *Etudes*, 384:161–171.
Mazive, E, ed. 2009. *Mortalidade em Moçambique – Inquérito Nacional sobre Causas de Mortalidade 2007/8*. Maputo: National Statistics Institute.
Medeiros, E. 2007. 'Os sino-moçambicanos da Beira. Mestiçagens várias'. *Cadernos de Estudos Africanos*, 13/14:157–187.
Negrão, J. 2003. 'On Relations between the NGOs of the North and Mozambican Civil Society'. Paper presented at the master's course *Alternative Globalization and Non Governmental Organisations in the Realm of Portuguese as Official Language*. Economics Faculty of Coimbra University, 1–22.
New York Times. 2008. 'UN grants China permission to import African ivory'. *The New York Times online*, 16 July. Available from: www.nytimes.com/2008/07/16/world/asia/16iht-ivory.4.14552709.html [Accessed on 1 May 2009].
Notícias. 2007a. 'Ambientalistas desencorajam barragem de Mphanda Nkuwa', 18 May. Available from: www.jornalnoticias.co.mz/pls/notimz2/getxml/pt/contentx/40383 [Accessed on 8 May 2011].
Notícias. 2007b. 'Numa afronta à legislação em vigor: madeira não processada continua a ser exportada', 13 August. Available from: www.jornalnoticias.co.mz/pls/notimz2/getxml/pt/contentx/65026 [Accessed on 8 May 2011].
Notícias. 2007c. 'Para extracção e importação de barbatanas: Desconhecidos pescam tubarões em Pomene', 10 October. Available from: www.jornalnoticias.co.mz/pls/notimz2/getxml/pt/contentx/74750 [Accessed on 8 May 2011].
Park, Y. 2008. *A Matter of Honour: Being Chinese in South Africa*. Johannesburg: Jacana Media.
Portal of the Government of Mozambique. 2007. *Moçambique e China avaliam cooperação*, 9 February. Available from: www.portaldogoverno.gov.mz/noticias/news_folder_politica/fevereiro2007/nots_po_124_jan_07/ [Accessed on 8 May 2011].
Redacção. 2007. 'Empreiteiros Chineses ameaçam nacionais', *Patria*, 15: 1-4 November.
Sautman, B & Park, Y. 2009. 'Dragon Slayers: Political oppositions and anti-China / anti-Chinese mobilization in Southern Africa'. *Chinese in Africa / Africans in China – Conference Papers*, Centre for Sociological Research, University of Johannesburg, 255–291.
Sautman, B & Hairong, Y. 2009. 'African Perspectives on China-Africa links'. *China Quarterly*, 199:728–759.
Serra, C. 2006. *Fenómeno novo: tiroteio 'chinês' em Maputo*, blog. 'Diário de um Sociólogo', 19 December. Available from: oficinadesociologia.blogspot.com/2006/12/fenmeno-novo-tiroteio-chins-em-maputo.html [Accessed on 6 June 2009].
Serra, C. 2007a. 'Naturalizar o inatural'. *Diário de um Sociólogo*, 10 January. Available from: oficinadesociologia.blogspot.com/2007/02/naturalizar-o-inatural.html [Accessed on 6 June 2009].
Serra, C. 2007b. 'Os caçadores locais das feiticeiras de Salém (8) (ou os cinco mosqueteiros)'. *Diário de um Sociólogo*, 30 April. Available from: oficinadesociologia.blogspot.com/2007/04/os-caadores-locais-das-feiticeiras-de_30.html [Accessed on 6 June 2009].
Serra, C. 2007c. 'Filho de ministro e negócio ilegal de madeira exportada para a China'. *Diário de um Sociólogo*, 10 November. Available from: oficinadesociologia.blogspot.com/2007/11/filho-de-ministro-e-negcio-ilegal-de.html [Accessed on 6 June 2009].
Serra, C. 2007d. 'Florestas e madeira em Moçambique: Estrangeiros, "pessoas bem posicionadas" e chefes tradicionais envolvidos na ilegalidade (afirma um relatório)'. *Diário de um Sociólogo*, 28 February. Available from: http://oficinadesociologia.blogspot.com/2007/02/florestas-e-

madeira-em-moambique.html [Accessed on 6 June 2009].

Serra, C. 2007e. 'Terra amada, terra desmatada: o que acontece às nossas florestas em Cabo Delgado'. *Diário de um Sociólogo*, 30 January. Available from: oficinadesociologia.blogspot.com/2007/01/terra-amada-terra-desmatada-o-que.html [Accessed on 6 June 2009].

Serra, C. 2007f. 'Afinal há desmatação no país, segundo o Ministro do Ambiente! (postagem especial para os mosqueteiros do tudo-está-bem)'. *Diário de um Sociólogo*, 21 August. Available from: oficinadesociologia.blogspot.com/2007/08/afinal-h-desmatao-no-pas-segundo-o.html [Accessed on 6 June 2009].

Serra, C. 2007g. 'Estamos a ser asiaticamente barbatanados em prol da sopa'. *Diário de um Sociólogo*, 10 October. Available from: oficinadesociologia.blogspot.com/2007/10/estamos-ser-asiaticamente-barbatanados.html [Accessed on 6 June 2009].

Serra, C. 2007h. 'De novo o síndrome da mão estrangeira'. *Diário de um Sociólogo*, 14 January. Available from: oficinadesociologia.blogspot.com/2007/02/de-novo-sndrome-da-mo-estranha.html [Accessed on 6 June 2009].

Serra, C. 2007i. 'Sim senhor: futebolizemos a vida'. *Diário de um Sociólogo*, 11 February. Available from: oficinadesociologia.blogspot.com/2007/02/sim-senhor-futebolizemos.html [Accessed on 6 June 2009].

Serra, C. 2007j. 'Trabalhadores sofrem? Mas patrão é patrão, canta o Mc Roger'. *Diário de um Sociólogo*, 22 August. Available from: oficinadesociologia.blogspot.com /2007/08/ trabalhadores-sofrem-mas-patro-patro.html [Accessed on 6 June 2009].

Serra, C. 2007l. 'E continua o saque desenfreado da nossa madeira'. *Diário de um Sociólogo*, 13 August. Available from: oficinadesociologia.blogspot.com/2008/04/segundo-mediafax-barco-com-armas-para.html [Accessed on 6 June 2009].

Serra, C. 2007m. 'Os caçadores locais das feiticeiras de Salém (3) (Lázaro Mabunda) (continua)'. *Diário de um Sociólogo*, 28 April. Available from: oficinadesociologia.blogspot.com/2007/04/os-caadores-locais-das-feiticeiras-de_28.html [Accessed on 6 June 2009].

Serra, C. 2007n. '21 de Março, Dia Internacional da Floresta: programa-se marcha em Maputo'. *Diário de um Sociólogo*, 4 February. Available from: oficinadesociologia.blogspot.com/2007/02/21-de-maro-dia-internacional-da.html [Accessed on 13 July 2012].

Serra, C. 2007o. 'Empreiteiros chineses'. *Diário de um Sociólogo*, 7 November. Available from: oficinadesociologia.blogspot.com/2007/11/empreiteiros-chineses.html [Accessed on 6 June 2009].

Serra, C. 2007p. 'Justiça Ambiental desencoraja Chineses na construção da barragem de Mphanda Nkuwa'. *Diário de um Sociólogo*, 18 May. Available from: oficinadesociologia.blogspot.com/2007/05/justia-ambiental-desencoraja-chineses.html [Accessed on 6 June 2009].

Serra, C. 2008a. 'E agora os elefantes'. *Diário de um Sociólogo*, 17 July. Available from: oficinadesociologia.blogspot.com/2008/07/e-agora-os-elefantes.html [Accessed on 6 June 2009].

Serra, C. 2008b. 'Atenção: Cadbury e melamina'. *Diário de um Sociólogo*, 6 October. Available from: oficinadesociologia.blogspot.com/2008/10/cadbury-e-melamina.html [Accessed on 6 June 2009].

Serra, C. 2008c. 'Leite para bebés com melanina'. *Diário de um Sociólogo*, 17 September. Available from: oficinadesociologia.blogspot.com/2008/09/leite-para-bebs-com-melamina.html [Accessed on 6 June 2009].

Serra, C. 2008d. 'Barco com armas para Zimbabué: Editorial do "Mediafax" critica China, SADC e regime de Mugabe'. *Diário de um Sociólogo*, 21 April. Available from: oficinadesociologia.blogspot.com/2008/04/barco-com-armas-para-zimbbu-editorial.html [Accessed on 6 June 2009].

Serra, C. 2008e. 'As mãos africanas de Pilatos (13)', *(fim)*. *Diário de um Sociólogo*, 12 July.

Available from: oficinadesociologia.blogspot.com/2008/07/AS-MOS-AFRICANAS-DE-PILATOS-13-CONTINUA.HTML [Accessed on 6 June 2009].

Serra, C. 2008f. 'Nampula: Situação dos trabalhadores nas empresas madeireiras'. *Diário de um Sociólogo*, 8 December. Available from: oficinadesociologia.blogspot.com/2008/12/nampula-situao-dos-trabalhadores-nas.html [Accessed on 6 June 2009].

Serra, C. 2008g. 'Celeiro chinês em Moçambique?'. *Diário de um Sociólogo*, 21 July. Available from: oficinadesociologia.blogspot.com/2008/07/celeiro-chins-em-moambique.html [Accessed on 6 June 2009].

Serra, C. 2008h. 'China coloniza África e, claro, Moçambique – escritor Henning Mankell'. *Diário de um Sociólogo*, 11 January. Available from: oficinadesociologia.blogspot.com/2008/01/china-coloniza-frica-e-claro-moambique.html [Accessed on 6 June 2009].

Sousa Santos, B. 2003. 'O Estado Heterogéneo e o Pluralismo Jurídico'. In: B Santos & J Trindade, eds. *Conflito e Transformação Social: uma paisagem das justiças em Moçambique*. Oporto: Afrontamento, 47–128.

Taylor, I. 2006. *China and Africa: Engagement and compromise*. London: Routledge.

Vircoulon, T. 2009. 'Chinese Ways to Survive in Kinshasa, Democratic Republic of Congo'. *Chinese in Africa / Africans in China – Conference Papers*. Centre for Sociological Research, University of Johannesburg, 308–317.

Xinhua. 2007. 'China, Mozambique sign cooperation agreement'. *China Daily*, 28 September. Available from: www.chinadaily.com.cn/china/2007-09/28/content_6143005.htm [Accessed on 8 May 2011].

Zamparoni, V. 2000. 'Monhés, Baneanes, Chinas e Afro-maometanos – Colonialismo e racismo em Lourenço Marques, Moçambique, 1890–1940'. *Lusotopie*, 191–222.

Chapter 10
Migrants or Sojourners? The Chinese Community in Maputo

Sérgio Chichava and Jimena Durán

Chinese migration to Africa has been increasing rapidly since the turn of the millennium, supported by the intensification of commercial and diplomatic ties. Mozambique is no exception and the Chinese presence is noticeable on arrival at Maputo's International Airport where, besides the large number of Chinese nationals entering the country, the Chinese group Anhui Foreign Economic Construction Co Ltd is building the new airport terminal, funded by a China Exim Bank loan. Furthermore, Chinese migration is made palpable by the existence of numerous small Chinese shops and restaurants, and even of some religious sites. This growing connectedness and economic exchange between Mozambique (and Africa in general) and China has resulted in an important wave of economic migration.

In spite of that, no one can estimate the number of Chinese citizens actually living in Mozambique, since there are no reliable data locally as is the case for Chinese migration in other African countries. What is certain is that the data available on estimates for Chinese in Africa show an important increase since 2001 and this coincides with the growth of Chinese foreign direct investment (FDI) and trade in Mozambique and across Africa (Mohan & Tan-Mullins 2009:6).

Most of the Chinese that come to Africa are temporary migrants and are employees of state-owned enterprises (SOEs) or independent private Chinese companies and businesses (Park 2009; Mohan 2009; Tan-Mullins 2009). Generally, they come with two- to three-year contracts and they have limited contact with the locals. Most of the temporary migrants return to China, but small portions decide to settle and start their own businesses across the continent after the end of their contracts. Besides this type of temporary migration, the arrival of independent settlers seeking new and better economic opportunities is increasing too.

Nonetheless, the recent studies on China-Africa renewed relations have focused on a 'globalisation from above' approach: state projects, bilateral aid, etc. In consequence, there is little information concerning the 'everyday' exchanges among members of the Chinese diaspora and the local hosting societies, despite the growing number of independent entrepreneurial Chinese migrants. Moreover, the diaspora studies have had the tendency to focus on south-to-north migration (Mohan & Kale 2007) and not on south-south migration. This question is part of a broader problem regarding the assimilation and integration of the Chinese into the host society that will be essential to understanding the implications of China migrating to Africa and their impact on the continent's economic and social landscape. Indeed, not only is it necessary to distinguish between different Chinese development actors when we look at China-Africa relations, but it is also important to keep in mind that 'the behaviour of thousands of newly settled Chinese businessmen and the conduct of the African communities in which they live and work will matter as much as the diplomacy and concessions made at the government level' (Alden 2007:128).

Our study focuses on intra-community relations with the Chinese community of Mozambique. To do this analysis we carried our research with the members of the Association of the Chinese Community of Mozambique (ACCM) in Maputo, during six months in 2012. In fact, the ACCM or the former the Chinese Pagoda – closed in 1975 by the newly independent Government of Mozambique and reopened in 1998 – is the place where the Chinese community in Maputo meet to celebrate China, their Chinese identity or to socialise. Two groups that are part of the ACCM in Maputo are discussed. The first is the 'Sino-Mozambicans', who divide themselves into two sub-groups: the Chinese born in Mozambique from a Chinese father and a Mozambican mother, and the Chinese born in Mozambique with both parents of Chinese nationality. The other group consists of the Chinese born in China and who have arrived in recent years with the wave of Chinese migration resulting from Chinese economic expansion. For lack of a better term, we are calling this latter group Sino-Chinese.

If, as is demonstrated in our research, the Sino-Mozambicans claim their 'Mozambicanity', they also identify themselves as Chinese, despite the fact that they do not speak Mandarin, Cantonese or other Chinese languages and may have never been to China. However, the 'Sino-Chinese' do not consider them Chinese, which creates some discomfort or tension between them. Also, the Sino-Chinese migratory wave do not consider themselves as immigrants but as sojourners. Why and how do Sino-Mozambicans claim Chinese identity? Why are they not accepted as Chinese by the Sino-Chinese?

To answer these questions, this chapter focuses on a brief historical introduction of the Chinese community which explains how a Sino-Mozambican community developed in Mozambique and how it was broken down by the independence of the African country in 1975. Secondly, we will look at the relationships between the Sino-Mozambicans and the Sino-Chinese members of the ACCM, which, as we said, is the main place of encounters between the two groups and of celebration of Chinese identity. Finally, we conclude with a brief synthesis of the central ideas of our study.

The Association of the Chinese Community of Mozambique: a place of encounters and celebration of Chinese identity

Established in 1903 as the Chinese Pagoda,[1] the ACCM was one of the most active among the Chinese associations in the Portuguese colony. It was created to promote the well-being of the community through education, organisation of festivals, sports and games. It also gave special attention to its poorest and sick members. It is important to note that even if the Chinese had considerable presence in the construction sector during the colonial period[2] they were excluded from the respective workers' associations (as were the Indians and Arabs who even though they had strong presence in the commerce sector were also excluded from these respective representative associations). This forced these communities to create their own associations in order to protect themselves from discrimination in the sector (Zamparoni 2000:210).

During this period, the Chinese associations in Lourenço Marques (now Maputo) were: Hoong Che Sha (1908),[3] the Club Fiel Observante do Direito (Chee Kung Ton), Clube chinês de Lourenço Marques (the Chinese Club of Lorenzo Marques, with a representation of the Chinese Nationalist Party)[4] (Kuo Min Tang), the Chinese Pagoda which, from 1938, also hosted the Chinese School, the Associação d'Operários Chinezes Beneficente 'Boa União'[5] in 1911 and the Big Desire Society (1908), which became the Chinese Nationalist Association. According to Zamparoni (2000:210), the changes in denominations of the Chinese associations were brought about by the political changes in China: on 10 October 1911, the Wuchang rebellion against the Qing dynasty started and in 1912, the last Qing emperor was overthrown.

At that time, the Chinese Pagoda was, as mentioned, earlier in charge of securing the welfare of the community by organising parties, games, social assistance for the unemployed and sick, Portuguese and Mandarin, etc. Indeed,

---

1 While established in 1903, the Chinese Pagoda was officially recognised in 1924 by the colonial authorities.
2 They were also involved into commerce activities, firstly for the native population and then specialised in commerce of Chinese crafts for tourists, but to a lesser extent than Indians and Arabs.
3 Later Hwoc Man Tong. According to Zamparoni (2000) there was probably a mistake; the name of the association was Kwo Min Tang not Hwoc Man Tong.
4 The Chinese Nationalist Party or Kuo Min Tang was one of the dominant parties of the early Republic of China, from 1912 onwards, and remains one of the main political parties in modern Taiwan.
5 Chinese Association of Workmen Bountiful 'Boa Uniao'. Later this association was called the Chinese Republic Association of Lourenço Marques.

during the 1950s and 1960s the emergence of a Chinese elite was made possible through accumulation of capital and, as a result, manifested in the diversification of economic activities, schooling, sport and cultural activities (beauty contests, for example) performed by the second and third generations. The majority of Chinese descendants (from Chinese and mixed origin) who attended the school entered the public service and had liberal professions (Medeiros 2007:171).

The identity of the Chinese established in Mozambique from the colonial period and of their descendants today in the country was and is highly related to their Cantonese origin (south and south-east China). Their language (Cantonese), their food and cultural habits differentiate them from the other Chinese and reinforce the sentiment of a diaspora community. From colonial times, while the Chinese community might seem to outsiders to be uniform, there were nevertheless important social and economic differences among them. Medeiros (2007) explains how the differences in status of their arrival (running away from political persecutions, or as coolies, slaves, free settlers, etc.) allowed the maintenance of the social fractures.

With the independence of Mozambique in 1975, the development of the Chinese community stopped completely as the former colonial society and its economy collapsed. At that time the Chinese community was characterised by the liberation movement as collaborators with the colonial regime or as 'people's exploiters' because they held private properties. The Chinese community were also affected by the nationalisation policy and policies such as the interdiction of the freedom of assembly (Macagno 2012; 2010). As was the case with the other associations, the Chinese Pagoda and the building were used to host a state school, the Maputo School of Visual Arts. The majority of Chinese descendants left the country for Macau, Taiwan, Portugal, Brazil, China, Canada or the United States (Macagno 2010). The Chinese Pagoda's nationalisation left an indelible mark on the spirits of the few Chinese descendants who had stayed in Mozambique, who felt betrayed by Frelimo, a movement supported by China in the colonial war. Fua, a Sino-Mozambican, describes the nationalisation of the Chinese Pagoda:

> With the independence, Frelimo nationalised our building. They took everything from us and we couldn't do anything about it. We didn't understand why they punished us, the country that helped them. It was China who helped and supported economically Frelimo, during the independence war. Two years after independence, they took our school. But, they didn't nationalise everything, for example, they didn't take away the Muslims' churches.

But then he says:

> When Mozambicans won independence they attacked and started to treat badly the white people, especially the Portuguese, but we didn't have any problems. We (had) always treated well the blacks. And, we were the only race and country that supported Frelimo and Mozambique to get independence.

The Sino-Mozambicans also felt discriminated against by Frelimo when they compare themselves with other 'minorities', particularly the Indian community, which, according to them, benefitted from the nationalisation process despite the fact that India — unlike the People's Republic of China — had not offered material support for the liberation struggle (though Delhi had in fact been an ardent critic of Portuguese colonialism). According to Yok, a mixed Sino-Mozambican, the nationalisation of the buildings and the departure of the majority of Chinese from Mozambique meant a loss of the gained status the Chinese elite had won during colonial times. Zhang (a translator for the Chinese medical mission for four years in Mozambique) says:

> The problem that Sino-Mozambicans have with the Indians is that during the colony, the Indians performed basic works. The elites, according to them, were the Portuguese, the white people and the Chinese community. After independence, the Chinese and the white left Mozambique and went to Portugal or Brazil. The Indians profited from this situation and bought houses and shops at a very good price. So, today they are a very powerful community.

The fear of Frelimo's Marxism-Leninism, or of Communism, as it is sometimes called, was, in their words, one of the main factors explaining the departure of the majority of Sino-Mozambicans from Mozambique. In António's words:

> I ask myself why all the Chinese left and not the Indians? The Chinese in Mozambique were running away from communism and when Frelimo took power and implemented communist reforms, the Chinese had to run away. Frelimo was a photocopy of Mao Tse Tung and they had in their mind all what they suffered with Mao's revolution.

Moreover, some Sino-Mozambicans living in Mozambique had Portuguese nationality. After independence they were accorded the right to choose between their Mozambican and Portuguese nationalities. According to Sino-

Mozambicans, choosing Portuguese nationality instead of Mozambican caused them to be perceived and treated as foreigners by local authorities in their own country. This left them disappointed and discouraged, as is explained by HL, one of the oldest and most well-known Sino-Mozambicans:

> We didn't know what was going to happen with Mozambique and if one day we would be forced to leave. Also, we didn't want our kids to go to war. So we chose to stay with the Portuguese passport. Today even if we never left the country we are treated as foreigners here. Every time we have problems with the DIRE [Identification and Residence Documents for Foreigners] we have to pay under the table. You know how it is in this country where everything is under the table. I was born in Mozambique from Chinese parents, I'm the only Chinese descendant with a machambas [plot, farm] and still I have to pay under the table!

With the political and economic changes in the 1990s, thanks to the new pluralistic constitution and the new wave of Chinese migration, the Sino-Mozambicans seized the opportunity to reactivate their association, which took placed in 1998. It should be stressed that this was a laborious task in itself and made all the more complex because the building of the former Chinese Pagoda had become the site for a state school. Facing enormous difficulties, the Sino-Mozambicans used the political influence of some of their well-placed members within the Mozambican government, like the current finance minister, Manuel Chang and current vice president of Maputo Municipal Assembly, both sons of Chinese fathers and Mozambican mothers.

> The Chinese descendants decided to create the association to recover the building… the objective of the association was to have a common front to negotiate with the government. The process was very long and we tried everything. For example, when we heard that Manuel Chang was named minister of finance we decided to invite him to join the association. We pressured him to join us. We knew that having someone high-ranked in the government could help our cause. Nevertheless, it took almost 15 years to get the building back. (Interview, António, Maputo, May 2012)

It was in that way that the Sino-Mozambicans recovered the building in 2007, opening it to all Chinese citizens as well as to their Mozambican descendants. In return, the Chinese government built a new school of visual arts in the Aeroporto neighbourhood, on the outskirts of Mozambique's capital, Maputo,

It was officially given to the Mozambican authorities in 2010 (AllAfrica 2010).

Reasons behind the ACCM reactivation
It is important to understand the reasons behind the reactivation of the ACCM, a process that was led by the Sino-Mozambicans. According to them, the main objective was to stay close to Chinese culture and society through interaction with new Chinese migrants, especially for their children:

> Our main motivation is to forward the Chinese culture and language. We are especially concerned by Chinese descendants that have no contact with China, its culture and its language. We want to send their Chinese culture.

This reinforces the idea that they want to recover the legacy of their parents, which has been damaged by the Mozambican government. So they seized the process of denationalisation of properties, especially those of the Catholics and the Muslims started by the Mozambican authorities, to claim their building back. Amélia, who joined the community when she arrived in Maputo from Marromeu, Sofala well before the ACCM was re-established, declares:

> This was our parents' association and we wanted it back. Our parents built it. When the government announced to give back the nationalised buildings and when we saw that the Muslims were getting back buildings, we (the Chinese of Mozambique) decided to make something ourselves. (Interview, Amélia, Maputo, 10 August 2012)

When we asked why she had joined the association, considering her limited links with China or with the Maputo Chinese Community, she answered:

> What I feel towards the Chinese culture and community, I call it blood. I feel good around Chinese-Mozambicans. I want to promote the teaching of the Chinese language even though I don't speak it myself. I want my children and grandchildren to learn what I didn't learn. I feel that I missed something.

There is no doubt that the resurgence of the ACCM is also due to the increased arrival of Chinese citizens to Mozambique and to the growing political and economic influence of China. We think another reason could be the will to use the association as a place of encounters between the children of the Sino-Mozambicans and Chinese partners from China, in order to avoid the extinction of the community and in order to obtain economic advantages. Also, the ACCM is used by the Sino-Mozambicans to express their citizenship and loyalty to the People's Republic of China (PRC). For example. in September 2012 the ACCM organised a meeting to support China in its conflict with Japan on the Senkaku islands. The Chinese Embassy in Mozambique, which is not directly involved in the activities of the ACCM, participated in this meeting. According to ACCM members, even if the Chinese Embassy is not directly engaged, it has participated in the local parties or festivals, like the Chinese New Year.

So, as can be seen, China is considered by the Sino-Mozambicans as their 'second homeland' after Mozambique:

> I went to China twice... I went because I wanted to know this country... I went to Guangzhou [Guangdong province]. I really love China... You know, I have seven brothers and some of them have Chinese names. So when I walked in the streets and I suddenly seen a name such that of one of my brothers on the streets, I really felt that I was Chinese. (Interview, Amélia, Maputo, 10 August 2012)

Thus even if Sino-Mozambicans consider themselves settlers, they think that China has an obligation to take care of them. Also, China should use them as a gateway to Mozambique instead of entrusting this task to the Chinese from China who know little or nothing about Mozambican reality (interview, HL, Maputo, August 2012).

Contrary to the Sino-Mozambicans, most of the Chinese who migrated to Mozambique after 2000 consider themselves sojourners. Most of them are of Chinese origin (Fujian province and northern China), only speak Mandarin and have their families in China. As a Chinese entrepreneur stated:

> Mozambique and Africa is good for business. I make money here while my family is in China. But, is not good to become old here. I will come back to China. (Interview, Li 2012)

Most of the time, their contact with the host society is very limited or non-existent; the work schedules and conditions are very strict. Derik, a Chinese businessman who owns a massage shop and a consultancy firm has been in Mozambique for more than ten years and explained:

> I have a Chinese massage shop in Maputo. So, I hire Chinese women to come to Mozambique for two years. They come here alone working

for me and I pay everything for them, except their private things. Every two years I change my staff... Here, they don't have any place to go and they don't speak Portuguese... The construction companies hire a lot of Chinese even though it's more expensive, because locals don't work hard so when you hire locals you lose money and time. They have very strict conditions, they cannot go out often and they are not allowed to have local partners. I don't allow my employees to have local partners either. It would be very irresponsible because imagine how bad for China, if they abandon their kids here. (Interview, Derik 2012)

Mozambique is not a singular case. Other scholars (Park 2009) have arrived at the same conclusion while they were studying the Chinese migrants in other African countries. As stated by Park (2009:9), 'most of Chinese in Africa cannot, as yet, be defined as settlers (with the exception of some Chinese in South Africa); rather, they fit in one of two categories: modern-day sojourners or transnational citizens.'

Relationships between the Sino-Mozambicans and the Sino-Chinese
If the association has become a place of encounters of the different waves of Chinese migration in Maputo, there are some tensions among them, essentially over their status in Mozambique and their degree of 'Chinesity'. The main tension among the Sino-Mozambicans and the Sino-Chinese revolves around the management of the building and the association itself. The 'new Chinese' have also organised associations: with the Fujian Association the most important one. According to the Sino-Chinese, they expected to use the building when they wanted, and they thought it was their own building too. In Amélia's words:

> There have been some misunderstandings with the other associations. The building belongs to the Chinese Association of Mozambique and their descendants. This means it belongs to the Chinese community living in Mozambique. As they are also Chinese, they wanted to make usage of our building. So, we had to explain to them that we are the Chinese resident community in Mozambique and we are the ones managing the building. They thought that the building was for everybody, maybe because they had seen the ambassador coming here to the parties.

Along with this quarrel, the relations remain distant among the different migration waves, especially the Cantonese descendants who arrived before independence and the 'new Chinese' because of the cultural and language differences. This diversity of members creates some language barriers among the members of the association. The mixed Sino-Mozambicans do not speak any Mandarin or Cantonese; the Sino-Mozambicans from Chinese parents speak Cantonese (but no Mandarin) or only Portuguese (depending on the generations and the families) and some members speak only Mandarin and some basic Portuguese or English. It is also interesting to see how the Sino-Mozambicans and the Sino-Chinese perceive each other. In what remind us of the Portuguese colonial racial discourse towards the Chinese, the Sino-Mozambicans think that the 'new arrivals' are not clean or that they are only interested in money and do not care about Mozambique or Mozambicans. In Yok's words:

> I believe that there is a difference between the first wave of Chinese in Mozambique and the Chinese arriving today. The behaviour is different. For example, the shops are not pretty and clean, or organised in a nice way. They just want to make money. This is not specific to Chinese but also Indians, Nigerians, etc. Unfortunately, I was hoping for a different attitude. Not even the Portuguese think like that.

Moreover, the Sino-Mozambicans complain because the Sino-Chinese perceive them as 'black':

> With the 'new Chinese' I don't have any connections. They are very reserved and they don't like mixing with us. They think we are black; they look at us like we were black. You feel it in the skin. And we don't speak their language so it's worst. (Interview, Gilberto)

In short, the Chinese community in Mozambique is very heterogeneous. There are, as we have stated, members who were part of the Chinese Pagoda during the colonial times and that were born in Mozambique; members who arrived in Mozambique 15 to 20 years ago with the first aid missions from the PRC and decided to stay; and those who have arrived very recently with the new Chinese engagement in Mozambique. From this perspective, the collective identity of the Chinese of Mozambique is not based on a linguistic identity but in the recovery of the association and of the status of the Chinese of Mozambique in comparison with other ethnic communities (Indians or Muslims) and even the 'new Chinese'. This shows how complex it is to define the Chinese of Mozambique.

Conclusion

With the increased arrival of Chinese in Mozambique there has been a revitalisation of the local Chinese community. This chapter has analysed the factors influencing the construction of Chinese identity or community in Mozambique. Broadly speaking, two factors influencing development and reconfiguration of the Chinese community in Mozambique, particularly in Maputo, can be identified: (i) the renewal of the Chinese Association of Mozambique and the claim of the Chinese identity by the Sino-Mozambicans and (ii) the relations between the Sino-Mozambicans and the Sino-Chinese, in particular the conflictual relationship and mutual representations.

The classifications 'Sino-Mozambican' and 'Sino-Chinese' are not based on strict criteria and neither category is homogenous. As shown, the 'Sino-Mozambicans' base their identity on how they lived and survived in the different moments of Mozambican history, where independence is considered as a central moment for the community. Also, the nationalisation and recovery of the association building is perceived as exclusively Sino-Mozambican combat, what gives them legitimacy to claim a Chinese identity, for example. It is useful to think that this classification system creates their objective reality. As stated by Bourdieu (1980), *'practical classifications are always subordinated to practical functions and oriented towards the production of social effects'*.

References

Alden, C. 2007. *China in Africa: Partner, competitor or hegemon?* London: Zed Books.

AllAfrica. 2010. 'Mozambique: New school of visual arts inaugurated in Maputo'. Available from: allafrica.com/stories/201011120476.html [Accessed on 12 November 2013].

Bourdieu P. 1980. 'L'identité et la représentation'. *Actes de la recherche en sciences sociales*, 35, November, 63–72.

Macagno, L. 2010. 'Os "bons portugueses" do Atlético Chinês: desporto e fotografia no Moçambique tardo-colonial, Lisbon'. Document presented at the 7th Congress of Iberian Studies.

Medeiros, E. 2007. 'Os Sino-moçambicanos da Beira. Mestiçagens Várias'. *Cadernos de Estudos Africanos*, 13/14:157–187.

Mohan G & Kale, D. 2007. *The Invisible Hand of South-South Globalisation: Chinese migrants in Africa, a report for the Rockefeller Foundation*. Milton Keynes: Open University.

Mohan, G & Tan-Mullins, M. 2009. 'Chinese Migrants in Africa as New Agents of Development? An analytical framework'. *European Journal of Development Research*, 21(4):588–605.

Park, Y. 2009. 'Chinese Migration in Africa'. *SAIIA Occasional Paper* 24, January.

Zamparoni, V. 2000. 'Monhés, Baneanes, Chinas e Afro-maometanos. Colonialismo e racismo em Lourenço Marques, Moçambique, 1890–1940'. *Lusotopie 2000*:191–222.

Conclusion
Reflections on a Changing Relationship

Sérgio Chichava and Chris Alden

The aim of this conclusion is twofold. The first is to reflect upon the detailed examination of the Mozambican case found in this book and draw out from these specificities some of the broader themes that underpin the emergence of China as a significant actor in Africa. Starting from an historical assessment of relations between China and Mozambique, the various chapters, with their distinct approaches, provide another perspective on the Chinese reality on the African continent and contribute to the debate on this new area of study that is often fed more by rumours than by empirical research. Throughout the book, the authors discuss the pattern and the trends of Chinese investment in the various sectors, particularly in banking and in agriculture, the social representations of various groups of Mozambicans of the Chinese and the profile and motivations of Chinese migrants.

Rather than just drawing up a balance sheet on what is discussed in the various chapters, the purpose of this conclusion is to focus on points that were not discussed or were only partially developed. These are some of the unavoidable or almost omnipresent themes when one speaks of the Chinese presence in Africa, namely land grabbing by the Chinese, the existence of a Chinese 'master plan' for expansion into Africa, the nature of labour relations between African workers and their Chinese counterparts, and the conduct and meaning of China as a new donor.

The second aim of this conclusion is to critically examine the content of the emerging Mozambique-China relationship. This reflection is divided into two parts: (i) looking at the recent evolution and trends of Chinese foreign direct investment in agriculture, building and mineral resources, and (ii) discussing the business alliance between Chinese investors and the Mozambican political and military elite. While nascent, these latter developments are harbingers of a general redirection of Mozambique's ties with the West towards China but one which, through elite interaction and collusion, is beginning to reproduce and localise social features of the Chinese development experience.

The Chinese and land grabs in Africa

Regarding land grabbing, we should mention the constant publication of news stories, sometimes without concrete evidence, concerning the acquisition of huge areas of land by the Chinese, as a rule in connivance with the local political elites, in order to develop agricultural activities intended to supply the Chinese market, but which do not contribute towards reducing food insecurity in Mozambique, or which leave African peasants without land (their main wealth).

The persistence of news stories about the Chinese grabbing African land has obliged the Chinese authorities to react, always stressing the positive side of this country's aid and investment in Africa. According to Hong Lei, spokesperson for the Chinese Foreign Ministry, not only is the much publicised Chinese land grab false, but Chinese involvement in African agriculture seeks to provide technical agricultural assistance to Africans, thus contributing to the development of agriculture on the continent (*Xinhua* 2011).

With regard to Mozambique, as mentioned in the chapter in this volume by Sigrid Ekman, in the academic arena the debate was launched by Loro Horta (2007, 2008), who announced a huge Chinese plan to occupy the Zambezi valley for agricultural purposes. Taken up by Deborah Bräutigam (2012), Bräutigam & Ekman (2012) and by Ekman herself (2010; 2012), in an approach which essentially calls into question Horta's claims, this debate has been at the centre of discussions. Ekman's chapter in this book, rather than seeking to demystify the debate on Chinese aid and investment in Mozambican agriculture, has the merit of insisting on the need for a more cautious and informed approach to these matters, since it has so far been impossible to confirm what Horta claimed.

To complete Ekman's analysis on agriculture in Mozambique, it is important to mention the current pattern of Chinese agricultural investment in Mozambique and compare it with the rest of the foreign direct investment (FDI) in this sector. As Chichava (2012) shows, from the data from the Investment Promotion Centre (CPI), between 2000 and 2010 Chinese investment in agriculture followed the same pattern as the rest of the FDI, in that it concentrated on forestry, and not on producing food or any other kind of crops. Indeed, of the eight projects authorised by the CPI, four were linked to the forestry sector – more specifically, the exploitation and trade in timber – and two were linked to food production. At the same time, Chinese investment in agriculture accounted for just 4% of total Chinese investment over this period (Chichava 2012.). This pattern of Chinese investment in Mozambican agriculture is no different from other FDI in this sector. Indeed, in the 2000–2010 period, although agriculture and natural resources were the sectors that attracted most investment, the greater part of the FDI in agriculture was concentrated on forestry (67%) and on biofuel production (18%).

A Chinese plan to colonise Africa?

The possibility that there exists a Chinese master plan for expansion into Africa is, as has already been mentioned, one of the themes that appears frequently whenever the presence of this Asian country in Africa is discussed. However, a large study undertaken by a team of researchers in some African countries showed that many of the Chinese in Africa, particularly those involved in petty trade, came under their own steam, and never contacted the Chinese embassies in these countries (McNamee et al 2012). Following this study, the work of Mikkel Bunkenborg in this book once again demystifies the idea that there is a vast Chinese plan to expand into Africa. However, we still need to explore the role of family ties in migration to Africa a little further. Are some Chinese coming to Africa thanks to their relatives who are already living on the continent? Chris Alden (2007) puts the Chinese migrants to Africa into three groups: the first consists of Chinese who emigrated at the end of the 19th century, attracted by colonial capitalism, particularly in South Africa and in French Equatorial Africa; the second consists of those who fled from the collapse of the Republic of China and the establishment of the People's Republic in 1949; and the third group can be divided into three sub-groups, namely: (i) workers on Chinese government projects; (ii) those who use family ties and come to work in establishments owned by their relatives (iii) and those who come at their own risk, legally or illegally, in search of new opportunities.

In the case of Mozambique, a country which, in the second half of the 19th century, accommodated a significant wave of Chinese emigrants, who came mostly from Guangdong in southern China and who were concentrated in Lourenço Marques (today's Maputo) and particularly in the city of Beira (Macagno 2010; Medeiros 2007), it would be interesting to see whether some Chinese have been using family ties with relatives resident in Mozambique and who did not leave the country at the time of independence in 1975. Although almost all the Chinese left the country in 1975, this analysis would still be pertinent because many of the Chinese emigrants who came to Mozambique at that time were single men who formed liaisons with Mozambican women, and thus created an important community of Sino-Mozambicans (Medeiros 2007).

Labour disputes, poor working conditions and failure to respect labour legislation

The difficulty in the relationship between Chinese companies and Mozambican workers, the failure to respect local labour legislation and the payment of low wages are also recurrent themes when one speaks of the Chinese presence in Mozambique. Discussion of this matter appears in several chapters in this book, notably those by João Feijó and Morten Nielsen. This issue, which some believe is the result of cultural differences in attitudes towards work, or communication difficulties,[1] is regarded as one of the greatest challenges that Chinese companies face in Africa. Alongside these reasons, others may be invoked, namely the poor supervision and control capacity of the Mozambican authorities.

In this discussion, one should not lose sight of the fact that precarious work and working conditions, as well as the ill treatment inflicted on Mozambican workers, have been an almost daily occurrence in Chinese companies. But this is not specific to Chinese investment in Mozambique. It happens to some extent all over Africa – for example, in Zambia and Zimbabwe. Furthermore, although the Chinese companies are at the centre of attention, poor working conditions and low wages are not exclusive attributes of these companies but also occur in companies managed by Westerners and even by Mozambicans.

Quality of infrastructures built by the Chinese

Although this is not the central theme of his analysis, this question is also present in Nielsen's chapter, when he discusses the use of unskilled Chinese labour in building infrastructure in Mozambique. While from the Chinese point of view this strategy may prove less expensive, it has negative effects on the quality of the infrastructures built in Africa, which also contributes to China's negative image on the continent. With regard to the quality of the public works built by the Chinese in Mozambique, it would have been interesting to show that this question is much more complex than it may appear at first sight. For it is not just to do with the Chinese, but also with the weaknesses of the Mozambican state in carrying out effective supervision, and with the corruption that characterises this sector in Mozambique. In fact, a study held in some African countries showed that in cases where there was strong and responsible supervision, respect for the legislation governing this sector, and less corruption, namely in South Africa and in Zambia, the quality of the work undertaken by the Chinese was high when compared with those countries where such factors did not apply, such as Sierra Leone and Angola (Centre for Chinese Studies 2006; Corkin et al 2008:7).

---

1 Interviews by João Feijó with various Mozambican officials. Some academics such as Anshan (2007) as well as some Chinese officials, such as Zhong Jianhua, the former Chinese ambassador to South Africa (*Wall Street Journal* 2012), have also put this thesis forward.

China: a donor different from the others?

As mentioned by some authors, notably Bräutigam (2009), while in the 1950s Chinese aid to Africa was guided more by solidarity with the 'non-aligned' (for ideological reasons), China's transition to a market economy ensured that its aid came to be a mixture of diplomacy and trade.

Even if China wants to bring a different approach to that of the West in its relations with Africa, declaring that it offers aid unconditionally, the current logic of its economic orientation contradicts this intention. There is an enormous juggling act between development aid and the logic of the market. In the case of Mozambique, an example that shows this new facet was mentioned in this book: China's reluctance to finance the Mphanda Nkuwa and Moamba Major dams, which form key parts of the Mozambican government's ambition to become a regional leader in the energy sector, on the pretext that Electricidade de Moçambique (EDM) did not offer sufficient guarantees that buyers would be found for the electricity generated by these dams. This situation illustrates the end of the epoch of the logic of 'solidarity', and the entry into the epoch of the logic of 'business', consistent with the current orientation of the Chinese economy.

Recent developments and trends in Mozambique-China relations

Having made some comments on various chapters in the book, we will now discuss some aspects of China-Mozambique relations, in the context of an increasingly strong Chinese presence in Mozambique.

Agriculture, mineral resources and construction: a new Chinese focus in Mozambique?

To highlight the recent development and trends of Chinese investment in Mozambique, three sectors are taken as examples: agriculture, mineral resources and construction.

The acquisition of the shares of the Mozambique Lianfeng Agricultural Development Company Ltd, a company that was producing rice in the Ponela irrigation scheme in Xai-Xai, in Gaza, by Wanbao Africa Agriculture Development Limited (WAADL), a subsidiary of the Wanbao Grain and Oil Co Ltd, seems to be changing the trend for the bulk of Chinese investment to be concentrated in the forestry sector. Indeed, in what is regarded as the largest Chinese investment in agriculture in Mozambique, perhaps one of the largest in Africa, or the success of Hubei province in following the Chinese government's 'going out' strategy (*Hubei Daily* 2012; Danqing & Yongsheng 2012), WAADL is undertaking a colossal investment, estimated at around US$95 million, in the production, storage and processing of rice in Gaza province. In addition to WAADL, the Lianhe Africa Agriculture Development Co Ltd, another company from Hubei, will also invest in food production (Chichava & Durán in this volume). It should be stressed that these companies managed to penetrate the Mozambican market thanks to the establishment of the Centre for the Demonstration and Transfer of Chinese Agricultural Technologies (CITAU), which shows the Chinese interest in investing in Mozambican agriculture. So these recent developments are set to radically alter the current pattern of Chinese investment in agriculture in Mozambique.

However, it should be said that while Chinese interest in investing in Mozambican agriculture is now a reality, Chinese companies are also turning their attention to mineral resources, a sector where this country will find two other BRICS (five emerging national economies; Brazil, Russia, India, China and South Africa) countries, Brazil and India, at the forefront, particularly in exploiting coal reserves. Indeed, many Chinese companies were formed in 2011, all of them with the purpose of exploiting mineral resources: heavy sands, titanium, zircon, gold, limestone and assorted other ores. Just as an example the Jinan Yuxiao Group Lda, in partnership with China Yuxiao Resources Holdings Lda, has set up a series of companies to exploit these minerals in various parts of Mozambique, including Inhambane, Sofala, Zambézia, Tete and Nampula. These are companies such as Africa Great Wall Mining Development Company, Future Metal Mining Co Ltd, Africa Yuxiao Mining Development Co Ltd, the China-Mozambique Mining Development Co Ltd, Mozambique Heavy Sand Mining Co Ltd, Africa Ocean Non Ferrous Metal Mining Co Ltd, and Africa Rare Metal Mining Development Co Ltd. A news item published in 2009 revealed that the Jinan Yuxiao Group had won the right to operate 20 zircon mines in Mozambique (*Metalnewsnet* 2009). A further news story, published in 2011, indicated that the Jinan Yuxiao Group had won ten licences to explore for zircon and 40 for titanium in Mozambique, making it one of the major players in Africa in exploiting these minerals, and the largest in Mozambique (*Asian Ceramics* 2011). This article also stated that the demand for zircon and titanium in China was growing at an average of 5% a year, but that these resources were increasingly rare in China, so that 95% of the zircon and 64% of the titanium consumed there came from imports. Added to this is the already mentioned interest of the China Qingho Group in coal (Chichava, chapter 2 in this volume).

A further aspect which deserves mention and which shows changes in the trends in Chinese FDI in Mozambique concerns the growth in investment in the construction sector. Indeed, while, between 2000 and 2010, Chinese FDI was dominated by the manufacturing industry, things seem to be changing. In 2011, the CPI approved 11 Chinese investment projects valued at

US$312 882 974, a much larger investment than that in the 2010 financial year, which was only US$38.6 million. It should be stressed that in this year, Chinese FDI was far greater than all the investment made by Chinese companies since 2007, the year when CPI sources put China on the list of the ten largest investors in Mozambique. A further important fact to be stressed is that in 2011, for the first time since 2007, China headed the list of the largest investors in Mozambique. Its FDI amounted to about 32% of total FDI in 2011, calculated at US$974 492 541.

Meanwhile, in sector terms, 85% of the Chinese FDI was concentrated in construction. About 14% of investments went to the manufacturing industry. It was thanks to the project of the Housing Promotion Fund (FFH)[2] and of the Chinese company Henan Guoji Industry and Development Co Ltd, to set up the limited liability partnership Henan Guoji Imobiliária (HGI), in order to build 5 000 houses in Matola, Maputo province (an investment valued at US$250 million – about 80% of the Chinese FDI in 2011) that the construction sector has undergone unprecedented growth, putting construction at the head of the sectors most sought after by Chinese FDI. This is a major development, bearing in mind that during the 2000–2010 period, Chinese FDI in the construction sector only amounted to US$9 million. We should add that the FFH and HGI project, according to the local authorities, seeks to provide housing for the poorer strata of the population. This is the first major investment by a Chinese company in the construction sector in Mozambique. The Henan Guoji Industry and Development Co Ltd, the first Chinese company to make an investment on this scale in the sector, is very active in some African countries, such as Zambia and Sierra Leone. However, it should also be stressed that while it is clear that there are many Chinese companies involved in construction in Mozambique (which local contractors do not look upon favourably), this arises under aid and cooperation projects between China and Mozambique, and so cannot be regarded as investment.

Will the Mozambican mamba be swallowed by the Chinese dragon?
While there is no doubt that Mozambique, like many other African countries, has benefitted enormously from Chinese aid and investment, we should reflect on some points that could cast a shadow over the relationship between the two countries. To illustrate this point we can look at the alliance between Chinese investors and the Mozambican political and military elite. Party-to-party relations have certainly expanded since their formalised agreement in 2008, but, just to underscore what we have been saying above, this issue is

---

2 A public institution set up by the Mozambican government in 1995.

not necessarily specific to Chinese investment in Mozambique. In most cases, an alliance with the emerging local bourgeoisie, linked to the Frelimo party directly in the form of joint ventures or a position on the board or indirectly through support for this party, is an imperative for anyone who wants to be successful in business in Mozambique. Some Chinese companies have already understood the importance of favours from Frelimo: in the 2009 general elections, Tenwin International Group offered 30 motorcycles to support the Frelimo election campaign.

The best known alliance, and the one most publicised in the media, occurs in the timber sector, with some segments of Mozambican society considering the Chinese timber business in Mozambique as nothing short of looting. But these alliances also exist in other areas, such as banking (Alves in this volume) and construction (Chichava, chapter 2 in this volume).

At the same time, there are other alliances between Chinese companies and the Mozambican bourgeoisie which merit a rather detailed analysis, namely between the China International Fund (CIF), a Chinese company based in Hong Kong, and SPI-Gestão e Investimentos, SARL, a Frelimo party holding company. The two companies have set up CIF-Moz, with various interests, including in agriculture, tourism, mineral resources, trade, construction, the import and export of various products, as well as the provision of services. CIF, a controversial company, is cited as being close to some corrupt and dictatorial African regimes (Weimer & Vines 2011:93–98). In collusion with these regimes it is said to be involved in business deals that are less than clear, notably with high-ranking figures of the MPLA, in Angola, where it set up a joint venture in partnership with the Angolan oil company, Sonangol, in 2004. This joint venture was also involved in business in Guinea (signed with the regime of the former dictator Dadis Camara) and in Zimbabwe. Likewise, CIF, without any history in the construction sector, won the right to build or rehabilitate important infrastructure in Angola. This deal was also not very transparent, and there were accusations of missing deadlines, and of delivering low quality work (Marques 2010; Bräutigam 2011; Croese 2012).

What is critical here is not the alliance in itself, but the way it relegates to a secondary position the interests of the majority of the population of African countries. In Mozambique, given the fact that most of the emerging Mozambican bourgeoisie is a product of links with the state and with Frelimo, the question is how these alliances could be used for the benefit of the majority, and not just for a group of people interested only in accumulation of wealth without regard for the interests of the majority. This is underscored by actions of local and provincial party officials in the case of WAADL rice farm in Xai-Xai, who have sought to monopolise the opportunities presented by the rice cultivation scheme for personal gain (Chichava, chapter 8 in this volume).

Mozambique has one of the highest growth rates in Africa, and is becoming one of the priority destinations for investment. But this growth has not necessarily resulted in the welfare of the majority of the population improving, and the gulf between rich and poor is widening. Between 2001 and 2010, the Mozambican economy grew at an average rate of 7.9% a year, one of the ten highest growth rates in the world (Africa Progress Panel 2012:8). Between 2011 and 2015, on a list headed by China, it is estimated that Mozambique, with a projected average annual growth rate of 7.7%, will be among the five countries that will grow fastest in the world.

At a time when, on the one hand, China is becoming an increasingly active partner in Mozambique and, according to the CPI data, was the country that undertook the most investment in Mozambique in 2011, and, on the other hand, several important mineral resources have been discovered in Mozambique, notably coal and natural gas, it is imperative to discuss what Mozambique can gain from its relationship with China. This is all the more imperative when one considers how, despite extraordinary advances in the fight against poverty, the gulf between rich and poor is widening in China too, leading the Chinese authorities to regard it as a threat to the country's stability.

So how can the enthusiasm of the Mozambican elites towards the Chinese presence in Mozambique be harnessed to bring benefits to the country, and not just for a handful of individuals? How can one ensure that there is no misalignment between the political will of the elites and actions on the ground, as has been the practice so far? Will the party-led development model in China, with increasing evidence of elite acquisition and even opulence through their privileged position and ability to mobilise state resources, be emulated in Mozambique? Ensuring that the mamba is not devoured by the dragon, that Mozambique does not become a simple exporter of raw materials and receiver of finished goods – in what would be a replay of the status quo in relations between Africa and the West – is the great challenge for Mozambique in its relationship with China.

References

Africa Progress Panel. 2012. 'Jobs, Justice and Equity: Seizing opportunities in times of global change'. *Africa Progress Report 2012*.

Alden, C. 2007. *China in Africa*. London: Zed Books.

Anshan, L. 2007. 'China and Africa: Policy and challenges'. *China Security*, 3(3):69–93.

Asian Ceramics. 2011. 'Jinan Yuxiao in Mozambique'. September. Available from: content.yudu. com/Library/A1tw08/ASIANCERAMICSSEPTEMB/resources/65.htm [Accessed on 26 June 2012].

Bräutigam, D. 2009. *The Dragon's Gift: The real story of China and Africa*. New York: Oxford

University Press.
Bräutigam, D. 2010. 'Was Guinea Bought by Beijing?' 5 March. Available from: www.chinaafricarealstory.com/2010/03/earlier-this-week-chatham-house-british.html [Accessed on 27 June 2012].
Bräutigam, D. 2011. 'Chinese Aid and Luanda General Hospital in Angola: Still falling down?' 21 April. Available from: www.chinaafricarealstory.com/2011/04/chinese-aid-and-luanda-general-hospital.html [Accessed on 27 June 2012].
Bräutigam, D. 2012. 'The Zambezi Valley: China's first agricultural colony? Fiction or Fact?'. Available from: www.chinaafricarealstory.com/2012/01/zambezi-valley-chinas-first.html [Accessed on 21 June 2012].
Bräutigam, D & Ekman, S. 2012. 'Briefing Rumors and Realities of Chinese Agriculture Engagement in Mozambique'. *African Affairs*, 483–492.
Centre for Chinese Studies. 2006. *China's Interest and Activity in Africa's Construction and Infrastructure Sectors*. Stellenbosch University.
Chichava, S. 2012. 'Investimento directo estrangeiro e o combate à pobreza em Moçambique: Uma leitura a partir do investimento chinês na agricultura'. In: L de Brito et al, eds. *Desafios para Moçambique 2012*. Maputo: IESE, 411–426.
Corkin et al. 2008. 'China's Role in the Development of Africa's Infrastructure'. SAIS Working Papers in *African Studies* 04-08.
Croese, S. 2012 'One Million Houses? Chinese engagement in Angola's national reconstruction'. In Marcus Power and Ana Cristina Alves. *China and Angola: a marriage of convenience?* Nairobi: Pambazuka, 125–144.
Danqing, X & Yongsheng, C. 2012. 'Xiangyang's First Overseas Investment of $95 Million in Agricultural Project in Mozambique'. *Xiangyang Daily*. Available from: en.xiangyang.gov.cn/publish/cbnews/201205/04/cb416_1.shtml [Accessed on 21 June 2012].
Ekman, S. 2010. 'Who is Loro Horta?' *Shanghaisigrid*, 4 May. Available from: http://shanghaisigrid.typepad.com/blog/2010/03/who-is-loro-horta.html [Accessed on 21 July 2012].
Ekman, S. 2012. 'Searching for Loro Horta', 23 April. Available from: starvingcritic.wordpress.com/2012/04/23/searching-for-loro-horta/ [Accessed on 21 July 2012].
Horta, L. 2007. 'China, Mozambique: Old friends, new business', 13 August. Available from: www.isn.ethz.ch/isn/Security-Watch/Articles/Detail//?id=53470&lng=en [Accessed on 26 June 2012].
Horta, L. 2008. 'The Zambezi Valley: China's first agricultural colony?', 20 May. Available from: csis.org/publication/zambezi-valley-chinas-first-agricultural-colony [Accessed on 26 June 2012].
Hubei Daily. 2012. 'Hubei Achieves Progress in Overseas Agricultural Development', 1 June. Available from: english.rikes.gov.cn/4/288/291/4085.html [Accessed on 21 June 2012].
Macagno, L. 2010. 'Os "bons portugueses" do Atlético Chinês: desporto e fotografia no Moçambique tardo-colonial, Lisbon'. Document presented at the 7th Congress of Iberian Studies.
Marques, R. 2010. 'The New Imperialism: China in Angola'. *World Affairs*, March/April. Available from: www.worldaffairsjournal.org/article/new-imperialism-china-angola [Accessed on 27 June 2012].
McNamee, T. et al. 2012. 'A Study of Chinese Traders in South Africa, Lesotho, Botswana, Zambia and Angola'. Discussion Paper 2012/03. Johannesburg, the Brenthurst Foundation.
Medeiros, E. 2007. 'Os Sino-moçambicanos da Beira. Mestiçagens Várias'. *Cadernos de Estudos Africanos*, 13/14:157–187.
Metalnewsnet. 2009. 'YuXiao Group has in Succession Bought 20 Zircon Mines in Mozambique", 29 December. Available from: www.metalnewsnet.com/Zirconium/frz7ogaLC9PI.html

[Accessed on 26 June 2012].

Sigrid, E. 2010. 'Who is Loro Horta?' *Shanghaisigrid,* 4 May. Available from: shanghaisigrid. typepad.com/blog/2010/03/who-is-loro-horta.html [Accessed on 21 June 2012].

Sigrid, E. 2012. 'Searching for Loro Horta', 23 April. Available from: starvingcritic.wordpress. com/2012/04/23/searching [Accessed on 21 June 2012].

Wall Street Journal. 2012. 'Zhong Jianhua: Chinese Enterprises in Africa', 17 April. Available from: www.focac.org/eng/jlydh/sjzs/t923570.htm [Accessed on 28 June 2012].

Weimar, M. & Vines, A. 2012. 'China's Angolan Oil Deals, 2003–2011'. In: Marcus Power & Ana Cristina Alves, eds. *China and Angola: A marriage of convenience?* Cape Town: Pambazuka, 85–104.

Xinhua. 2011. 'China refutes "land grab" claims in Africa'. Available from: news.xinhuanet.com/ english/china/2011-12/08/c_131295942.htm [Accessed on 6 June 2012].

Index

A

Action Plan for the Reduction of Absolute Poverty (PARPA) 15
Administração Nacional de Estradas (ANE) *see also* National Road Administration 67
Africa Forest Law Enforcement and Governance (AFLEG) 12
Africa Great Wall Cement Manufacturer 30, 34
Africa Great Wall Mining Development Company 204
Africa Ocean Non Ferrous Metal Mining Co Ltd 204
Africa Rare Metal Mining Development Co Ltd 204
Africa Yuxiao Mining Development Co Ltd 204
African National Congress (ANC) 3
African Union xii
Agência de Desenvolvimento do Vale do Zambeze (AGZ) 46, 123
agflation (food inflation) 86
aggression towards workers 173
Agrícola CCM 95, 127, 128, 143
agricultural demonstration centre *see also* Chinese
    agricultural centres 4, 92, 93, 107, 108, 118, 120
        aid viii, 107
        colony 104, 141, 143, 145, 208
        cooperation xv, 89, 91, 95, 96, 102, 121
        development 17, 27, 90, 96, 118, 120
        expertise 85
        experts 114, 115, 120, 139
        exports 89, 126
        imports 98, 126
        infrastructure 123
        investment 6, 41, 85, 87, 90, 95, 97, 101, 103–105, 132, 200
        mechanisation 46, 147
        potential 15, 87
        production 3, 84, 87, 89, 91, 97, 111, 120, 157, 164
        productivity 89, 92, 93
        products 26, 90, 98, 126, 165
        project 15, 16, 85, 96, 97, 101, 107, 120, 123, 124, 140, 143
        research 16, 110, 153
        sector 15, 16, 84, 85, 88, 89, 91, 92, 96, 100, 102, 107, 120, 125, 137, 139
        technology 16, 96, 97, 99, 107, 109, 114–119, 129, 137
        technology centres 27, 28, 89, 92, 96, 102, 105
        trade 89
        training centre 162
Agricultural Technology Demonstration Centres 107, 109, 119, 124, 125
agriculture 15, 32, 56, 85, 97–99, 165, 203, 206
    African 27, 90, 120, 200
    Chinese 115, 116, 139
    colony 139, 141
    cooperation xv, 5, 7, 26, 92, 95, 122, 142, 153
    credit 134, 141
    equipment 46, 133
    expertise 89, 100
    investments 8, 30, 39, 43, 93, 97, 101, 127, 149, 152, 164, 182, 199, 201
    Mozambican 22, 94, 96, 97, 102, 115, 121, 125, 126, 128, 133, 135, 164, 200, 204
    potential 44
    projects 133
    regions 124
    sector 16, 31, 47, 107, 121–124, 127, 142
    Zambézia 95, 140, 141
agro-industry 4, 30, 32, 44, 45, 117, 127
airport construction 6
Albino, Roberto 46
Alden, Chris vii, xi, xiv–vi, 1, 19, 20, 22, 48, 51, 65, 86, 93, 103, 106, 142, 143, 183, 189, 198, 199, 201, 207
Ali, Prime Minister, Aires 8, 24, 25
All-Africa Games 9, 22
aluminium production 110
    smelter 11
Alves, Ana Cristina vii, xv, 15, 20–22, 39, 42, 48, 124, 142, 206, 208, 209
Angoche district 35
Angola xi–iv, xvi, 1, 2, 21, 43, 60, 69, 104, 147, 173, 184, 202, 206, 208, 209

Index

Angónia district 27
Anhui Foreign Economic Construction (Group) Co Ltd (AFECC) 6, 41, 56, 80, 188
anti-China sentiment/feeling 148
anti-colonial struggle xii
anti-malaria medicines 4
aquaculture 7, 14, 30–32, 109, 127
Argentina 84, 85
Aruangua Agro-Industrial Limitada 127
Associacção d'Operários Chinezes Beneficente 'Boa União' 190
Associação dos Agricultores e Regantes do Bloco de Ponela para o Desenvolvimento Agro-Pecuario e Mecanização agrícola de Xai-Xai 129, 131, 142
Associação dos Agricutores e Regantes de Ponela see Ponela Association of Farmers and Irrigators
Association of the Chinese Community of Mozambique (ACCM) 189, 190
Attorney-General's Office 27, 28, 152
Australian 11, 34, 39
automobile assembly industry 17, 35

B

Banco Austral 40
Banco Comercial de Investimento (BCI) 40
Banco Comercial Português (BCP) 40, 44
Banco da África Ocidental 43
Banco de Moçambique 45
Banco Espírito Santo (BES) Africa 15, 45
Banco Espírito Santo Group 15
Banco Privado Atlantico 43
Banco Timorense de Investimento 44
Bandung conference 51
Bank of China 46
Bank of Mozambique 15, 124
Bank of Portugal 26, 36
Barclays Bank Moçambique 40
Barué 128
BBC News 98, 103, 159, 183
Beijing xii–iv, 1, 2, 5, 7–9, 15, 16, 25, 28, 39, 42, 62, 64, 94, 99, 101, 112, 119, 120, 151
Beijing Consensus 51, 66
Beijing Summit 107
Beira 9, 11, 16, 22, 28, 34, 47, 57, 59, 128, 146, 171, 185, 198, 201, 208
Beira-Machipanda road 11
Beluluane Industrial Park 18
Benga mining concession 39
Benin 108
bilateral cooperation 4, 26, 121, 122, 151
Bill & Melinda Gates Foundation 94, 129, 143
biodiesel production 94
biofuel 43, 84, 103
  industry 102

production 127, 201
projects 15
Biworld International Limited 126
Boane district 27, 92, 96, 110, 111, 114–117, 119, 125, 153
Bräutigam, Deborah xi, xvi, 26, 36, 51, 52, 65, 92, 93, 96, 98, 103, 106, 107, 119, 121, 122, 129, 130, 140, 143, 200, 203, 206–208
Brazil vii–ix, 6, 10, 41, 43, 91, 00, 137, 146, 150, 153, 165, 182, 191, 204
Bretton Woods 1, 3
BRICS countries 204
Broadman, Harry xi, xvi, 21
Brown, Lester 84, 103
Who Will Feed China 84, 103
Brown, William 19, 21
Brussels Institute of Contemporary China Studies 101
Bunkenborg, Mikkel vii, xv, 50, 67, 201
Buque, Adelino 163, 183
Bureau of Complaints of Hubei 132
Buzi 11

C

Cabo Delgado province 12, 14, 30, 33, 34, 36, 57, 59, 91, 123, 124, 126, 158, 186
Cahora Bassa dam 10, 44
  hydro-electric plant 11, 44
Caixa Economica 43
Caixa Genral de Depositos 40
Camara, Dadis 206
Camargo Corrêa 6, 10, 41, 91
Cameroon 27, 107, 108, 148
Canal de Moçambique 38, 136
Cantonese 189, 191, 196, 197
Cape Verde 43
Capitais de Moçambique 45
cassava 16, 110
Catembe 11, 47, 139
Center for Agricultural Investment Promotion (CEPAGRI) 95
Center for Chinese Agricultural Policy 99
Centre for Chinese Studies, Stellenbosch University 20, 21, 22, 37, 65, 82, 103–106, 150, 184, 202, 208
Centre for Police Civic Cooperation 61, 62
Centre for the Demonstration and Transfer of Chinese Agricultural Technologies (CITAU) 204
Centro de Investigação e Transferência de Tecnolgias Agrárias do Umbéluzi (CITTAU) 109, 118
Centro de Promoção de Investimentos (CPI) 125, 127, 143
Chamei Agricola 95
Chang, Manuel 193

Cheringoma 34
Chichava, Sérgio vii, xi, xv, xvi, 1, 2, 4, 7, 8, 21, 24, 68, 82, 94–96, 103, 107, 120, 125, 128, 142, 143, 149, 153, 182, 183, 188, 199, 200, 204, 206–208
Chidenguele 73, 77, 78
Chifunde district 35
Chimbonhanine 138
China Begbu Lisheng Chemical Technology Development Co Ltd 127
China Daily 11, 21, 64, 65, 100, 103, 187
China Development Bank (CDB) 8, 18, 40, 120, 143
China Engineering Co Ltd (CAMCE) 123
China Grains and Oils Group Africa (CGOG Africa) 16, 126, 127, 142
China Henan International Cooperation Group Co Ltd (CHICO) xv, 7, 9, 56, 67
China International Fund (CIF) 31, 206
China Minmetals 140
China National Petroleum Corporation (CNPC) 34
China Qingho Group 6, 12, 28, 34, 36, 37, 204
Safari 53, 66
China Tong Chain Investments 17
China Tong Jian Investment Co Ltd 26, 35, 36
China Yuxiao Resources Holdings Lda 204
China-Africa Cooperative Partnership for Peace and Security xiii
China-Africa Cotton 18
China-Africa Cotton Development Ltd 128, 143
China-Africa Cotton Moçambique Ltd (CACM) 128
China-Africa Development Fund (CAD Fund) 8, 120, 143
China Export-Import (Exim) Bank 4, 6, 8, 10, 11, 18, 21, 26, 27, 29, 40, 41, 46, 69, 90, 91, 103, 123, 124, 140, 152, 159, 163, 164, 188
China-Mozambique cooperation xv, 7
  engagement 6
  interactions 125
  relations 7, 8, 21, 25, 39, 203
China-Mozambique Mining Development Co Ltd 204
Chinese Academy of Agricultural Sciences (CAAS) 94, 99, 129, 143
  agricultural demostration centres (CADC) *see also* agricultural demonstration centres 108, 109, 112
  century 62
  construction companies 9, 10, 56, 67, 78, 80
  embassy 60–63, 89, 96, 104, 147, 151, 182, 195, 201
  emigrants 201
  engagement with Africa xii, 22, 52, 62, 86

FDI *see also* foreign direct investment xi, 8, 26, 30–35, 105, 127, 188, 204, 205
Foreign Ministry 200
foreign policy xiii, 87
immigrants 146, 148, 176, 177
investment xv, 7, 8, 24, 25, 29–31, 34–37, 39, 40, 43, 47, 97, 121, 125–128, 140, 147, 149, 150, 153, 155, 165, 181–183, 199, 200, 202–204, 206
leadership style 172, 175
master plan 50–53, 62, 63, 65, 199, 201
medicine 53, 65
migrants xiv, 194, 196, 199, 201
migration xiv, 147, 188, 189, 193, 196
Ministry of Commerce (MOFCOM) xi, 101
Model of Development 51
National Petroleum Corporation (CNPC) 11
Nationalist Party 190
Pagoda 189–191, 193, 197
policy banks *see also* China Development Bank, Exim Bank 40
polity 51, 64
shops 60, 61, 188
Chipata Cotton Company Moçambique 128
Chipembe 91, 123, 124
Chissano, Joaquim 8, 9
Chissibuca 67, 69, 71, 73, 79, 80
Chitima 69
Chokwé 123, 124
Chokwé Agro-Processing Complex 124
civil war 2, 3, 64, 68, 121, 122, 124
Club Fiel Observante do Direito (Chee Kung Ton) 190
Clube chinês de Lourenço Marques (the Chinese club of Lorenzo Marques) 190
coal power plant 12
  reserves 11, 39, 204
Cold War 2
colonisation 88, 161
commercial banks 40
commercial fishing 14
Communism 192
Companhia Nacional de Algodão (CAN)
Confucius Centre 4
Congo (Brazzaville) 108
Construction and Agriculture Machinery Import and Export 140
construction industry 20, 175, 179
construction sector 4, 10, 31, 129, 161, 172, 190, 204–206
Construções CCM Limitada 128, 143
consumer price index (CPI) 24, 25, 31, 34, 35, 69, 86, 125–127, 129, 132, 143, 147, 200, 204, 205, 207

coolies 146, 171, 191
Corporate social responsibility (CSR) xiii, 139
Corridor Sands Titanium project 11
corruption 12, 13, 202
cotton plant 8, 41
Council of Ministers 17, 28, 38
cultural barriers 118
Cultural Revolution 53, 54

D
Darfur xiii
d'Almeida Santos, António 124
Daqing Oilfield Drilling Engineering Company 34
Dar es Salaam 18, 62
de Sousa Santos, Boaventura 155, 156
deforestation 162
democracy 156, 158
Democratic Republic of Congo (DRC) xi, 132, 148, 187
developing country 87, 103, 167
Dhlakama, Afonso 182
Diario de um Sociólogo 150, 153, 155, 156, 158, 162, 164, 185–187
diaspora 147, 188, 189, 191
Dingsheng International Investments 17
Diogo, Prime Minister Luísa 28, 29, 37, 152
Direcção Provincial da Agricultura de Gaza see also Provincial Department of Gaza Agriculture 135
direct foreign investment (FDI) 25
Directorate for Land and Forestry 90
Durán, Jimena viii, xvi, 107, 125, 128, 143, 188, 204
Durban 19, 160

E
Economia e Negócios 165
Economic Affairs Department xii
 Counselor 4, 11, 18, 23
 economic cooperation 51, 107
 development 9, 51, 64, 181
 exchange 188
 exploitation 158
 growth 4, 43
 influence 163
 interests xiii, 50, 162
 migration 188
 motivation 118
 power 4, 181
 reform 3
 relations 25, 147, 183
 rewards 165, 166
 threats 158
 trade theory 85

Eduardo Mondlane University 4, 16, 150, 175, 184
education xiv, 4, 5, 26, 56, 177, 190
Egypt xii
Ekman, Sigrid-Marianella Stensrud viii, xv, 84, 122, 129, 140, 143, 144, 200, 208
Electricidade de Moçambique (EDM) 91, 203
emerging countries 24
employment contracts 76, 77
energy xi, 11, 22, 35, 43–45, 147
 companies 6, 41
 sector 11, 43, 47, 203
enforcement of regulations 13
Environment Ministry 14
environment policies 12
environmental consequences 10, 162
 impact xiii, 10, 149
Environmental Justice 159, 163
environmental organisations 59, 155
 practices 183
 problems 158, 163
 standards 159
environmentalists 10, 156, 157, 163, 164
Equatorial Guinea 173, 183
Ethiopia xii, xiv, 84, 108, 148
Europe 2, 148
European colonial experience 163
 concern 162
 descent 175, 176
 languages 169
 origin 168
 Union xi
 workers 146
Europeans 117, 176
exploitation 13, 31, 149, 153, 158, 200
 of forestry resources 7, 156, 157, 182
 of raw materials 156
Exploração, Transformação e Comércio de Madeira 126
exploration licence 12
 of gas fields 11, 12
 of natural resources 5
Export and Import Bank 10, 46
Export Buyer's Credit 29

F
Feijó, João viii, xvi, 146, 149, 154, 168, 173, 175, 182–184, 202
FIFA World Cup 9
Financial Times, The 37, 100, 103
Finland viii, 91
Fiscal Benefits Codes 25
fish farming 109
fisheries 8, 10, 12, 14, 30–32, 39, 101, 127
flood victims 27
flooding 10

floods 94, 152, 160
Food and Agriculture Organisation (FAO) 104, 120, 153
food crisis 86, 89, 92, 93, 104
    insecurity 15, 107, 111, 127, 200
    prices 86, 98, 101, 102
    processing 18
    production 84, 87, 97, 100, 102, 128, 165, 200, 204
    scarcity 120
    security 84, 85, 88–91, 93–95, 97–100, 104, 120, 144
    supply 84, 88, 89, 94, 96, 100–102
foreign aid 1, 36
    capital 30, 40, 124, 182
    companies 11, 58, 153
    construction companies 9
    currency reserves 8
    debt 25
    direct investment (FDI) *see also* Chinese FDI xi, 8, 25, 86, 127, 188, 199, 200
    employees 154, 170, 179
    exchange xi, 14, 110, 164
    farming 101
    influence 2
    interests 20
    investment 11, 17, 24, 29, 82, 91, 121, 179
    investors 13, 16, 69, 88, 136, 147, 152
Foreign Ministry 9, 161, 164
foreign policy viii, xiii, xvi, 7, 42, 87
    workers 179, 181
foreigners 13, 148, 168, 179, 180, 193
forestry 7, 12, 21, 58, 59, 89, 97, 101, 122, 127, 141, 157, 162, 200, 201, 203
    exploitation 156
    officials 13
    resources 156
forged documents 158
Fórum das Organizações Não-Governamentais Nacionais de Gaza (FONGA) 136, 144
Forum on China-Africa Cooperation (FOCAC) xii–iv, 16, 25, 27, 37, 92, 105, 107, 119, 120, 144, 149
France 68
Freemantle, Simon xi, xvi
Frelimo party 1, 2, 6, 7, 10, 23, 30, 31, 39, 43, 45, 68, 121, 122, 124, 127, 133–136, 142, 145, 147, 155, 191, 192, 206
French Equatorial Africa 201
Front for the Liberation of Mozambique (Frelimo) *see also* Mozambique Liberation Front 2
Fujian Agriculture and Forestry University 108
    Association 196
    province xiv, 63, 148, 195
Fundo de Desenvolvimento Agrário (FDA) 139

Fundo de Investimento de Iniciativa Local (OIL) 136
Fundompara o Fomento da Habitação (FFH) 31
Future Metal Mining Co Ltd 204

G
Gabinete do Plano de Desenvolvimento da Região do Zambeze (GPZ) *see also* Zambezi Valley Planning Office 45, 46, 49, 87, 90, 91, 93, 104, 106, 123, 144
Gabinete de Promoção do Zambezi Vale (GPZ) 88
Gabon xii, 159
Gaza province xv, 27, 33, 94, 95, 111, 121, 123, 126, 128–130, 133, 135, 142–144, 203
General State Budget 28
Geocapital 14, 15, 40–48, 93, 124, 142, 144
Geopactum Oriente 43
Ghana 6, 41, 148
global financial crisis xi, 1, 8
global friction 81
Global Hunger Index (GHI) 88
Global Pactum 43
global warming 84
Go Global strategy 101
Going Out Strategy 147, 203
Golden Peacock 34
Gorongosa district 35
governance 28, 50, 164, 172, 183
Government of Mozambique (GoM) 5, 21, 22, 26, 37, 69, 152, 185, 189
green revolution 88, 93, 100
Green Super Rice Project 129, 143
Grenada 55
gross domestic product (GDP) 14, 98
Guangxi 57
Guangxi Bagui Agricultural Science and Technology Co Ltd 108
Guangzhou 65, 141, 195
Guebuza, President Armando 8, 9, 15, 21, 24, 28, 29, 37, 40, 41, 46, 48, 68, 92, 103, 111, 112, 137, 151
guerrilla training 2, 68
Guinea-Bissau 43
Guro district 27, 96, 123

H
Hang Seng Bank 42
Haoping, Luo 132
Heavily Indebted Poor Country Initiative 3
Henan Guoji Industry and Development Co Ltd 31, 205
Henan Haode Mozambique Industrial Park 31
Henan Guoji Imobiliária (HGI) 205
HI-virus 54
HIV-positive patients 54
HIV/AIDS 178

Ho, Stanley 14, 22, 42, 43, 93, 124
Holland 26
Hong & Binga Development Fishery Company 31, 36
Hong Kong 42, 45, 63, 141, 184, 206
Hoong Che Sha 190
Horta, Loro 15, 16, 21, 69, 82, 84, 89–92, 104, 139–141, 144, 145, 157, 164, 184, 200, 208, 209
Housing Promotion Fund (FFH) 205
Hu, President Jintao xiii, 4, 8, 25–27, 92, 107, 109, 112, 118, 140, 151, 152, 157
Huawei xi, 4
Hubei Agriculture University 4
Hubei Daily 132, 145, 203, 208
Hubei Liafeng 94, 95, 97, 113, 128, 129, 131
Hubei Liafeng Agricultural Development Corporation 108, 111
Hubei Lianfeng farm 95, 96
Hubei Lianfeng Mozambique Co Lda (HLMO Co Lda) *see also Moçambique Lianfeng Desenvolvimento de Agricultura co Limitada* 121, 126, 128, 143
Hubei province 92, 94, 96, 125, 128, 129, 132, 203, 204
human rights 51, 153, 156, 158, 160, 164
Human Rights League 180
Hunan Hybrid Rice Institute 16
hydro-carbon exploration 11
hydro-electric project 11, 152, 185
hydro-power 9, 10, 44

I
Identification and Residence Documents for Foreigners (DIRE) 193
illegal aliens 56, 63
illegal export 13, 14, 59, 157, 158
illegal logging 12–14, 39, 158
ill-treatment 161, 162
Imensis 158, 163, 184
immigrants 146–148, 176, 177, 189
Inchope 9, 69
Incomati river 8, 69, 82
India 29, 99, 146, 153, 157, 165, 192, 204
India Export and Import Bank 46
Indian Ocean 87, 146
Industrial Association of Mozambique (AIMO) 149
industrial centre 110
  fishing 14, 31
  machinery 126
  park 17
  sector 30, 35
industry xi, 17, 32, 35, 58, 108, 149, 157, 169
infrastructure 1, 2, 7, 9–11, 16, 18, 19, 26, 27, 41, 46, 47, 50, 56, 87, 141, 152, 160, 162, 164, 202, 206

projects xii, xiv, 67, 69, 73, 81, 90
Inhambane 12, 33, 128, 204
Inhassoro 11
Insitec 10, 40, 91
institutional incoherence 112, 118
Instituto de Algadão de Moçambique (IAM) 123
Instituto de Cereais de Moçambique (ICM) 123
Instituto de Investigação Agronómica de Moçambique (IIAM) 109
Integrated Road Sector Programme 69
International Development Association (IDA) 69
International Food Policy Research Institute 88, 106
International Monetary Fund 68
international tenders 9, 10
investment banking 14, 45
Investment Promotion Centre (CPI) 24, 69, 147, 152, 200
irrigation 98, 125, 131, 138, 141, 142, 203
  channel network 16
  infrastructure 94
  systems 17, 110, 116, 121, 124, 128, 130, 135, 141
Italy 68
ivory 156, 158, 185

J
Japan 6, 17, 137, 195
jatropha cultivation 94, 165
Jian, Hong 55, 62, 65
Jiang, President Zemin 4
Jiang, Lu viii, xvi, 107
Jinan Yuxiao Group Lda 204, 207
Joaquim Chissano International Conference Centre 9, 56, 152, 161, 164
job creation 7, 94, 164
jobs generated 30, 33
Joint Economic and Trade Commission 4, 25

K
Kachamilla, John 128
Kenmare mineral sands 11
Kenya xi
Khan, Obed 165
Kuo Min Tang 190

L
labour conflicts 52
  discipline 173
  disputes 153, 174, 201
  inspectors 149, 151, 167, 171, 180–182
Labour Law 154, 167, 170
labour laws 77, 137
  legislation 178, 201, 202
  politics 52

relations 149, 155, 161, 165, 172, 174, 175, 181, 182, 199
unions 8
requirements 10
land grabbing 84, 90, 91, 94, 95, 102, 103, 139, 141, 144, 199, 200, 209
leases 85, 88–91, 97, 100
language barrier 115, 116, 170, 173, 196
law enforcement 13, 181
Lee, Ching Kwan 52, 65
Lei, Hong, 200
Le Nouvel Observateur 161
Lemos, Annabela 13, 21, 149, 184
Lenovo 17
Lesotho xvi, 148, 172, 208
Li, Sien-nien 122
Lianfeng Farm 92, 95, 96
Lianfeng Overseas Agricultural Development Co Ltd 128, 143, 203
liberation movement 2, 3, 121, 191
war 39
Liberia xiii, 27, 108, 109
Libya xiv, 64
Limpopo rice 129
Liugong 132, 143, 90
local elites 40, 58–60, 121, 136, 137
Lourenço Marques 146, 190, 201
low-income housing 9, 41
Luso-Chinese 40, 43, 44
Lusophone business culture 41
Lusophone Africa 14

M

Mabunda, Lázaro 162, 186
Macau 14, 41–44, 47–49 82, 93, 191
Forum 42, 44
Macauhub 4, 8, 16, 21, 39, 41, 44–46, 48, 68, 69, 82, 84, 89, 92, 93, 105, 140, 145, 164, 184
Machel, Samora 2, 124
Mackenzie, Catherine 24, 37, 58, 65, 149, 156, 184
Madagascar 55, 146
Magazine Independente 140
Mágoé 69
maize 16, 18, 90, 96, 99, 110, 117, 122, 123, 125
Malawi 11, 18, 24, 128
Mali xi, xiv, 148
Maluana 35
Mananga-Mungassa 18
Mandarin 171, 177, 180, 189, 190, 195, 197
Manica province 18, 27, 33, 48, 87, 90, 95, 96, 123, 128, 158
Mankell, Henning 161, 187
manufacturing industry 30, 31, 166, 172, 177, 182, 204, 205
Mao, Chairman Tse Tung 54, 192

Maputo xvi, 2, 7, 18, 33, 63, 171, 173, 201
agricultural demonstration centre 112
Chinese ambassador 59
Chinese community 188, 189, 190, 194, 195, 196, 198
Chinese doctors 55
Chinese embassy 96, 182
Chinese investment 30, 31, 36
City Police 61
cotton plant 8
diplomatic ties 39
embassy complex 4
hospital 53
industrial park 17
infrastructure projects 11, 47, 69, 90
International Airport 6, 27, 29, 41, 47, 53, 56, 82, 152, 188
investors 44
low-income housing 9, 31, 41
military housing 5
Municipal Assembly 193
Province 27, 30, 31, 34, 35, 41, 61, 69, 129, 205
Province Police 61
rehabilitation of port 19
relationship with donors 1
School of Visual Arts 191
shoe shop 60, 61, 62
Umbeluzi centre 16
Maputo-Catembe bridge 47
Marracuene 30, 31
Marxist-Leninist 2, 121, 122, 147
master plan *see* Chinese master plan
Matama state farm 122
Matola 17, 31, 110, 205
Matutuíne 31, 35
Mauritius 31, 146
Mavalane airport 176
mechanised farms 122
Mediafax 160, 186
Memorandum of Understanding (MoU) 12, 16, 39, 44, 90, 96, 122, 130, 132, 140, 141, 155
Meng, Dr 53, 55
Meuser, Heike E 158
migrants xiv, 146, 188, 189, 194, 196, 198, 199, 201
migration xiv, 63, 147, 148, 157, 188, 189, 193, 196, 198, 201
military assistance 5
cooperation 5
elite 199, 205
equipment 5, 160
support 2, 68, 147
training 147

Millennium BIM 40
mineral extraction 4
  resources 8, 30, 31, 34, 35, 39, 44, 124, 199, 203, 204, 206, 207
minimum wage 59, 78, 137, 166
mining industry 58
Ministry of Agriculture, Finance and Development 17, 90, 100, 101, 109, 113, 122, 151
Ministry of Commerce xi, xii, xvi
Ministry of Finance 37
Ministry of Foreign Affairs and Cooperation 22, 26, 37, 41, 56, 151, 152
Ministry of Health 54
Ministry of Industry and Trade (MIC) 25, 26, 151
Ministry of Labour 174
Ministry of Mineral Resources 128
Ministry of Planning and Development (MPD) 24, 35, 37, 46, 69
Ministry of Public Works and Housing 11, 151
Ministry of Science and Technology 92, 96, 109, 125
Ministry of Youth and Sport 152, 154, 155
Moamba 110, 123, 129
Moamba Major dam 11, 28, 29, 203
Moamba state farm 122
Moamba Technolgy Park 93
Moatize 29
Moatize coal mines 11
Moçambique Lianfeng Desenvolvimento de Agricultura Co Limitada see also Hubei Lianfeng Mozambique Co Lda, HLMO Co Lda 128
Mocumbi, Pascoal 122
Mombasa Port 18
Mondlane, Eduardo 2, 147
Mongolia 50, 82
Monte Binga, SA 31
Montepuez 57
Morais, José 151
Mosse, Marcelo 157
Movement for Democratic Change (MDC) 160
Moza Banco 6, 14, 15, 45, 48, 123, 124
Moza Bank 15, 43, 46
Moza Capital 15, 43, 45, 49
Mozal 110
Mozal aluminium smelter 11
Mozambican Armed Forces (FADM) 5
  banking sector xv 40
  bourgeoisie 30, 124, 106
  independence 1, 2, 39, 68, 89, 121, 124, 136, 138, 146, 147, 189, 191, 192, 196, 198, 201
  Insitec 10, 40, 91
  Ministry of Agriculture, Finance and Development 17
  Ministry of Health 54
  Ministry of Science and Technology 92, 96

National Directorate for Land 90
Planning Ministry 18
Police 61, 62, 64, 181
Poverty Reduction Action Plan 120
Mozambique Heavy sand Mining Co Ltd 204
Mozambique Lianfeng Agricultural Development Company Ltd 203
Mozambique Liberation Front (Frelimo) 1, 2, 6, 7, 10, 23, 30, 31, 39, 43, 45, 68, 121, 122, 124, 127, 133–136, 142, 145, 147, 155, 191, 192, 206
Mozambique National Resistance (Renamo) 2, 3, 68, 136
Mozambique-China relations xvi, 199, 203
Mozcapital 93
Mphanda Nkuwa dam 6, 10, 28, 29, 41, 47, 89, 91, 96, 139, 152, 157, 163, 203
Mphanda Nkuwa Hydroelectric Company (HMNK) 29, 91
Mugabe, Robert 160
Mutanguro, Taurai 72
Muthisse, Gabriel 162–165
mutual benefit xii, xiii, 87, 89, 130, 167
Muxungwe 9, 69

N
Nacala 13, 17, 18, 47, 137
Namacurra district 27
Namibia xii, 27, 148, 172–176, 179, 183
Nampula province 12, 16, 18, 27, 28, 33, 35, 95, 109, 123, 126, 141, 178, 204
Nanjing Construction Group 128
National Agricultural Programme (PROAGRI) 15
National Development and Reform Commission 98, 100, 107
National Directorate of Geology (DNG) 34
National Food Security and Long-term Planning Framework 100
National Front for the Liberation of Angola (FNLA) 2, 147
National Highway No 1 152
National Road Administration (ANE) 67
National Union of Hotel, Tourism, Building, Timber and Mine Workers of Mozambique (SIMTICIM) 149, 169, 174, 175, 180
natural disasters 94, 160
  gas 8, 11, 12, 19, 34, 39, 207
  resources 5, 11, 16, 28, 42, 44, 45, 50, 58, 64, 84, 85, 87, 88, 127, 136, 156, 200
neo-colonialism 86, 87, 91, 96, 102, 149
Netherlands 46
New York Times 158, 185
Nguri 91, 123, 124
Nhantumbo, Isilda 158, 162
Nhemachena, Samuel 70, 71, 73, 75, 79

Niassa province 12, 27, 31, 33, 34, 36, 122, 144, 158
Nielsen, Morten ix, xv, 50, 57, 67, 77, 79, 82, 202
non-governmental organisations (NGOs) 1, 59, 149, 150, 155, 183
Norway 46
Notícias 27, 35, 37, 124, 142, 158, 159, 162, 163, 165, 183, 185

O

O País 5, 22, 24, 37, 48, 162
Office for Accelerated Development Economics Zones (Gazeda) 17
Official Development Assistance (ODA) 3
offshore natural gas 19
Ogle, Alan 158, 162
one-party state 2, 172
Organisation for Economic Cooperation and Develop-Development Assistance Committee (OECD-DAC) 3, 7, 22, 36
Organisation of Mozambican Workers (OTM) 166

P

Pande 11
paternalist management 167
Pátria 158, 159, 164, 185
pay slips 77, 78
Pemba 18, 22, 58, 59, 62
People's Liberation Army 64
People's Republic of China (PRC) 37, 42, 147, 192, 195, 201
personal connections (guanxi) 41–44, 47
plastics industry 166, 171, 181
poaching 14
Police and Citizen Joint Defense Mechanism 61
political allies 64, 68
    backing 60
    connections 40, 43, 46
    elites 19, 21, 28, 30, 68, 121, 124, 142, 199, 200, 205
    influence 42, 113, 136, 163
    prominence 113
Poly Fuzhou Hongyong Pelagic Fishery Co Ltd 31
Ponela 121, 125, 128, 130, 131, 134, 135
Ponela Block Association of Farmers and Irrigators for Agri-Livestock Development and Mechanization in Xai-Xai (ARPONE) 121, 129, 130, 131, 133–136, 139, 142
Ponela irrigation scheme 130, 203
Ponta do Bela 17
Portugal 2, 14, 42–44, 68, 146, 150, 152, 157, 191, 192
Portuguese colonisers 68

Portuguese Socialist Party 43
Portuguese Banco Espírito Santo Group 15
Portuguese Parliament 43
Portuguese Private bank (BPI) 40
poverty 3, 12, 15, 51, 59, 107, 111, 115, 120, 163, 165, 207
    alleviation 15
printing industry 168, 177
private investment 42, 125, 141
    investors 18, 47, 56, 94
privatisation 3
Promotion and Reciprocal Protection of Investment 25
Prosavana 137
protected areas 159
    species 158
Provincial Department of Gaza Agriculture (DPAG) 135
public health 146, 159
    care 55

Q

Quelimane 9, 18

R

Ramo, Joshua 51, 66
Rapid Intervention Force 61
Ratilal, Prakash 15, 45, 46, 48, 124
REN (national electricity grid company) 44
Republic of China 190, 201
research methodology 149
Reunion 146
Rhodesia 2
Ribeiro, Daniel 13, 21, 59, 66, 149, 159, 168, 184
Ribeiro, Jorge Ferro 42, 43
rice 16, 18, 79, 90, 95, 96, 99, 100, 110, 117, 120, 123, 128, 129, 131, 133, 134, 138, 142, 157, 164
    consumption 16, 20
    farming xvi, 4, 121, 125, 206
    production 15, 92–94, 104, 111, 122, 132, 138, 139–141, 164, 203
Riversdale 39
Riversdale Mining Limited (RML) 34
Riversdale Mining Ltd 11
road marking 70–73
Robinson, David Alexander 4, 15, 22, 64, 66
Roque, Paula Cristina ix, xv, 1, 14, 19, 22, 68, 82, 87, 89, 91, 105
Rovuma Basin 11
Rwanda 108

S

safety conditions 165, 171
Sasol natural gas pipeline 11
Scott Wilson Ltd 69–72, 75–77, 82

seed 17, 88, 92, 98, 114, 115, 117, 131, 134
   cultivation 107
   production industry 29
Serra, Carlos 150, 156–165, 168, 184–187
Shanghai viii, 17
Sheng, Mr Wu Jinhou 70
shoes 60, 62, 171
Sichuan 53
Sierra Leone 202, 205, 132
Sino-African relations 86, 87
   -Chinese 189, 196–198
      -Lusophone private investment fund 42, 43
   -Mozambican relations 147, 150
   -Mozambicans 2, 189, 191–198, 201
   -Soviet 2
SINTICIM *see* National Union of Hotel, Tourism, Building, Timber and Mine Workers of Mozambique
SINTIHOTS *see* Union of Hotel, Tourism, Restaurant and Allied Workers
So, Ambrose 43
Sociadade de Gestao Integrade de Recursos (SOGIR) 45, 46, 93
social benefits 166, 167
   relationships xiv, 79, 80, 81
   services 5
   unrest 84, 86
   welfare 117
Sofala province 8, 12, 18, 27, 28, 30, 33–35, 41, 87, 126, 128, 158, 194, 204
soft loan 6, 10, 26, 27, 29, 41, 90, 96, 97
Sogecoa 35, 55, 56
Sogecoa Hotel 62
sojourners 188, 189, 195, 196
solidarity xii, 2, 39, 122, 203
Sonangol 43, 206
South Africa xi, xiii, xiv, xvi, 2, 8, 9, 17, 19, 26, 27, 31, 39, 40, 58, 60, 63, 87, 91, 108, 109, 112, 146–148 152, 160, 173, 174, 182, 196, 201, 202, 204
South China Sea 53
Southern African Development Community (SADC) 3, 17, 19, 22, 160
Southern China 53, 201
South-South Cooperation 20
Soviet Union 2, 147
soybean 99, 122
Special Economic Zones (SEZs) 15, 17, 18, 22
SPI-Gestão e Investimentos 206
spraying machine 70–74
Standard Bank (South Africa) xi, xvi, 40
State Security and Information Service (SISE) 28
State-owned enterprises (SOEs) xiii, 3, 44, 127, 129, 188
Stevens, Jeremy xi, xvi
strikes 8, 57, 77, 182

sub-Saharan Africa 50, 67, 68
Sudan xi, xiii, 27, 69, 108, 148
Sunway International Mozambique Lda 95, 126
sustainable development 12
sustainable forest management 12, 15
Swaziland 87
Sweden 91

T
Taipei xii
Tanzania 11, 17, 18, 52, 54, 108, 128
technical cooperation 4, 89, 90, 94, 96, 116,
Technical Unit for the Implementation of Hydropower Projects (UTIP) 10
technology transfer 92, 94, 111, 115, 118, 129–131, 134
telecommunications xi, 149, 152, 170, 182
Temane 11, 29
Tenwin International Group 206
Tete province 11, 34, 35, 39, 45, 69, 82, 87, 90, 123
Thailand 84
timber 7, 24, 26, 57–59, 126, 127, 160, 182, 200
   illegal export of 12, 14
   illegal extraction 13
   looting of 156
   processing 59
   sector 30, 124, 158, 161, 206
Timor Leste 44
titanium 11, 204
Togo 108, 148
tourism 32, 35, 43, 44, 58, 126, 206
   destination 4
   sector 31, 32
trade union 149, 155, 160, 165, 166, 174
traditional donors 1, 28, 29
healer 178
medicine 53, 178
partners 29
transportation corridor 18
Treaty of Friendship 2
tropical hardwoods 12
Tsing, Anna 81, 83
TTTimber 13

U
Uganda xi, 6, 41, 107–109, 129, 148,
Ulongué 90, 96, 123
Umbeluzi 92, 93, 96, 110
Umbeluzi Agricultural Station 110
Umbeluzi Institute of Agricultral Research 16
Umbeluzi River 110
UN Peacekeeping Operation xiii, 3
União dos Trabalhadores de África (UTA) 126
União Nacional dos Camponeses (UNAC) 137
Union of Hotel, Tourism, Restaurant and Allied

Workers (SINTIHOTS) 149, 174
United Arab Emirates 31
United Kingdom 91
United Nations (UN) xiii, 3
United States (US) xi, 147, 148, 191
unprocessed wood 13, 59, 157, 158
urban water supply systems 9
urbanisation 98

V
Vala, Rafik 153
VARILOG 43
vegetables 110, 112, 126
VEM 43
Vieira, Sérgio 44, 46, 140
Vietnam 17, 85, 91, 147

W
Wanbao Africa Agriculture Development Limited (WAADL) 132, 203
Wanbao Oil and Grain Co Ltd 94, 95, 128, 131, 132, 203
Wate, Clóvis 75
Weng Chen Liao 126
Western donors 1, 6, 7, 19
wind energy 147
work contracts 179
    culture 154
    ethic 57, 80, 115
    permits 115, 179
working conditions 57, 67, 79, 171, 173, 201, 202
World Bank 3, 6, 9, 10, 23, 41, 46, 57, 164
World Bank-China Exim Bank cooperation 6
Wuhan Iron and Steel Corporation (WISCO) 11, 34, 39

X
Xai-Xai xvi, 67, 69, 79, 97, 111, 133, 136, 140, 203, 206
irrigation system 121, 125, 128, 135, 138, 141, 142
rice farm 94, 120, 121, 129, 131
xenophobia 163
xenophobic attacks 148
attitudes 13
Xi, President Jinping 18

Xiangyang city 132
Xie, Guoli 101
Xin Jian Companhia 126

Z
Zacarias, Felício 151, 152
Zambezi river 6, 10, 41, 44, 45, 47, 87, 91, 152, 159
    valley 6, 15, 16, 27, 29, 44–46, 87–91, 93, 96, 97, 157, 165, 200
    Chinese interest in 141
    development 123, 124, 128
    investment 140
    transformation 139
Zambezi Valley Planning Office (GPZ) *see also* Gabinete do Plano de Desenvolvimento da Região do 44
Zambézia province 6, 18, 28, 33, 90, 95, 126, 139–141, 204
    agricultural development 27, 41, 123
    production 87
    as Chinese province 157
    forestry 12, 13
Zambia xi, xii, xv, 107, 108, 128, 157, 172–177
    anti-China relations 148
    Chinese investment 11, 205
    Chinese migration xiv
    copper mines 52, 165
    development corridors 17, 18, 87
    supervision of infrastructures 202
Zamcorp 15, 43, 45, 93, 94
Zhan, Mei 53, 66
Zhang, Xiaoqiang 98, 100
Zhao, Ziyang 3
Zhen Hwa Harbour Construction 140
Zheng, Admiral He xii
Zimbabwe xii, 2, 11, 18, 24, 26, 55, 87, 128, 206
    agriculture demonstration centres 107, 108
    anti-China sentiment 148
    weapons from China 160
    working conditions 202
Zimpeto 9, 53, 55, 56, 151, 153, 155, 161, 172